at home in
the whole food
kitchen

WITHDRAWN

at home in the whole food kitchen

celebrating the art of eating well

AMY CHAPLIN

ROOST BOOKS

Boston

2014

Roost Books
An imprint of Shambhala Publications, Inc.
Horticultural Hall
300 Massachusetts Avenue
Boston, Massachusetts 02115
roostbooks.com

9 8 7 6 5 4 3
Printed in the United States of America

♾ This edition is printed on acid-free paper that meets the American National Standards Institute Z39.48 Standard.
♻ Shambhala Publications makes every effort to print on recycled paper. For more information please visit www.shambhala.com.

Distributed in the United States by Penguin Random House LLC and in Canada by Random House of Canada Ltd

Art directed and designed by Stephen Kent Johnson

Library of Congress Cataloging-in-Publication Data

Chaplin, Amy.
At home in the whole food kitchen: celebrating the art of eating well / Amy Chaplin.
    pages   cm
Includes index.
ISBN 978-1-61180-085-2 (alk. paper)
1. Cooking (Natural foods) 2. Natural foods. I. Title.
TX741.C463 2014
641.3'02—dc23
2013043411

for
Jacqui,
with all my love, x

CONTENTS

introduction

My relationship with food and nature goes further back than I can remember. I suppose I really did inherit my love of good food from my mother and father. I was raised in a remote area of rural New South Wales, Australia, by vegetarian parents who grew and cooked everything we ate. My parents migrated up the coast to a developing community farm before I could walk, because they wanted to live off the land as much as possible.

Our family home—an octagon-shaped, mud-brick house—was built around the kitchen. We all spent a great deal of time in that large open room washing, chopping, and cooking vegetables; sharing meals; and in winter, warming ourselves by the wood-burning stove.

My father designed and built the house with handmade, sun-dried mud bricks; reclaimed wood and windows; and antique doors. When I was an infant, my mother bathed me in the kitchen sink; once I could sit up on my own, she perched me on the counter to keep an eye on me as she cooked our daily meals. I sampled whatever she happened to be making, and as soon as I could hold a spoon, the job of stirring (and tasting) cake batters was mine. Before long, I graduated to using a small knife and chopped the chives and parsley picked from the garden that we added to almost all our meals.

As a child, a weekly high point for me was helping my father make our bread. He would set me up at a low table so I was able to knead the dough. I loved creating my own minirolls from the excess dough, which I filled with dried fruit and spices.

My sister and I were involved in everything my parents did: keeping bees, brewing ginger beer, making tofu, molding the mud bricks to build the house, creating biodynamic preparations for the property, and grinding wheat into flour. We were also part of the process of planting, harvesting, and cooking the food we ate; inevitably composting our food scraps, which were eventually used to fertilize the garden.

There were no stores within a thirty-mile radius of where we lived, so being well prepared on the food front was ingrained from an early age. Besides growing fruits, vegetables, and herbs on our land, my parents ordered bulk grains, nuts, seeds, dried fruits, and olive oil, which sat in jars on a big old dresser in the kitchen. The image of those large jars filled with wholesome ingredients has been central to inspiring me to create new recipes over these many years as a chef.

In addition to having a well-stocked pantry at home, we packed meals whenever we went on road trips; my mother still travels with a picnic blanket and a "billy can" (Australian campfire kettle) in her trunk. Sipping tea and eating delicious homemade food out in nature—on remote beaches or in subtropical rain forests—is something we frequently did. Today, I do this as often as possible and think of it as one of life's greatest luxuries.

It never occurred to me when I was growing up that as we ate from the garden, collected milk in jars from a local bio-dynamic farmer, composted and collected rainwater, we were living an ecofriendly lifestyle. This cycle of growing, harvesting, cooking, eating, composting, and fertilizing was deeply rooted in us. Even now, though I live in downtown Manhattan, I continue to compost every food scrap that is created in my kitchen by making biweekly trips to the Lower East Side Ecology Center's compost bins at the Union Square farmers' market. After lightening my load, I then fill my bags with fresh vegetables, and the ever-rewarding cycle begins again.

I attribute my reverence for nature and obsession for seeking out the best-tasting whole foods to spending countless hours in our garden as a child. There I sampled everything we grew and often made herb-vegetable combinations in my mouth as I walked the paths that divided the tiered garden beds. Those vegetables I casually sampled on a daily basis made a huge impact on my taste buds. I am always seeking ingredients that match the integrity of the produce I grew up with and honoring it with recipes that bring out its best qualities. This is what I strive for as a chef.

The first time I set foot in a working kitchen was at my favorite café in inner-city Sydney. I got a job there through word of mouth (and lots of enthusiasm!) working the espresso machine and waiting tables. I often found myself helping out in the busy kitchen during the lunch rush and would step in when they were short-handed, making the daily specials.

I worked hard and learned a lot in that bustling little café.

During this period, I was living with friends who followed a macrobiotic diet. Through them and the local macrobiotic restaurant (which quickly became my favorite), I was introduced to the idea of food as medicine. In the short time I lived in Sydney, I cooked a lot and shared many meals with both new and old friends: we ground millet for porridge, roasted copious amounts of vegetables, discovered the endless possibilities of tahini sauce, and experimented with vegan desserts—just because my awareness for healthy ingredients was expanding, I still didn't consider missing out on dessert! I found I actually preferred the flavor of desserts made with natural sweeteners, nuts, and fruit. The challenge of creating a delicious dessert in its own right, without using animal products or refined ingredients, captivated my interest.

I was itching to travel, and less than a year later, I arrived in Amsterdam and continued my food journey, this time in a Japanese macrobiotic restaurant, once again waiting tables. Eating the daily staff meal was an education in home-style Japanese food and kept me curious; on my days off, I replicated what I ate for friends and continued my exploration of vegan, whole-food desserts. To my delight, the owner of the restaurant noticed my interest and zeal for cooking and offered me a position as pastry chef. I was given a few training sessions on traditional Japanese desserts, which solidified my understanding for the way agar and kuzu work and gave me the keys to create any vegan dessert I could imagine. Once my foot was in the kitchen door, I got the chance to learn from some very talented macrobiotic chefs, and in addition to the desserts, I started preparing the daily "bento box" specials.

Though I still didn't consciously realize that I was moving deeper and deeper into a career in food, it did excite me that I had built a small following, and my desserts started selling out nightly. Planning menus and envisioning new flavor combinations occupied my mind and started keeping me up at night. I was inspired by the endless possibilities that food held and bounded out of bed at five a.m., when the quiet kitchen gave me the space to create. I felt so happy and fortunate to be able to dream up desserts and then create them at work.

Through these early years in my career, I knew I wanted to eat food that tasted great and nourished my body (with indulgences, of course!) while having a minimal environmental impact. I also remained strongly drawn to honoring a connection to nature and the way food has the ability to act as a catalyst for this. As my knowledge about the benefits of vegan and macrobiotic diets deepened, the world of plant-based whole foods commanded my full attention; its seemingly endless possibilities still inspire me as much today as they did when I was first starting out as a chef. Though the structure of cooking this way grabbed my attention, I also wanted to find ways to infuse my food with the element of celebration with which I was raised, the festive quality that I think defines many Australians' approach to food.

Some of my most vivid food memories are of my mother's parties. She routinely invited people to celebrate holidays and special occasions, setting long tables with antique plates and linen napkins, serving champagne, and often entertaining with live music. All the food was either made by us or prepared by the neighbors and friends in attendance. I took to the role of hostess at a young age and, along with the rest of the family, was involved in every aspect of the party from cocktails to dessert. Besides food for the main event, my mother would often prepare late-night pastas and breakfast the following day for the guests who had stayed over.

Looking back, it's no surprise that I moved from Amsterdam to London to found a catering business with my dear friend, Rosada Hayes. The business was based on our shared passion for vibrant, delectable, healthy food and lavish vegan and wheat-free desserts. Together we constantly created new dishes and planned seemingly endless menus for all sorts of events and parties. In that highly creative time, I finally and fully embraced my life path as a chef.

My journey deepened further when I followed my heart to New York City and moved to an apartment a block from the Union Square farmers' market. Although I had grown up eating homegrown vegetables, food miles and microseasons were not concepts I had been aware of, and never in my life had I seen such an abundance of local, organic produce. To this day, I am able to stay intricately connected to the seasons through that market and feel blessed to live just a short walk away.

One of my first meals in New York was at Angelica Kitchen, the city's most famous and long-standing vegan restaurant. I got a job working there not long after, first as pastry chef and then as executive chef. At Angelica Kitchen, I experienced the most challenging and rewarding restaurant work I have done. I got down to the nitty-gritty of using truly local food and took great care to center the daily meals around seasonal ingredients, while keeping them healthy, tasty, and beautiful. I learned firsthand what it means to build relationships with growers and how those relationships are imperative to sustaining ethical business practices. Some farmers have been providing Angelica Kitchen with produce, tofu, or sea vegetables for more than thirty-five years; it was an honor to witness those deep ties and to cook with the freshest, locally grown produce available. In that busy 24/7 kitchen, I was fortunate to be able to absorb the exceptional knowledge of the many past and present chefs who have cooked there. The culinary challenges that I was faced with at Angelica pushed me out of my comfort zone and helped solidify my approach to food.

I moved on from Angelica Kitchen to work as a recipe developer and private chef and have had the pleasure of cooking for people who value the thought and effort that goes into sourcing sustainable organic ingredients and preparing them in ways that enhance nutrition. Again, the farmers' market is central to what and how I cook, be it a cleansing diet or special multicourse dinner. The produce there is my trusty guide and barometer, as well as my primary source of inspiration.

Ultimately, my favorite thing about working with food has been sharing my knowledge with others, whether by teaching cooking classes or through my blog. I love introducing people to the nightly rituals of soaking grains, beans, and nuts and how the routine of cooking can inspire and delight not just the cook but everyone involved. Today, nothing gives me greater pleasure than seeing people excited by a trip to the farmers' market, what they can make, how they feel, and a new practice that enriches their life.

Cooking is something I began doing to make a living and to nourish and ground myself in different parts of the world while I was looking for the career I really wanted—at that time, I didn't realize cooking would be that career. The pleasure of choosing ingredients and creating meals kept me company in the early days of navigating new cities, whether it was Sydney, Amsterdam, London, or New York. Then and today, food continues to keep me connected to nature, to my past, and to the people I cook and eat with. The more I learn about the nutritional benefits of eating a diet of real whole foods, the more I want to cook—and vice versa.

The recipes in this book, like my diet, are over 90 percent vegan. I always choose real whole-food ingredients over anything processed and would rather leave the cheese out than eat a processed vegan cheese with questionable ingredients—when given the choice, I will always choose real butter over a processed (vegan) margarine. I use local goat dairy products and occasionally yogurt as a garnish and a way to enrich meals; this way I'm not always relying on avocados, nuts, and seeds to add richness (none of which are local to the region where I live). So choosing a vegetarian diet over a vegan one means that I can support a variety of local farmers and artisans.

Through this book, my intention is to inspire you to seek out ingredients that have been grown with reverence for the environment, find a deeper connection to the natural world, and above all else, to cook more. This way we can participate in a healthy, sustainable food system that truly nourishes us all. This book is the culmination of my life with food thus far, and I hope it will inspire you on your own food journey.

Amy Chaplin
NEW YORK CITY

PART ONE

the pantry

A well-stocked whole-food pantry has always been a place of inspiration and magic for me. As a small child, I was mesmerized by the stories in Jill Barklem's book series Brambly Hedge. Her tales about a community of mice living in roots and tree trunks, in harmony with nature, are beautifully illustrated with detailed drawings of their day-to-day activities. The cozy, productive kitchens she conjured captured my attention—especially the tall, wooden dressers lined with the jars of berries, roots, and nuts that the mice collected. There was bread rising by the stove, cakes on stands, pots of bramble jelly, bunches of drying herbs, steaming cups of tea, and a kettle always boiling on the open fire.

These scenes evoked in me a desire to participate in the wholesome culinary adventures of the characters. The fact is that a well-stocked kitchen and pantry still induces a deep urge in me to create nourishing food. When faced with jars of grains, beans, nuts, and seeds, I see not only their beauty but also their potential to nourish and heal while being pleasurable and delicious to eat.

The ingredients in my pantry are not confined to the shelves and cupboards; they are also part of a well-stocked fridge, carrying a wealth of nutritious condiments, hardy greens, and fermented vegetables that I turn to when creating quick meals on a daily basis. The pantry also includes vegetables and fruits that sit out on the kitchen counter—here you'll find bowls and platters filled with local produce that changes depending on the season.

Having a well-stocked pantry is vital for creating delicious and varied meals, whether you're planning ahead or you need something fast.

my pantry essentials

Storing your pantry ingredients in glass jars is the best way to see (and use) what you have on hand. Having a collection of jars in all sizes means that you can purchase items in bulk, which is more environmentally sound and economical. You can recycle empty jars from condiments or whatever you happen to have finished. (To remove labels, soak jars in hot, soapy water; some come off more easily than others!) A good stockpile of recycled jars is also handy for storing prepared food—like soaked chia seeds, chopped parsley, almond milk, and leftover soups, stews, and grains—in the fridge. You can also use them as to-go containers for taking meals to work or sending friends home with leftovers. Since whole grains are more nutritious than refined grains, bugs are drawn more to whole grains. A tightly sealed jar is the best way to keep critters out.

I don't label my grains, except for brown basmati and jasmine rice, because they look so similar. If you have a variety of whole grains that are new to you, then labeling is a good idea.

Store any grain and nut flours that you don't use frequently in the freezer because keeping them cold ensures a longer life and fresher taste. Place them in reusable containers and label them. If you have space in the freezer, store nuts that you don't use regularly there as well.

In the Resources section at the back of this book, you'll find the brands that I seek out and use in my own kitchen.

WHOLE GRAINS

For thousands of years, ancient people cultivated grains from common grasses which contain nutrients essential for human development, vitality, and prevention of disease.

—**PAUL PITCHFORD,** HEALING WITH WHOLE FOODS

I find whole grains infinitely intriguing, as well as delicious, and have never come across one I didn't like. The vast array of textures, colors, flavors, and nutrients that are available through grains are immense. They each have their own unique healing properties and contain all necessary nutrient groups—carbohydrates, protein, fats, vitamins, minerals, and fiber—that help boost immunity and maintain health and balance. In addition to the grains listed here, some others I have in rotation are hulled (whole-grain) barley, brown jasmine rice, brown basmati rice, red rice, wild rice, and emmer wheat, an Old-World grain that is the original farro.

1. FORBIDDEN BLACK RICE 2. AMARANTH 3. WHEAT BERRIES 4. BUCKWHEAT 5. TEFF 6. MILLET 7. SPELT BERRIES 8. BLACK QUINOA 9. SWEET BROWN RICE 10. SHORT-GRAIN BROWN RICE 11. CORN GRITS 12. ROLLED OATS 13. EMMER 14. WILD RICE 15. QUINOA

AMARANTH

Amaranth is a flowering plant whose tiny seeds can be eaten as a grain. Like quinoa, amaranth is an ancient grain from the high valleys of the Andes, a richly nutritious food that is exceptionally high in protein and calcium. It has a delightfully sweet and nutty flavor with an enchanting corn-like aroma. When cooked with brown rice or quinoa, it adds a sticky quality; when cooked alone, it is best served as a porridge or "grits." Amaranth also pops like popcorn, as you'll find in the Amaranth Muesli (page 130) and Golden Amaranth Superfood Bars (page 347). You can even eat amaranth's pretty pink leaves; look for them at farmers' markets in summer and early autumn.

BUCKWHEAT

Buckwheat is not technically a grain—it is the seed of a plant related to rhubarb—but it is used like one. It is sold both toasted, which is called kasha, and raw. I like both but usually choose the untoasted buckwheat so I can soak it to activate the nutrients (see page 61) or toast it myself. Buckwheat is a gluten-free, blood-building food that helps clean and strengthen intestines and lower blood pressure. Its flavor is robust and earthy, which goes perfectly with the sweetness of onions (page 65). Buckwheat is fast cooking, with a light texture that is surprisingly substantial and warming.

CORN GRITS

Corn grits are slightly coarser than Italian polenta (in both the grind of corn and the finished dish) but can be used in the same way. I had never cooked with corn grits until moving to the United States; there are far fewer varieties of corn products in Europe and Australia. When using corn grits to make polenta, I find their coarser texture more interesting, and it is less likely to become lumpy. Look for local stone-ground corn grits at farmers' markets, and always buy organic corn products—anything else is most likely genetically modified. Keep corn grits on hand for times when you forget to soak grains; they cook in 20 minutes and are great with sautéed greens, beans, tomato sauces, and even a simple drizzle of olive oil and chopped parsley. I also grind them (in a spice grinder) to make cornmeal for the Blackberry Cornmeal Muffins (page 133).

FORBIDDEN BLACK RICE

Black rice has all the health-promoting properties of brown rice but with the added benefit of anthocyanin, a plant-based pigment also found in dark berries and acai. This pigment is what gives the rice its gorgeous deep purple color and its antioxidant and anti-inflammatory properties. Although the color is dark and dramatic, the flavor is mild, nutty, and slightly sweet. I use it in many different ways, as in the recipes for Black Rice Breakfast Pudding with Coconut and Banana (page 145) and Black Sesame Rice Crackers (page 218), or as a side dish for Coconut Curry with Tamarind Tempeh (page 274).

MILLET

Millet is a lovely, sunny-colored, fast-cooking, gluten-free grain with a high amino-acid protein profile. It has a nutty, earthy flavor and is the only grain that has an alkalizing effect on the blood due to its high alkaline ash content, which also makes it easy to digest. Millet also helps strengthen kidney function and contains more iron than any other cereal grain. Cook millet up light and fluffy like in Plum Millet Muffins (page 142) or soft as in the Millet, Squash, and Sweet Corn Pilaf (page 138); it can also be cooked for longer with extra water and set like polenta. Of all the grains I keep on hand, I make sure millet is stored with a very tight seal, as it tends to attract bugs. It has a natural protective bitter coating called saponin, so be sure to wash it thoroughly before cooking.

QUINOA

Quinoa is one of my favorite grains. It's a nutrient-rich, energy-building food that contains more calcium than milk and all nine essential amino acids, making it a complete protein. Originally from the highlands of the Andes, quinoa is an ancient grain that was first cultivated more than six thousand years ago and was considered a sacred staple food of the Incas. It cooks fast, and it has a light texture and mild, nutty flavor that works well in both sweet and savory preparations. I reach for pearl quinoa regularly, as it cooks up softer than red or black quinoa, which I find are best added to dishes that benefit from a seedlike crunch. Like millet, quinoa is coated with saponin, a bitter-tasting natural substance that protects it from bugs, so it needs to be washed thoroughly before cooking. Soaked quinoa will sprout quickly (see sprouting instructions on page 79).

ROLLED OATS

Oats help soothe and restore the nervous system, lower cholesterol, and regulate weight. In traditional Chinese medicine, they are used as a qi (energy)-building tonic. I use rolled oats in many dishes; primarily, as part of my daily breakfast, ground in tart crusts, and added to cookies. I prefer the texture of regular rolled oats or old-fashioned rolled oats over quick oats, which are cut smaller and cook faster. Choose old-fashioned rolled oats if you like a heartier textured oatmeal. Oats are naturally gluten-free but are usually processed in facilities that also process wheat and other gluten grains, so look for certified gluten-free oats if you are allergic to gluten.

SHORT-GRAIN BROWN RICE

Besides being my favorite grain, brown rice is also one of the most nutritious; it contains more than seventy antioxidants, all necessary amino acids, magnesium, iron, minerals, and the highest amount of B vitamins of any grain. It helps to purify the blood, expel toxins, and balance blood sugar levels. Short-grain brown rice is nuttier and stickier than the long-grain variety, and I'd happily eat it every day.

SPELT

Spelt is an ancient, unhybridized wheat that is higher in protein and fiber, lower in gluten (though not gluten-free), and easier to digest than regular wheat. I love the chewy texture and nutty flavor of whole spelt berries in salads like the Herbed Spelt Berry Salad with Peas and Feta (page 183) or stirred into stews such as the Roasted Fall Vegetable Cannellini Bean Stew with Spelt Berries and Kale (page 269). Like millet, spelt tends to attract bugs more than other grains, so be sure to store it in a tightly sealed jar.

SWEET BROWN RICE

I add this grain to my regular pot of brown rice for a wonderfully sweet and sticky result. It is easy to digest, strengthening for the kidneys and stomach, and higher in protein than short-grain brown rice. When cooked alone, it is best served as a porridge, as it can be quite wet. Sweet rice can also be cooked and pounded to make mochi, a sticky Japanese rice cake.

TEFF

Teff is a tiny (smaller than amaranth), ancient seed that is native to Ethiopia, where the flour is used to make a fermented pancake called injera. Like quinoa and amaranth, teff is rich in protein and calcium. When cooked alone, it can be eaten as a porridge or set like polenta. When cooking brown rice or quinoa, I like to add a few tablespoons of these tiny seeds for protein and texture. Teff flour is fun to experiment with; its rich, earthy, and chocolaty flavor is great in waffles. You can replace all the flour with teff flour in most recipes with good results. Since teff is gluten-free, start by replacing a small amount of the flour in your recipes.

WHOLE-GRAIN CRACKERS

Crackers are always good to have on hand to enjoy with soups or spreads and for snacking. My favorites are rye crackers, brown rice crackers, and black sesame crackers. You can also make your own Black Sesame Rice Crackers (page 218).

WHOLE-GRAIN NOODLES AND PASTAS

It's a good idea to keep a selection of whole-grain pasta on hand, I especially like spelt, kamut, and whole-wheat for last-minute, pasta dinners. Whole-wheat udon noodles are lovely for cooling summer salads like the Whole-Wheat Udon Noodle Salad with Sautéed Peppers, Sweet Corn, and Spicy Sesame Marinade (page 188). When it comes to soba noodles, look for those made with 100 percent buckwheat; otherwise they are combined with more than half refined wheat flour.

BEANS AND LEGUMES

Although I stock just about every bean you can find, this is a short list of my must-haves. Since all beans benefit the kidneys, I like to think of them not only as an excellent healthy source of protein but also as a way to support kidney-adrenal function, which is increasingly important in our fast-paced lives.

The flavor of home-cooked beans is far superior to anything you'll find in a can, although I do keep a few cans on hand for making quick pâtés and spreads (see page 45 for hints on how to improve the flavor of canned beans). Cooking beans yourself is very simple and fast if you invest in a pressure cooker (the Equipment section has suggestions on choosing pressure cookers; and cooking instructions for beans are on page 68). Once you get the basic method down, the possibilities are endless—marinated with olive oil, mashed, puréed, or made into warming soups or stews.

When beans are stored in clear glass jars, not only can you enjoy their beauty, but you'll also get inspiration for what to cook just by looking at the variety of colors and shapes. I purchase 4 to 6 cups of beans at a time and usually use them within six months, but they'll keep a lot longer. The older the bean, the longer it takes to cook, so it is best to buy them in bulk from a place with a high turnover to ensure that they are fresh and will cook evenly, with a creamy interior. In addition to the beans and legumes listed here, I also like to have pinto, cannellini or navy, green split peas, and beluga lentils on hand.

1. SCARLET RUNNER BEANS 2. MUNG BEANS
3. CHRISTMAS LIMA BEANS 4. CHICKPEAS
5. BLACK BEANS 6. RED LENTILS 7. FRENCH LENTILS
8. FRESH CRANBERRY BEANS 9. ADZUKI BEANS
10. BLACK CALYPSO BEANS 11. CRANBERRY BEANS
12. KIDNEY BEANS 13. GREEN SPLIT PEA
14. WHITE RUNNER BEANS

ADZUKI BEANS

Adzuki beans are small, deep purply red beans with an earthy, slightly sweet flavor. They cook faster than most other beans and do not require a pressure cooker to achieve a soft, creamy texture. They are used in traditional Japanese medicine to tonify kidney-adrenal function and also appear in Japanese desserts. I love them warm, seasoned with tamari, or combined with sweet rice (page 280). They are also great in soups, especially the Hearty Winter Miso Soup with Adzuki Beans, Squash, and Ginger (page 174).

BLACK BEANS

According to Traditional Chinese Medicine, the color black is beneficial in supporting healthy kidney function (see black sesame seeds) and since all beans support the kidneys, these beans, being black have double the strength. I especially love using black beans in soups and stews, like Spicy Black Bean Stew (page 264) or partially mashed in a simple sauce for rice or tacos.

BABY LIMA BEANS

Baby limas are perfect for making soup, because they cook relatively fast and melt partially, creating a great creamy background for any vegetable you choose to add. They are wonderful paired with squash and sage in autumn and with dill and tomato in summer. Limas are one of the few beans I don't cook in a pressure cooker, as their skins separate and can block the pressure valve.

CHICKPEAS

Chickpeas are my all-time favorite bean. When cooked well, they are creamy, rich, and tasty, requiring little to enhance their flavor. They contain more iron and vitamin C than any legume, and according to Traditional Chinese Medicine, they support the stomach, spleen, pancreas, and heart. Try them mashed, marinated, in salads, or smashed and shaped into savory cakes. You'll find plenty of recipes in this book celebrating the greatness of chickpeas.

HEIRLOOM BEANS

Heirloom beans, like other heirloom plants, come from seeds that have been grown for generations and remain untouched by genetic science and modern technology. These plants have all their inherent intelligence and nutrition intact and are exactly as nature intended. Including a couple of heirloom bean varieties in your pantry is a great way to add excitement to your weekly bean-cooking routine: their flavor, colors, and textures are sublime and make any simple soup, salad, or stew special.

Look for heirloom beans in health-food stores, gourmet food shops, or online. My favorites are all the runner beans—scarlet, white, black, and purple—Anasazi, borlotti, Christmas lima, rio zape, and cranberry. You can also find fresh heirloom beans at farmers' markets in late summer and early fall. These are a real treat and need nothing more than a drizzle of olive oil and a pinch of salt to highlight their flavor. No need to soak them, just shell them and simmer until tender.

FRENCH LENTILS

Lentils have one of the highest protein contents of all legumes; they also have no sulfur, making them a great transitional food for people new to digesting beans. French lentils cook up quickly and maintain their lovely, symmetrical, pebble-like shape and color. They are incredibly delicious in a simple marinade of lemon and olive oil (page 71). Their earthy flavor is perfect for autumn soups like the French Lentil Soup with Rosemary, Squash, and Rainbow Chard (page 167).

MUNG BEANS

Easily digested, soothing, and detoxifying, mung beans also support healthy liver and gallbladder function. Olive green in color and similar in size and shape to adzuki beans, they are also quick to prepare and are better cooked by simmering than by pressure-cooking. My favorite way to eat them is in dals or in Kitchari (page 175). They also sprout easily (see page 79 for instructions).

RED KIDNEY BEANS

Deep red and larger than most common beans, kidneys have a luscious, creamy smooth texture that is perfect for marinating, as they hold their shape and absorb flavors well. They are great in hearty stews, soups, and salads. When large heirloom beans are not available, I substitute kidney beans in the Heirloom Bean Bourguignon with Celery Root Mash (page 283).

RED LENTILS

Red lentils have the outer hull removed, which means they don't contain phytic acid and do not need to be soaked (see page 58). Red lentils cook fast and become creamy in very little time, making them great for quick soups, dals, and sauces. You can't go wrong when seasoning them, because they seem to go with everything from aromatic spices, chilies, curry blends, and coconut to lemon, mint, garlic, and any fresh herb you may have on hand. I never seem to tire of the Simple Red Lentil Soup with Spinach, Lemon, and Pepper (page 91).

NUTS AND SEEDS

A whole-food pantry isn't complete without a good variety of nuts and seeds. Not only do they enrich and add interest to everyday meals and snacks, but they are also an essential part of many of the cookies and desserts in this book. Organic nuts and seeds can sometimes be costly, but seek them out when possible, as pesticides concentrate in their oils. I highly recommend purchasing them raw, so you can decide whether you want to soak them for making milks or toast them for other uses.

As with anything oily, it is best to store nuts in glass; their high oil content can leach toxins from the plastic (see page 53). Store nuts or seeds that you don't use frequently in the fridge or freezer to keep them fresh. In addition to the nuts and seeds listed in this section, I also like to stock pecans, pine nuts, hazelnuts, and macadamia nuts.

1. PINE NUTS 2. WALNUTS 3. SUNFLOWER SEEDS
4. CASHEWS 5. PUMPKIN SEEDS 6. AUSTRIAN
PUMPKIN SEEDS 7. PISTACHIOS 8. HAZELNUTS
9. MACADAMIA NUTS 10. ALMONDS 11. BLACK
SESAME SEEDS 12. UNHULLED SESAME SEEDS
13. PECANS 14. BRAZIL NUTS

ALMONDS

I use almonds more than any other nut—they're high in calcium, iron, vitamin E, and several B vitamins; they're also the only nut that has an alkalizing effect on the blood. Like most other nuts and seeds, their nutrients are activated after being soaked overnight. This makes them easier to digest (see the notes on phytic acid on page 58). For this reason, it's important to seek out unpasteurized almonds; otherwise, they are not truly raw and can't be activated. Almonds labeled raw from California are now legally required to be pasteurized. At this time, unpasteurized almonds can only be sold direct from farmers (see the Resources section). Organic almonds from Italy and Spain are not required to be pasteurized before being packaged and sold, and they can be found in some health-food stores and co-ops. Ayurvedic medicine recommends that you remove the skin from almonds after soaking for easier digestion; I do this in a couple of desserts, since it's difficult to find organic blanched almonds, and it's really easy to slip off their skins after an overnight soak.

My favorite way to enjoy the naturally sweet taste of almonds is in a nut milk made from soaked almonds, cinnamon, and vanilla (page 74). Almonds are also scrumptious toasted (page 77) and blended into Toasted Almond Butter (page 117).

BRAZIL NUTS

These nuts from the Amazon basin are one of the richest sources of selenium, a mineral that helps regulate thyroid function; promote healthy skin, hair, and nails; and protect cells from free radical damage. In the rare case that I need a change from almond milk, I make a batch of Brazil nut milk for a subtle, tropical-tasting treat.

CASHEWS

Originally from Brazil, cashews are rich in zinc, magnesium, and selenium. Since cashews don't have a skin, they don't need to be soaked overnight to remove phytic acid (see page 58). However, soaking them for a few hours helps to achieve a silky smooth consistency when making nut milk. Cashew milk requires no straining, as the nut completely dissolves when blended. Cashews are great for adding a rich, creamy quality to vegan desserts like Vanilla Chia Pudding (page 111) and Cashew Cinnamon Cream (page 322), and can also be made into a tangy cheese (page 217). Most cashews labeled as raw are not truly raw because they are heated to remove them from their shells—for superior flavor and nutrition, seek out truly raw cashews from specialty raw food suppliers.

PISTACHIOS

The vibrant green and pink colors of pistachios add effortless beauty and interest to sweet and savory dishes alike. They're also a great source of potassium, iron, and calcium. Pistachios are wonderful to have on hand for jazzing up simple meals—

for example, try toasting them and sprinkling them over cooked quinoa with olive oil, lemon juice, and lots of chopped fresh herbs. Purchase pistachios raw, with or without their shell.

PUMPKIN SEEDS

Pumpkin seeds, when toasted until crisp and fragrant, make the perfect snack—they have a satisfying, nutty flavor without being too rich. I also love sprinkling them over grains and salads or toasting them with cayenne and lime (page 77). They're a good source of omega-3 fatty acids, zinc, and iron, and they are higher in protein than many other seeds. Look for Austrian pumpkin seeds, an heirloom variety with a beautiful dark green color and larger size than most pumpkin seeds—they make a striking garnish or addition to granola and mueslis. The oil from Austrian pumpkin seeds is fragrant and richly textured, great for drizzling over soups and salads.

SESAME SEEDS

I love toasted sesame seeds for their rich flavor and the way they make any simple bowl of grains or steamed vegetables look appealing. Always seek out unhulled black or brown sesame seeds rather than the hulled white variety; the nutritious hull helps the liver metabolize their high fat content. Since tahini made from unhulled sesame seeds is rare in the United States, I've included a recipe (page 115) so you can make your own. Black sesame seeds have a stronger flavor and are higher in minerals than brown; they're used in Traditional Chinese Medicine to strengthen kidney function. I keep a jar of toasted black sesame seeds in the fridge for sprinkling over quick meals or for making Black Sesame Gomasio (page 114).

SUNFLOWER SEEDS

High in protein and a good source of calcium and iron, sunflower seeds are an excellent addition to your pantry. They can be soaked and activated (see page 73) to use in seed milks or stirred into oatmeal, or you can toast them for a light, sweet flavor and crunchy texture that elevates grain-based dishes and salads such as Parsley Brown Rice Salad with Seeds (page 97).

WALNUTS

Walnuts are highly regarded in Traditional Chinese Medicine for their kidney-toning properties. High in omega-3 oils, they also support brain function and can help reduce inflammation. Walnuts have a rich texture, making them great as a substitute for pine nuts in pesto and as the base of a lovely nut butter. Although they can also be soaked before eating, I enjoy them most toasted (page 78) and combined with goji berries as a snack and in desserts, cookies, or salads.

SUPERFOODS

In a healthy whole-food kitchen, so many of the foods stocked in the pantry and fridge can be categorized as superfoods. These are functional foods that have been used to promote health and healing by traditional cultures for millennia; they are often from remote regions at high altitudes and have only recently become more widely available. Here is a short list of items that are particularly dense in nutrients, with abundant antioxidants, minerals, phytochemicals, and vitamins. Since many of these foods come from developing nations, be sure that the products you purchase are certified fair trade.

1. SOFT-DRIED GOJI BERRIES 2. CHIA SEEDS
3. BEE POLLEN 4. GOJI BERRIES 5. MACA ROOT POWDER
6. FRESH GOLDEN BERRIES 7. GOJI POWDER
8. GOLDEN BERRIES 9. HEMP SEEDS 10. DRIED
MULBERRIES 11. POMEGRANATE POWDER 12. FLAX
SEEDS 13. POMEGRANATE JUICE

BEE POLLEN

Bee pollen is a potent, nourishing food that has been used throughout history to increase energy and vitality and to promote growth and development. Bee pollen provides nearly all the nutrients necessary to humans, including protein, B vitamins, antioxidants, and amino acids. Because it comes from the pollen of trees and flowers, eating local bee pollen can be an effective treatment for seasonal allergies. Bee pollen has a strong, bittersweet, honey-like taste, and as with honey, its flavor and color vary depending on the plant pollen from which it originates. To incorporate bee pollen into your diet, try sprinkling it over smoothies, fruit, yogurt, or your favorite breakfast dishes.

CHIA SEEDS

Chia seeds are the second highest plant source of omega-3 fatty acids (after flax); one of the most digestible plant proteins; and an excellent source of amino acids, minerals, and antioxidants. They were used by ancient Native American civilizations as an energy-boosting endurance food. Chia seeds should be eaten raw after being soaked in liquid to "bloom" (page 73). They thicken any liquid they are added to, creating the luscious consistency of my most popular dessert, Vanilla Chia Pudding (page 111), and my summer breakfast staple, Soaked Oats and Chia (page 88). Being mucilaginous seeds (those that thicken the liquid they're soaked in), they're great for intestinal health, and unlike flax, you don't need to grind them to benefit from their nutritional value.

DRIED MULBERRIES

Mulberries originate from the Far East and were used in Traditional Chinese Medicine to strengthen the liver and kidneys and to build blood. Like wine, mulberries contain the heart-healthy and antiaging antioxidant resveratrol. They also contain iron and calcium and have a sweet, caramel-like flavor when cooked. I use mulberries in my Superfood Oatmeal (page 87) and Golden Amaranth Superfood Bars (page 347). They also make a tasty addition to trail mixes.

FLAX SEEDS

Flax seeds are the highest known plant source of omega-3 fatty acids, which help support cardiovascular health, reduce inflammation, strengthen immunity, and contribute to healthy brain function. The seeds need to be ground for their nutrients to be absorbed—for the best flavor, grind half a cup at a time in a clean coffee or spice grinder, store it in a jar in the fridge or freezer to prevent oxidation, and use it within a couple of weeks. Enjoy their nutty flavor daily sprinkled over oatmeal, granola, fruit salads, and steamed vegetables. Whole flax seeds can be soaked in water overnight and added to smoothies for a thicker texture and nutritional boost. Ground flax seeds can be mixed with water and used in place of eggs in vegan baking (see page 73). If you are purchasing preground flax seeds, look for sprouted flax powder.

GOJI BERRIES

Goji berries are one of the most nutrient-rich foods available. Packed with antioxidants, trace minerals, essential amino acids, vitamin C, and beta-carotene and loaded with immune-boosting and antiaging properties, goji berries have been used in Asian herbal medicine for thousands of years to preserve youth and promote well-being. Earthy, slightly astringent, and mildly sweet, goji berries have a peculiar flavor that grows on you, especially when you know how potent they are—eating an ounce a day will allow you to benefit from all their nutrients. I stock goji berries in a few forms: dried berries for cooking in daily breakfasts or soaking and adding to smoothies; a soft-dried berry that's moist and chewy, making it perfect for snacking or adding to granola and muesli; and a goji powder that dissolves in cool or warm water for a vibrant orange immune-boosting drink.

GOLDEN BERRIES

Sometimes called cape gooseberries or Incan berries, golden berries can be found fresh in summer and fall at farmers' markets and are also available sun-dried. They taste sweet when eaten fresh and have a bright, sour flavor when dried. Golden berries are rich in antioxidants and beta-carotene and unusually high in protein. I keep dried golden berries on hand for snacking and enjoy them added to trail mixes and granola for a tangy surprise.

HEMP SEEDS

Shelled hemp seeds, also known as hemp hearts, are rich in digestible protein and contain all essential amino acids, omega-3 fatty acids, and gamma-linoleic acid (GLA)—an omega-6 fatty acid that helps reduce inflammation, improve brain function, maintain bone health, and facilitate weight loss. Hemp seeds have a great creamy texture and mild grassy flavor that complements both sweet and savory dishes. Sprinkle them over your daily breakfast, blend them into smoothies, or try the Simple Green Salad with Tangy Hemp Seed Dressing (page 94). To preserve the integrity of their polyunsaturated fatty acids, only consume hemp seeds raw. Like all hemp products (hemp oil and hemp butter), they should be stored in the fridge. Hemp seeds do not contain phytic acid (see page 58); therefore, they don't need to be soaked before they are added to meals or made into seed milk.

MACA ROOT POWDER

Maca is a potent superfood root native to Bolivia and Peru, where it was traditionally used as an endurance food to increase stamina and combat fatigue. Maca has adaptogenic properties that help our bodies adjust to stress, and the alkaloids in it support and nourish the endocrine system (thyroid, adrenals, and glandular system). It provides abundant minerals, vitamins, and fatty and amino acids and is also used to balance hormones and boost fertility. Maca root is eaten as a powder and can be purchased raw or gelatinized—gelatinized means that the starch is removed, which concentrates the active ingredients and makes it easier to digest. I really like the malty flavor of maca sprinkled over breakfast (Superfood Breakfast Sprinkle, page 117). Maca can also be added to smoothies and nut milks; start with a little until you get used to the flavor and then build up the amount to a teaspoon a day to enjoy all its benefits.

POMEGRANATE

Revered for millennia in traditional healing systems, pomegranates have been used to promote longevity and fertility. They contain abundant antioxidants and anti-inflammatory properties and are high in vitamin C, minerals, and amino acids. In the fall, when pomegranates are in season, add the seeds to salads or yogurt, or use them as a garnish for everything from breakfast to dessert. You can juice the fruit like you would an orange and drink it fresh, or use it to make Pomegranate Kanten (page 351). During winter, spring, and summer you can purchase pure, unsweetened organic pomegranate juice—not from concentrate—to drink as a health tonic. Freeze-dried pomegranate powder is handy for dissolving into warm or cool water for a refreshing drink or for adding to smoothies.

WHEAT GERM

Wheat germ is the most nutrient-dense part of whole wheat and is what is removed when whole-wheat kernels are refined into white flour. It contains a concentrated amount of essential nutrients: folic acid, magnesium, vitamin E and essential fatty acids, and B vitamins. I enjoy the light, nutty flavor and include it in my Superfood Breakfast Sprinkle (page 117). Wheat germ can be purchased raw or toasted; toasting increases its flavor, but the process causes it to lose some of its nutritional value. Keep either kind in the fridge to preserve freshness and nutrients.

OILS

Good-quality unrefined oils are an essential part of a healthy whole-food kitchen. Oil not only warms and energizes us, it protects and nourishes our vital organs; it also carries flavor and gives us a comforting, satiated feeling. Unrefined oils taste like the food they were pressed from and sometimes appear cloudy. They need to be stored in dark glass bottles away from heat and light. Some oils, like flax oil, must be refrigerated to preserve their high omega content. Store oils that you use infrequently in the fridge, and if the weather gets hot, it's a good idea to store all your unrefined oils there. If they're stored in wide-mouth jars, you can scoop out what you need rather than repeatedly melting the whole container (which can damage the oil).

Oils are refined to increase shelf life and keep them stable at high temperatures. At best, they lose all their flavor, aroma, and vital nutrients when repeatedly exposed to heat; at worst, they are extracted by petroleum-based solvents then bleached and chemically treated. Refined oils have an unpleasant mouthfeel and can have a seriously negative effect on your health, suppressing immune system function, compromising good digestion, and accelerating aging.

Eating good-quality oils is a challenge if you don't cook for yourself, as most restaurants and even "healthy" prepared-food manufacturers use refined oils in all or some stages of their food preparation.

Labeling can be confusing when it comes to oils, but the most important words to look for are unrefined (for sesame oil) and extra virgin (for olive and coconut oil).

Expeller-pressed simply means that the oil wasn't chemically extracted from the food.

Look for oils that are pressed below 120°F, away from heat and light. Many trusted producers put the press date on the bottle. As with nuts, pesticides concentrate in oils, so investing in organic oils is definitely worthwhile. It's also a good idea to get to know the smell of a fresh oil as it's the best gauge for rancidity. If oils don't smell fresh and nutty, don't use them. My list of oils is pretty short, because it's difficult to obtain truly unrefined oils, though I'm always on the lookout. In addition to those listed in this section, I occasionally use pumpkin seed oil and macadamia nut oil.

For high-heat cooking like panfrying, extra virgin coconut oil or ghee are the most stable oils to use. Extra virgin olive oil and unrefined sesame oil can withstand moderate heat, because they don't contain delicate omega-3 fatty acids. These oils should be heated just until fragrant—if the oil ripples in the pan or smokes, it has become toxic and should be discarded.

1. FLAX OIL 2. COCONUT OIL 3. UNTOASTED SESAME OIL 4. GHEE 5. TOASTED SESAME OIL 6. EXTRA VIRGIN OLIVE OIL 7. COCONUT BUTTER

COCONUT BUTTER

Coconut butter contains both the flesh and oil of the coconut, making it a whole-food product. Coconut butter can be made at home by blending dried coconut the same way you make nut butter. It's great for enriching desserts like Vanilla Chia Pudding (page 111) and is also good in smoothies and shakes such as the Peach Chia Breakfast Shake (page 137). It doesn't melt the same way coconut oil does and is therefore not good for sautéing or roasting. However, you can replace coconut butter with extra virgin coconut oil in the recipes in this book.

COLD PRESSED FLAX OIL

Flax oil has a rich, grassy flavor that's luscious drizzled over everything from greens and grains to toast and salad; it's the oil I use most in my day-to-day meals. Flax oil is a rich source of omega-3 fatty acids, which support healthy brain function, strengthen immunity, and help break down cholesterol. Flax oil should never be warmed or exposed to light, and it must be stored in a dark glass bottle in the refrigerator to preserve its nutrients.

EXTRA VIRGIN OLIVE OIL

Extra virgin olive oil has been used for thousands of years with appetizing and healthful results. It supports liver and gallbladder function and contains high levels of vitamin E. I love its rich, fruity flavor and versatility, and I use it to make everything from dressings to dessert. I keep two extra virgin olive oils on hand: a milder flavored one for general cooking, and a more assertive, grassy tasting one that is best used for drizzling, dipping, and dressings. Stored away from heat and light, olive oil will keep for about a year. Although the best olive oils are extra virgin, many are combined with refined olive oils. Look for labels that also say "unrefined."

GHEE

Ghee is made in a similar way to clarified butter—pure butter fat with the milk solids separated and removed. The difference with making ghee is that the butter is simmered longer, allowing the milk solids to caramelize. This process results in a uniquely aromatic butterscotch flavor. Ghee is used extensively in Indian and Ayurvedic cooking for its ability to enhance the healing benefits of food and aid in digestion. Since the milk solids are removed, ghee has a high smoke point, making it excellent for high-temperature cooking. I like the rich, soothing element it adds to Curried Socca with Cilantro Coconut Chutney (page 209) and Kitchari (page 175). Seek out ghee made from good-quality organic butter from pastured cows.

TOASTED SESAME OIL

Toasted sesame oil is great for adding an intense sesame flavor to dressings, marinades, and vegetables, as well as for finishing Asian-inspired dishes like Whole-Wheat Udon Noodle Salad with Sautéed Peppers, Sweet Corn, and Sesame Marinade (page 188). A little of this pungent oil goes a long way, so taste as you go. Although it is shelf stable, I keep mine in the fridge to extend its life, since a bottle tends to last a long time. You can also purchase hot pepper–infused toasted sesame oil, which adds a lively kick to noodles and dressings.

UNREFINED EXTRA VIRGIN COCONUT OIL

Coconut oil in its purest form has antioxidant and anti-bacterial properties and contains 50 percent lauric acid, a medium-chain fatty acid also found in breast milk. Lauric acid boosts immunity and supports healthy brain function. Coconut oil is one of the only oils that is not damaged by high temperatures, making it ideal for high-heat cooking—sautéing, roasting, and panfrying. Although cholesterol-free, it is a saturated fat (solid at room temperature) and should be used sparingly by people with high cholesterol. Its saturated fat content makes it a great butter replacement in baked goods, especially crusts and cookies. It has a subtly sweet and fragrant taste that goes well with many flavors. (Extra virgin coconut oil is also a great makeup remover and moisturizer.) Since coconut oil is solid at room temperature, it needs to be melted first for accurate measuring. To melt it, place the jar in a bowl of hot water for a few minutes, then pour out what you need. You can also scoop out a little into a small pot and warm it until liquid; anything left over can be poured back into the jar.

UNREFINED SESAME OIL (UNTOASTED)

Unrefined sesame oil is to Asian cultures what olive oil is to the Mediterranean. Sesame oil has a lovely mild fragrance and toasty flavor and is perfect for medium-heat sautéing. Unre-fined sesame oil contains the antioxidants sesamol and sesamin that keep it from becoming rancid and make it shelf stable.

VINEGARS

Naturally fermented, unpasteurized, and unfiltered organic vinegars are an excellent pantry staple for tasty quick dressings, pickles, and marinades. Adding a dash of vinegar to bean dishes or other rich meals at the end of cooking enlivens and balances flavor. Traditionally brewed vinegar has many medicinal uses, both internally and externally, from providing relief from insect bites and sunburn to improving circulation and reducing toxic accumulations in the liver. High-quality vinegar contains amino acids and trace minerals; it also aids in digestion and detoxification. Besides the vinegars listed here, I often stock red wine vinegar too.

UNPASTEURIZED APPLE CIDER VINEGAR

Apple cider vinegar is my favorite everyday vinegar; its bright, fresh flavor is excellent as a seasoning, in dressings, and in marinades. As with all vinegars, make sure that the apple cider vinegar you purchase is naturally fermented, unpasteurized, and unfiltered to ensure you are getting all the healing benefits—restoring your internal acid-alkaline balance, boosting immunity, and normalizing weight. Apple cider vinegar is also used as a home remedy for soothing skin and disinfecting insect bites.

BALSAMIC VINEGAR (RED AND WHITE)

Red balsamic vinegar is great when you need to add richness and a touch of sweetness to dishes; I always add a splash to tomato-based soups and sauces and to caramelized onions. Traditionally made balsamic vinegar is aged no less than twelve years and up to fifty years, and it gets sweeter and more velvety with time. A good teenage balsamic is heavenly drizzled over anything from cheese to dessert. When purchasing balsamic (no matter what the age), make sure it doesn't have any thickeners or caramel coloring added.

White balsamic vinegar is lighter and sweeter than red, making it perfect for when you don't want to alter the color of a dish.

BROWN RICE VINEGAR

Traditionally brewed brown rice vinegar is a mellow, delicately flavored vinegar that is fermented with koji (a naturally occurring yeast used to make miso and sake) and perfect for everyday use. I love its refreshing flavor on brown rice and noodle salads, like the Parsley Brown Rice Salad with Seeds (page 97), and for adding a light tanginess to tofu cheeses. As with all fermented products, make sure you purchase a naturally fermented vinegar to avoid added sugars and chemical processes.

UME PLUM VINEGAR

Traditionally brewed ume plum vinegar (or *ume su*, in Japanese) is the treasured brine that is left after pickling umeboshi (Japanese ume plum with shiso leaves). It's the perfect seasoning, as it adds salt and tanginess at the same time. A few drops of ume plum vinegar is excellent for finishing bean soups and stews or in salad dressings; keep in mind that it's strong and you will need to reduce or eliminate the amount of salt you would normally use. Traditionally made ume plum vinegar has a delicate pink color from red shiso leaves; commercially manufactured versions contain red chemical dyes, preservatives, and additives and should be avoided.

SEASONING AND CONDIMENTS

Good-quality seasonings are just as important as good ingredients—they enhance flavors and add interest and depth without overpowering the food. I keep tamari, a pepper grinder, and a couple of different types of sea salt on the kitchen counter to use during cooking and for finishing dishes. Miso and umeboshi (paste, plums, or vinegar) are excellent alternatives to seasoning with salt.

MIRIN

Traditionally made mirin is a sweet rice cooking wine that is produced by brewing and fermenting sweet brown rice with koji (a naturally occurring yeast used to make miso and sake). While I generally prefer to keep my sweet ingredients out of savory food, I make an exception for mirin. Its delicate flavor pairs particularly well with seaweed dishes like Arame with Carrots and Sesame (page 107). Although more expensive, naturally brewed and fermented mirin is worth the cost, because a little goes a long way and most mirin found in Asian markets is sweetened with glucose or corn syrup and chemically brewed to speed production time.

MUSTARD

I love anything mustard: mustard greens, mustard seeds, and prepared mustard. A member of the cabbage family, mustard greens and the seeds are packed with anticancer compounds, promote circulation, and purify blood. Whole-grain Dijon mustard has a great texture and mild flavor and is by far my favorite for dressings and sandwiches. If I'm looking for something sharper, I opt for ground dijon, which is perfect in the Dijon Mustard–Marinated Tempeh (page 105). Many brands are available—just be sure to purchase one that is unsweetened and free of artificial preservatives. You'll also find black mustard seeds in my spice drawer for adding to curries, not only for their texture and pungent flavor, but also because they add a pretty color contrast.

UMEBOSHI PLUMS/PASTE

These salty, pickled Japanese plums are a great medicinal condiment to have around. A small piece on your tongue or a little paste dissolved in warm water helps relieve nausea, indigestion, and hangovers. You can purchase umeboshi plums whole or as a paste. I like cooking the whole plums into brown rice or congee in place of salt. Just like ume plum vinegar, a small amount of the paste adds a tangy and salty flavor to dressings and sauces and is great in nori rolls and rice balls. Make sure to buy umeboshi that is naturally fermented and additive-free. Once you open it, store the paste and plums in jars in the fridge, where they can last for years.

NATURALLY FERMENTED TAMARI OR SHOYU (SOY SAUCE)

I grew up with tamari always on the table; my family sprinkled it over everything we ate. I still use it almost daily and especially enjoy it on grains and steamed vegetables—a few drops can magically transform basic ingredients into something sublime. The best tamari and shoyu are made using traditional Japanese methods of fermenting soybeans for more than eighteen months in cedar kegs. Shoyu is fermented with wheat, while tamari is wheat- and gluten-free, but they both add a wonderful warmth and depth of flavor to savory food. Make sure you purchase naturally fermented tamari or shoyu, which contain amino acids and aid digestion.

SEA SALT

Unrefined, sun-dried sea salt contains important and easily assimilated trace minerals (including iodine) that are an essential part of a healthy diet. Regular, refined table salt is stripped of these important minerals and often has anticaking agents added. Good-quality sea salt not only enhances and deepens flavors, but a little added while cooking helps make food more digestible. Kosher salt is refined, but you can get sea salt that is kosher certified. My salt selection is pretty basic—I use a fine-ground Celtic sea salt in all my cooking and also like to have a fleur de sel or flaked sea salt like Maldon on hand for finishing some salads and desserts.

SEAWEEDS

Seaweeds have incredible healing properties and have been used throughout history to prevent disease, assist in detoxification, alkalize the blood, and impart beauty. They also remove the residue of radiation from the body, aid in weight loss, alleviate liver stagnancy, and help lower cholesterol and high blood pressure. A true beauty food, seaweeds contain thiamine and niacin, which promote lustrous hair and healthy nails, eyes, and skin. They are some of the most nutrient-dense food around, containing up to twenty times the minerals of land vegetables, and are rich in iron, calcium, and amino acids. Seaweeds can be added (in small or larger amounts) to many different foods, from soups to desserts. All dried seaweeds can be kept indefinitely in a dark, dry place. Look for sustainably harvested sea vegetables from the North Atlantic coast (see the Resources section). Many hand-harvested sea vegetable companies carry unusual varieties unique to their area that can be substituted for those listed here.

1. KOMBU 2. DULSE 3. ARAME 4. WAKAME
5. AGAR FLAKES 6. DRIED SHIITAKE MUSHROOMS
7. WAKAME FLAKES 8. NORI

AGAR

Agar is used as a vegetarian gelatin—it is clear, virtually flavorless, and contains no calories, making it perfect for use in desserts. In Japan, agar is used in a fruit dessert called kanten; I've included recipes for Strawberry Rose Kanten (page 326) and Pomegranate Kanten (page 351). Agar helps reduce inflammation, soothes the digestive tract, promotes good digestion, and like all seaweeds it's rich in iron and calcium, and it helps remove toxins from the body. You'll find many recipes for using agar in the dessert section of this book; for more information about how to use it, see page 292.

ARAME

Arame has a mild flavor, so I often cook it for people who are new to eating seaweeds. Its thin, black strands look pretty in salads and noodle dishes, and when cooked with carrots, sesame, and mirin (page 107), it makes a delicious side dish. Arame needs to be soaked and drained before using—the soaking water will be full of minerals and can be used to water houseplants. Soak it for 20 minutes if you plan to eat it uncooked, as in salads; soak it for about 10 minutes if you plan to cook it. Arame is particularly high in iron, calcium, and iodine.

DULSE

Dulse has a beautiful, deep purply red color and a salty, tangy flavor. It can be chopped and eaten as is; added to food during cooking; or toasted in a skillet and crumbled as a smoky tasting seasoning for salads, soups, and grains. Dulse is exceptionally high in iodine and makes a great salt substitute.

DRIED SHIITAKE MUSHROOMS

Dried shiitakes are by no means a seaweed, but I keep them alongside seaweed in my pantry and use them together in dashi, the stock base of my miso soups (pages 158 and 174). Shiitake have played an essential role in traditional Asian medicine for more than six thousand years. They have an abundance of health-promoting properties, including lowering cholesterol and reducing fat in the blood. Shiitakes are high in selenium; iron; and vitamins B, C, and D. The rich, woodsy flavor of shiitake mushrooms adds depth, interest, and abundant nutrients to meals. Rehydrated shiitakes have a much heartier texture than the fresh ones, but can be used anywhere you would use fresh mushrooms. Either soak them overnight or simmer them in water until soft before using.

KOMBU

Sometimes referred to as an Asian bay leaf, kombu is one of the easiest seaweeds to incorporate into your diet. A small piece can be simmered into stocks, soups, stews, beans, or grains, infusing dishes with minerals and greatly increasing their nutritional value. Kombu contains glutamic acid, which naturally enhances flavor and tenderizes food. I use it most for cooking beans, as the added minerals help balance and break down the proteins, oil, and carbohydrates in the beans, making them easier to digest.

NORI

Nori is most commonly used to wrap sushi and rice balls, but it also makes a lovely, simple garnish, like on the Bento Bowl (page 278) and Kabocha Chestnut Soup with Nori Sesame "Leaves" (page 171). Nori has the highest protein content of all seaweeds. You can buy sheets pretoasted or raw. Toasting nori enhances its delicate, grassy flavor and makes it crunchy rather than chewy—if you buy it raw, you can toast the sheets yourself by holding each one over a low flame until it changes from dark green to bright green. Look for nori "krinkles" or flakes to sprinkle over food, or simply tear a toasted sheet into squares and use it like flat bread when eating grains, vegetables, and salads. The versatility of nori makes it a tasty and convenient way to get the numerous benefits of seaweeds.

WAKAME

Wakame is the lovely emerald green seaweed most commonly used in miso soup. (See Spring Miso Soup with Lemon on page 158.) I like the delicate texture and ease of wakame flakes (also called instant wakame), which are simmered in seawater before being dried (see the Resources section). If you buy regular wakame, soak it until hydrated and soft, then remove the tough stem, slice the leaves, add it to simmering soups, and cook until tender. Wakame can also be used in place of kombu when cooking beans or grains.

SPICES

My spice drawer is jam-packed with spices from all over the world. I often open the drawer to see if something grabs my attention or gives me inspiration about what to cook. I find it so pleasing to see the brightly colored turmeric lying beside green cardamom pods and rich red chili flakes.

Apart from a za'tar blend from Israel and some Turkish oregano, I don't stock dried herbs, as fresh herbs taste better and will last weeks in the fridge—a good thing since I find the robust bunches of rosemary, thyme, and sage at the farmers' market irresistible! Likewise, it's best to buy most dried spices whole and grind them yourself, with the exception of (ground) turmeric, cayenne, cinnamon, and ginger. The fastest way of doing this is to use an electric spice or coffee grinder (see the equipment section). It takes a bit of extra effort, but the flavor of freshly toasted and ground spices is rich and intoxicating. I often grind a couple of extra tablespoons of a spice I'm using and store it in a small jar; it will stay fresh for a few months and always tastes better than purchased preground spices. Making your own spice mixes is also worth the extra effort—in this book, you'll find recipes for Curry Powder (page 112) and homemade Harissa (page 112). I purchase all my spices (whole and the necessary preground ones) from health-food stores that buy them in bulk; they taste much fresher and are much less expensive than the small bottled spices. The following is a short list of spices I use on a daily basis.

BAY LEAVES

Bay leaves add a mild, aromatic flavor to soups, stews, and beans. I use fresh bay leaves in place of dry whenever I have them on hand; I especially like the way their deep green color and shape look in Marinated Goat Cheese (page 116). Fresh bay leaves can be found in health-food stores and gourmet markets, and they last weeks in the fridge. Buying dry bay leaves in bulk is very economical, and they keep well for years in a jar away from heat and light.

BLACK PEPPER

My pepper grinder lives close to the stove, because I reach for it when finishing dishes that need a lift or added interest. When freshly ground, black pepper aids digestion, stimulates blood flow, and increases the liver's detoxification process. Most preground pepper not only tastes flat and harsh, but it's also often preroasted, and once roasted, black pepper becomes an irritant. You won't find many measurements for pepper in this book because I usually grind it directly into the foods I'm cooking. Start with a few turns of your grinder and add more to taste, but be aware that the flavor of black pepper changes as it cooks and can become stronger and slightly bitter, so it's best to add it at the end of cooking.

CINNAMON

Adding a pinch of cinnamon brings warmth, depth, and a sweet pungent flavor to both sweet and savory foods. Cinnamon has been used in traditional Eastern and Western medicines throughout history to stimulate circulation and digestion, to boost overall vitality, and for its antiseptic properties. I like to have cinnamon sticks and ground cinnamon on hand for many of my favorite recipes—I can't imagine my daily oats without it—and it's also a necessary ingredient in Curry Powder (page 112) and many desserts and sweet treats.

DRIED CHILIES

A pinch of dried chili provides a zesty kick to everything from soups and stews to dressings, marinades, and even drinks. Hot chili peppers have antioxidant and detoxifying properties; they also enhance circulation and stimulate digestion. Eating chilies causes perspiration, which ultimately cools the body. Keep in mind that the heat of dried chilies can increase as they cook, so it's best to add them toward the end of cooking.

Hundreds of types of dried chilies are available, but these are the three I always keep on hand:

- **Whole dried red chilies**, either Thai or other red chilies, for marinating olives and cheese (see Marinated Goat Cheese, page 116). They can also be crushed or rehydrated in water before they're added to food.
- **Red pepper flakes** for simple pasta dishes and homemade Kimchi (page 123). I like to add a pinch to tomato soups and sauces as they simmer for a zesty kick and for sprinkling over pizza.
- **Cayenne** is great for giving bean dishes a lift, and it's the chili I use in my homemade Curry Powder (page 112) and Harissa (page 112). Adding a pinch to miso soup clears your head when you're feeling under the weather.

TURMERIC

The aromatic flavor and color of turmeric is intoxicating, but what really inspires me are its amazing anti-inflammatory, antioxidant, and immune-boosting properties. Turmeric is the best-known source of beta-carotene and is effective in decongesting the liver, dissolving gallstones, and improving the digestion of protein. I often add a pinch when cooking red lentils and grains and, of course, in all my curries. In this book, you'll also find it added to lemon desserts for a soft golden hue and in Turmeric Lemonade (page 222). Look for fresh turmeric in Indian markets and health-food stores—it looks a bit like fresh ginger, but when the skin is scraped, its flesh is brilliant orange. The flavor of fresh turmeric is sweeter and brighter than dried. Peeled and finely grated, you can use about three times the amount of fresh turmeric as dried in cooked food.

PANTRY VEGETABLES

Since I see the fridge as an extension of my pantry, basic fresh vegetables that last a couple of weeks or longer are always on hand. I especially rely on these basics in the colder months when I don't have an abundance of seasonal vegetables available. As with all the other vegetables that sit out on my counter, these fridge basics are treated in similar ways: steamed, roasted, made into salads, marinated, and added to soups and stews. You'll find many recipes using these basics throughout this book.

AVOCADOS

With ripe avocados on hand, a flavorful meal can be made out of just about anything. I especially love them as a topping for quinoa with toasted black sesame seeds and tamari or slathered on toast with lemon and pepper. Rich in copper and good fats, avocados help build red blood cells and are a nutritious source of protein, magnesium, and vitamin B. Leave hard avocados out on the counter to ripen and place them in the fridge once they're ripe but still firm; they will last a week or longer.

BEETS

It's a blessing that beets grow so well through summer and fall and can be stored for most of the winter—they're flavorful, versatile, and incredibly rich in nutrients. You'll find plenty of recipes celebrating my love for beets in this book, but most often I simply cook and marinate them (see page 104)— prepared this way they can last up to a week in the fridge and add rich color and flavor when served as a side dish or appetizer or tossed with chickpeas and greens for a salad. Fresh beet greens cook up similar to Swiss chard, as in the Quinoa Beet Salad with Feta, Chili, Garlic, and Sautéed Beet Greens (page 191). Although I adore any color from red and golden to pink and candy striped, red beets have been used since ancient times for medicinal purposes. They purify the blood; build red blood cells; improve circulation; treat liver ailments; and are rich in silicon, calcium, and iron.

CABBAGE

Cabbage, like other members of the cruciferous/brassica family (which includes kale, broccoli, cauliflower, and turnips) is praised for its disease-fighting properties, especially related to cancer and heart disease. The outer leaves of the green cabbage contain more chlorophyll, vitamin E, and calcium than the paler leaves, so don't throw them away! I often reach for red cabbage for its gorgeous color, which is also responsible for its additional antioxidant properties. Green cabbage is a great addition to bean and lentil soups and tastes great steamed with Zesty Flax Dressing (page 92). I make Pink Kraut (page 121) with a combination of red and green cabbage, and when a simple meal needs enlivening, I whip up a batch of Quick Pickled Red Cabbage (page 102). Cabbage can last for weeks when kept in the fridge.

CARROTS

Carrots add sweetness, nutrition, and a bright shot of color all year round. They're perfect for lively last-minute side dishes like Carrot Parsley Salad (page 102) or steamed and tossed with Harissa (page 112) and are a reliably sweet ingredient when making stocks and soups. Best known for their high level of the immune-boosting and cancer-fighting antioxidant beta-carotene, carrots also tonify the kidneys, improve liver function, strengthen the spleen and pancreas, reduce inflammation, and clear acidic blood conditions.

CELERY

Celery adds an aromatic freshness to soups, broths, and stews and makes a lovely addition to winter salads. Celery has long been used to treat high blood pressure, improve digestion, and purify the blood. Its high silicon content helps build connective tissue, bones, and joints. It stores well in the fridge for weeks.

CITRUS

Lemons support healthy liver function, cleanse the blood, and promote weight loss. They are indispensable in dressings, sauces, soups, desserts, and the popular morning detox drink—lemon juice combined with warm water first thing in the morning. Keeping all kinds of citrus on hand is great for any spontaneous baking; I use fresh orange juice in muffins, cakes, and waffles to add flavor and to reduce the amount of concentrated sweeteners. I find it also adds a lovely sweet note and lift to salad dressings and sauces.

Peak citrus season is during the winter months, and these fruits can bring much needed brightness to heartier cold weather meals; they also add the freshness we crave as winter comes to an end. Look for blood oranges, Meyer lemons, and ruby red grapefruit to add color and new flavor to everything from breakfast to desserts. In a cool kitchen, citrus can be kept on the counter, but they'll last many weeks when stored in the fridge.

FRESH HERBS

Fresh herbs brighten the simplest foods and can last a long time in the fridge when wrapped in a cloth or paper towels (to absorb moisture) and stored in airtight containers. Rosemary and thyme can last weeks stored this way, and oregano and sage can also last well over a week. In summer, I keep pots of basil and mint (and the herbs already mentioned) on my fire escape; they're pretty and perfect for adding a pinch of flavor here and there.

GARLIC

Being the most potent of the onion family, the health benefits of garlic are vast—from protecting against infection and viruses, removing toxins, reducing cholesterol, and stimulating metabolism to promoting the growth of healthy intestinal flora, fighting cancer, and more. Garlic bought from the farmers' market at the end of autumn will last right into February and March when it's stored in an airy, dark place. Look for firm bulbs with tight, papery skin.

FRESH GINGER

Ginger is good in everything from curries, soups, and broths to teas and desserts. I buy big gnarly clusters of ginger and keep them out on the counter to use over the course of a week, but if you don't go through it fast, store it in the fridge, where it will last for up to a month. Ginger promotes warmth and circulation, stimulates digestion, and is widely used as a remedy for nausea and motion sickness.

GREENS

Kale and collards are my staple greens, especially in fall and winter; they are excellent sources of calcium, beta-carotene, chlorophyll, and iron. Being members of the cruciferous/brassica family, both have abundant anticarcinogenic properties, and their high sulfur content helps purify the blood and destroy common parasites. The calcium in these greens is higher and more absorbable than milk, and when eaten daily, they can help prevent osteoporosis and arthritis. They keep well for at least a week, and longer when locally grown and purchased fresh. I usually eat them steamed and drizzled with flax oil, Black Sesame Flax Dressing (page 93), or Zesty Flax Dressing (page 92). I also like to add them to soups and stews toward the end of cooking. Many recipes have you tear the leaves from the stem, but much of the nutrients are in the stem, so just cut off the tough bottoms and slice the whole leaf. Other members of the cruciferous family, like mustard greens, mitzuna, broccoli rabe, turnip greens, arugula, watercress, and bok choy can be prepared in similar ways and contain similar nutritional profiles; just keep in mind when you buy them that they don't last as long as the hardier kale and collard greens.

ONIONS

You can never go wrong when you have big bowl of onions sitting in your kitchen, especially if they're from the farmers' market—not only are they the base for many recipes, but in a pinch, caramelized onions added to simple marinated beans, chickpeas, or grains can turn these basics into something special. Onions are prized for their health-promoting properties. High in antioxidants and sulfur, they cleanse the blood, lower cholesterol, and sooth inflammation. Red and yellow onions can be used interchangeably unless you're cooking a light-colored dish, and then you should stick with yellow. Stock up on onions when they look their best in early fall—in a cool kitchen or the fridge, they will last weeks or even months.

PARSLEY

Although technically an herb, I use parsley more like a vegetable and always keep a bunch in the fridge. When there are no good-looking greens available, a big handful of chopped parsley brightens everything up, adding a fresh grassy flavor and lift to everyday grains, salads, pasta, and beans. Parsley is a blood purifier, rich in iron and calcium, and has three times as much vitamin C as citrus. Store parsley as you would other herbs (see Fresh Herbs on page 34), and it will keep up to two weeks. I often chop a cup or so at a time and keep it in a sealed jar in the fridge to sprinkle over meals before serving.

RADISHES

These pretty little vegetables are perfect for snacking, pickling, steaming, roasting, or adding to salads. The greens can also be sautéed or added to soups. Radishes keep well (without their leaves) for a couple of weeks in the fridge. Daikon, a long, white radish, is used in dipping sauce for tempura in Japanese cuisine, as it aids the digestion of fat. Radishes have detoxifying properties and are a traditional folk remedy for cleansing the gallbladder (eat two a day between meals for a month). Look for varieties like French breakfast, Easter egg, and the beautiful and robust watermelon radish.

SCALLIONS AND CHIVES

I always have either scallions or chives on hand, as they can magically turn any simple meal into something tasty and interesting. Like parsley, I chop about a cup at a time and keep them in a jar for easy use—chopped scallions will last up to four days; chives and garlic chives are best used in a couple of days. In spring and early summer, I love to use chives and their blossoms; the rest of the year, I keep scallions on hand. Like garlic, scallions have antifungal and antimicrobial effects and can help stop a cold (with chills) in its tracks if caught early.

WINTER SQUASH

From late summer into winter, you'll find a large variety of winter squash in my kitchen: dense-fleshed kabocha or red kuri, pudding-like delicata, smooth butternut, or emerald-skinned acorn—I love them all. Squash are an integral part of my cooking as soon as the crisp air sets in. Whether they're steamed, roasted and added to salads, velvety in soups, sweet and tender in nishime, or made into lasagna, I will never tire of them. They are among the vegetables that contain the highest amounts of carotenoids; they also contain vitamin C and magnesium and support healthy spleen and pancreas function. Winter squash can last months in a cool, dark spot in the kitchen and even longer in a cellar. In late spring and summer, look for the variety of different shapes and colors of zucchini and summer squash; all of them need to be stored in the fridge, where they will last a week or two.

COMPOST

When our food scraps break down in the absence of oxygen (like they do in a landfill), they create methane, a harmful gas that's similar to carbon dioxide and causes the greenhouse effect in the atmosphere that is leading to global warming.

Composting is perhaps the best and easiest action we can all take to reduce waste and greenhouse gasses while simultaneously nourishing the soil—which in turn increases the nutrients in our food. For these reasons, I feel very strongly about the importance of composting and suggest it every chance I get.

If you don't have the space to compost yourself, contact your local farmers' market or community garden to find locations and drop-off times. Storing food scraps in the freezer is a great way to prevent odor and messy transportation, and it also helps them break down faster.

IN THE FRIDGE

Even when I haven't shopped for fresh vegetables, my fridge—that great modern invention that enables consistent cold storage—is home to many foods that last weeks or months (and some, even years). When I need to make a fast meal, I dig out whatever vegetables I have and, depending on the season, either steam or roast them or use them in a salad, soup, or stew. If I have a grain cooking, I look in the fridge for ways to turn it into a meal by topping it with things like sauerkraut, chopped parsley and scallions, avocado, flax oil, and maybe a crumble of feta, if I have it on hand. The fridge not only keeps vegetables fresher longer but also prolongs the life of the ferments and condiments I make ahead—like Pink Kraut and Kimchi (pages 121 and 123), and Miso Mayonnaise (page 114). All these quickly and easily jazz up simple snacks, grains, and steamed vegetables.

FERMENTED VEGETABLES

Having a range of different ferments on hand adds flavor, live active enzymes, and color to everyday meals and snacks. Make sure that the sauerkraut, kimchi, pickles, and other fermented vegetables you purchase are naturally fermented and locally made, or learn to make your own (see pages 120–23). Because of the abundance of probiotics in fermented vegetables, adding just a half cup to your daily diet will improve digestion, nutrient assimilation, immunity, and more. These vegetables will continue to ferment and develop in the fridge, but at a much slower rate, and will keep many months. Save any of the juice left in the bottom of the jar to use in dressings—I love adding it to the Zesty Flax Dressing for steamed greens (page 92).

GOAT CHEESE

I buy locally made goat cheese (aged and fresh) to add richness and interest to simple meals and snacks. Goat milk is easier to digest than cow's milk because the fat globules are smaller. It has a chemical makeup that is closer to human breast milk than cows' milk and has been used as a remedy for weakened health conditions in many traditional cultures. When stored in brine, goat milk feta will last up to a month and tastes fantastic crumbled over grains, beans, or salads with lots of chopped parsley and scallions. Goat cheeses aged six months or longer can be used in the same ways you would Parmesan cheese.

MISO

Miso is made from beans and cultured grains that are fermented with koji (a naturally occurring yeast used to make rice vinegar and sake) for up to three years. Usually created from a combination of soybeans and rice or barley, you can also find miso made from chickpeas, adzuki beans, and millet. Unpasteurized miso, like other naturally fermented foods, contains abundant probiotics ("good" bacteria) that aid in digestive health. Miso is a complete source of protein and contains all the amino acids essential for human nutrition.

Miso has been used in traditional Japanese cooking for centuries for its role in maintaining good health and vitality. To get all the medicinal benefits (and the best flavor) from miso, make sure to purchase the naturally fermented and unpasteurized variety (see the Resources section). The color of miso is an indicator of its flavor and how long it has been fermented—lighter miso is sweeter and has been fermented for less time than darker miso, which tastes stronger and has greater medicinal properties. Miso's rich, unique flavor is great for seasoning dressings, sauces, stews, and soups. For a taste sensation, try Miso Mayonnaise (page 114). My favorite all-purpose misos are chickpea, white miso, and barley.

NUT BUTTERS

I adore nut butters, but Toasted Almond Butter (page 117) is my all-time favorite and is always in my fridge. I use it for simple things, like smeared over sprouted grain toast for breakfast or as a snack, and in more involved preparations, like Almond Butter Brownies with Sea Salt (page 340). I also keep raw cashew butter on hand for making dressings like Creamy Mustard Dressing (page 192) rich without overpowering them (like tahini can) and in sweet things like Cinnamon Caramel Popcorn (page 344). Macadamia butter has a delicately sweet flavor and is also rich and buttery. It's used in Macadamia Lime Sauce (page 206). Look out for sprouted nut butters made with activated nuts (see page 17) that are dehydrated before grinding. If you have a dehydrator you can make your own.

....

1. EGGS 2. UMEBOSHI PASTE 3. TEMPEH 4. TOFU 5. DILL PICKLES
6. WHOLE-GRAIN DIJON MUSTARD 7. ADZUKI-BEAN MISO
8. FRESH GOAT CHEESE 9. UMEBOSHI PLUMS 10. CHICKPEA MISO
11. AGED GOAT CHEESE 12. CASHEW BUTTER 13. FLAX OIL

PASTURED EGGS

Although I don't rely on eggs as a protein source or feel my pantry is bare without them, I do like to keep them on hand for use in pancakes, waffles, and some baked goods—and for the occasional perfectly poached egg with greens on toast. It is really important to make sure the eggs you purchase are not only organic and free-range but are also pastured; this means the chickens were outside getting vitamin D from sunshine and eating the bugs, worms, seeds, and grasses they need to produce flavorful and nutritious eggs. Free-range and cage-free chickens are not always out in daylight and may be on a diet of grains alone, which does not provide all necessary nutrients or happy, healthy chickens. A local farm or farmers' market is the best place to find pastured eggs—ask farmers about how they keep their chickens and buy from those who use the best practices.

REPLACING EGGS

Eggs provide moisture, leavening, and a binding quality to baked goods, but if you're vegan or simply prefer not to use eggs, here are two methods for substituting them in recipes.

- Whisk 1 tablespoon of ground flax seeds with ¼ cup filtered water. Set the mixture aside for 5 to 10 minutes, or until thickened. It can be stored for two to three days in the fridge.

- Whisk 1 teaspoon chia seeds with ¼ cup filtered water. Set the mixture aside for 15 minutes, or until thickened. It can be stored for up to four days in the fridge.

TEMPEH

Tempeh is a healthy and convenient protein to have handy for quick, nutrient-rich meals such as Quick Braised Tempeh (page 108). Originally from Indonesia, tempeh is made from whole cooked soybeans that are lightly crushed and fermented with a mold called rhizopus oligosporus. This white mold produces a natural (heat-stable) antibiotic that helps support immune system function and increases digestive ability. Tempeh is high in omega-3 fatty acids and B vitamins and has a nutty, rich flavor.

Commercially made tempeh is pasteurized and keeps for weeks in the fridge, or it can be frozen for up to six months. Homemade or unpasteurized tempeh is a heavenly culinary treat, so flavorful that it needs nothing more than a little oil to sauté it. Tempeh is available plain (my favorite) or with the addition of grains, seeds, and sometimes land or sea vegetables. Seek out local, handmade tempeh at farmers' markets and always buy organic—like corn, nonorganic soybeans are most likely genetically engineered.

TOFU

Making tofu is not unlike making cheese—soy milk is curdled, then pressed, drained, and shaped. With an ultrasmooth texture, a neutral taste, and an ability to absorb any flavor you add to it, tofu is a convenient way to get protein and minerals without any prior thought or preparation. Traditionally, tofu was eaten in small amounts—think miso soup in a Japanese restaurant—rarely was it eaten as a main course and never in such volume as in some Western diets. Because of their high phytic acid content (see page 58), soybeans are best eaten fermented (fermentation removes more phytic acid than soaking can) like in tempeh, miso, natto, or tamari, so I reserve tofu for occasional use as a last-minute protein or for times when I want a cheese-like texture in a dish without the dairy, for example, in Butternut Squash Lasagna (page 270). Garlic Tamari-Braised Tofu (page 109) is great on sandwiches, as a salad topping, or with grains. For a tasty warm weather meal, grill it along with lots of summer veggies and serve it with Chimichurri Sauce (page 118). Be sure to purchase water-packed organic tofu that is made with the traditional coagulant nigari, not a chemical version. Once opened, store tofu in a glass container covered with filtered water, change the water every couple of days, and use it within a week. As with any soy product, always buy organic tofu, as nonorganic soybeans are most likely genetically engineered.

IN THE FREEZER

The freezer is a great place for storing pantry items that you use less often, like whole-grain flours and nuts, as they'll keep fresher for a lot longer. I also keep some other basics in the freezer for adding to meals—things like frozen peas, corn, and berries that can save you when the fridge is bare. The freezer can also be used to store seasonal produce when it's at its peak. Freeze sliced peaches, corn cut off the cob, shelled fava beans, pitted cherries, and all kinds of berries for a taste of summer in the dark of winter. I also freeze Kaffir lime leaves and curry leaves; they can last for months and add interest and flavor to quick soups, stews, and curries. I don't store many cooked foods in the freezer, because I prefer to eat something fresh, even if it's super simple; however, puréed soups, cooked beans, and grains all freeze well.

BLUEBERRIES AND OTHER BERRIES

The gorgeous deep color of blueberries is due to anthocyanin, a pigment found in dark berries, black rice, red cabbage, and Concord grapes. This pigment is what gives these foods their extremely rich antioxidant content. Blueberries also help strengthen blood vessels and promote heart health. Although nothing beats the flavor and fragrance of fresh, juicy blueberries, they do freeze well and can be eaten year-round—stirred into oatmeal, pancakes, and muffins; simmered into a compote; or blended into smoothies. Although more delicate, raspberries, strawberries, and blackberries also freeze well, so stock up when they're at their peak and enjoy them throughout the winter. All berries are high in vitamin C and a great addition to your daily diet to help boost immunity.

CULTURED BUTTER

Cultured butter (also called "European-style" butter) is made from cream that is cultured first, the way butter was traditionally made—the naturally occurring bacteria in milk ferments the cream before it is churned into butter. This creates a product with fuller flavor that is easier to digest. Look for cultured butter that is organic and "pastured"—from cows that grazed outdoors on grass, resulting in higher levels of vitamins and CLA (conjugated linoleic acid). I store a few sticks in the freezer, where it keeps for months. Pastured butter is available only from spring to fall, so look for it at local farmers' markets and some health-food stores. While no recipe in this book requires butter—though the Date Pistachio Praline Tart (page 313) seriously benefits from it!—I do like to keep some around for those times when only buttered toast will do and when I have guests.

PEAS

English peas are one of the few frozen vegetables I keep on hand—peas, unlike many vegetables, freeze particularly well. They add a welcome burst of sweetness and jolt of bright green color to simple meals any time of year. Since fresh local peas have a short growing season and become mealy soon after they're picked, I purchase frozen peas and find they work well in all the pea-related recipes in this book.

SPROUTED BREAD, ENGLISH MUFFINS, AND TORTILLAS

Freezing bread is a good option if you don't eat it daily, as it won't get stale and can be toasted as needed. I keep sprouted bread and English muffins handy for quick breakfasts; I also freeze thinly sliced sourdough rye, which is terrific with poached eggs and roasted tomatoes or avocado. Sprouted whole-grain and corn tortillas are great for quick quesadillas or simply warming in a skillet, drizzling with flax oil, and eating with soups. Breads made from sprouted grains have higher nutrient and antioxidant levels, and the sprouting process breaks down enzyme inhibitors and increases digestibility. (See the Resources section for my favorites.)

SWEET CORN

Local sweet corn is abundant in late summer, and when it's available, I eat it as often as I can. Once it's at its peak, cut kernels off the cob and freeze them in airtight containers. I use frozen corn when I want to add some sweetness and color to quick meals like Curried Quinoa Pilaf with Toasted Cashews (page 108) and Crispy Sweet Corn Polenta (page 267). If I don't freeze enough, I purchase frozen corn and find it works just as well.

BAKING

Adding a small selection of baking ingredients to your whole-food pantry means you can whip up a batch of cookies or muffins and other breakfast treats at a moment's notice. Enjoying the occasional sweet thing is one of life's little pleasures, and when made with sprouted whole-grain flours, unrefined oils, and natural sweeteners, they don't have such a negative effect on your health. In addition to the flours listed in this section, others I like to keep on hand are brown rice flour and barley flour.

ALMOND MEAL

Almond meal, sometimes called almond flour, gives a moist and tender texture to cakes, muffins, and waffles. If you don't use almond meal regularly, storing it in the fridge or freezer will keep it fresher longer—sometimes hard lumps will form after it's been frozen, so break them up with your fingertips before measuring. You can also make your own almond meal by grinding cold or frozen blanched almonds in a food processor—be sure to keep an eye on them, as they can quickly turn into nut butter. However, it won't be as fine as commercially ground almond meal, and since it's hard to find organic blanched almonds, I opt to buy it already ground (see the Resources section).

ARROWROOT

Arrowroot is a powdered tropical root starch that is used as a thickener, and it's preferred over cornstarch as it is not genetically modified or highly processed. To use arrowroot, dissolve the powder in cool water or juice and add it to desserts or sauces at the end of cooking. It can also be tossed with fruit fillings for pies or crisps because it will thicken the juices as they are released from the fruit during cooking. You'll find more information and many recipes using arrowroot in the Desserts section on pages 287–353. Arrowroot has a soothing effect on the stomach, and is widely available and affordable.

BAKING POWDER AND BAKING SODA

Baking powder can contain aluminum compounds, which not only taste metallic but, once accumulated in the body, may cause neurological disorders. Look for aluminum-free baking powder that is also made without genetically modified cornstarch (see the Resources section). Store it in an airtight container in a cool place, and use it within a year. There are only a couple of cake recipes containing baking soda in this book, but having it around for nontoxic cleaning and deodorizing is a great idea.

DRIED UNSWEETENED COCONUT

Medicinally, coconut is warming and strengthening, and a good source of protein, fiber, and fatty acids. It builds blood, increases energy, and supports cardiovascular health. In the United States fresh coconuts are irradiated when imported, which is the reason I stick with using the dried version. I store dried, unsweetened coconut in two forms—shredded and flaked—to use in everything from breakfasts to desserts. Shredded coconut is easiest to measure, and I often add a handful when grinding ingredients for crusts, cakes, and cookies to add moisture, richness, and a sweet flavor. You can also use dried coconut to make coconut milk as in the Coconut Curry (page 274)—this milk is much lighter and less rich than canned coconut milk. A little dried coconut added to almond or Brazil nut milks makes a nice change

too. Since coconut is a fruit, it doesn't need to be soaked before using, although presoaking will help soften it when making milks. Toasting coconut enhances its sweet flavor and makes a nice crunchy garnish for Black Rice Breakfast Pudding with Coconut and Banana (page 145). I also stock coconut flour for use in gluten-free baking.

KUZU

Kuzu is a wild mountain root from Japan that is used as a thickening agent. Although it is used in similar ways as arrowroot, it tends to be stronger and creates more body; unlike arrowroot, it can also be simmered for long periods of time without the risk of becoming thin. Kuzu was introduced to the United States to help prevent soil erosion, but it is has grown out of control and is now classified as a noxious weed. Oddly, kuzu from America is not available for purchase. In traditional Asian medicine, it is used to treat indigestion, fevers, colds, hangovers, and headaches and to improve overall vitality. Kuzu comes in chalky white lumps that need to be dissolved in cool water or juice before adding it to simmering sauces, stews, or desserts.

SPROUTED FLOURS

Sprouted flours are ground from grains that are first sprouted and dehydrated. Sprouting activates enzymes and removes the phytic acid present in grains (which inhibits nutrient absorption; see page 58), transforming them into highly nutritious, easy-to-digest plants. Some people with gluten sensitivities find they can eat sprouted flours, as sprouting can reduce the gluten content. For all these reasons, I feel better about making and eating baked goods with sprouted flour. Sprouted flours have a pleasant, lightly fermented smell, not unlike sourdough bread, and I find they taste even better than regular whole-grain flours. Since it is a healthier option, all the breakfast recipes in this book call for sprouted flour, and while not specified in the dessert recipes, I often use sprouted flour there too—just keep in mind that crusts and cookies tend to need a few minutes longer in the oven. Sprouted spelt and wheat flour are sold in many health-food stores, and you can order an array of other sprouted flours online, including brown rice, barley, chickpea, and buckwheat.

WHOLE-GRAIN SPELT FLOUR

I keep whole-grain spelt flour on hand for times when sprouted flour isn't available. I find that any recipe containing wheat flour can be made successfully with whole-grain spelt flour. It yields a moister crumb in cakes, and because of its lower gluten content, baked goods usually don't rise as high. All recipes in this book that require sprouted spelt flour can be made with whole-grain spelt flour.

1. MEDJOOL DATES 2. TRADITIONALLY MADE BROWN
RICE SYRUP 3. COCONUT SUGAR 4. MAPLE SUGAR
5. BROWN RICE SYRUP 6. YAKON SYRUP 7. COCONUT
SYRUP 8. MAPLE SYRUP

NATURAL SWEETENERS

The deep, rounded, and complex flavors of natural unrefined sweeteners like brown rice syrup, dates (and other dried fruits), maple and yakon syrups, and coconut sugar are far more interesting and satisfying than white sugar. White sugar and other highly refined sweeteners are chemically processed and contribute to a slew of diseases; since they contain no nutrients, digesting them causes the body to draw on its own reserves of vitamins and minerals, creating deficiencies. Although most of the sweeteners listed here are concentrated, they still contain nutrients, and in the case of brown rice syrup, they enter the bloodstream much more slowly than refined sweeteners, preventing a blood sugar spike. That said, too much of any kind of sweetener does not promote health, and they are best reserved for occasional use.

Here is a list of the sweeteners I keep in the kitchen. I also stock raw honey from local beekeepers (and some found on my travels), which is my sweetener of choice for drinks. I opt not to bake with it, as the beneficial enzymes are destroyed when honey is heated.

BROWN RICE SYRUP

Brown rice syrup (sometimes called rice malt or rice nectar) is a whole-grain sweetener that's less destructive to the body's natural mineral balance than refined sugar and most other sweeteners. It contains 50 percent maltose, a slow-digesting carbohydrate that enters the bloodstream gradually. Traditionally made, brown rice syrup is created by fermenting brown rice with koji (a naturally occurring yeast that is used in miso and sake) and boiling it until it becomes a thick syrup. Many commercial brands of rice syrup use artificially produced enzymes that speed up the fermentation process. Brown rice syrup has a honey-like color and mild, malty flavor; you'll find it in this book in recipes like Cherry Coconut Granola (page 151) and Cinnamon Caramel Popcorn (page 344).

COCONUT NECTAR AND SUGAR

Coconut nectar and sugar (sometimes called coconut syrup and palm sugar or coconut crystals) is made by tapping the sap of the coconut blossom, then evaporating or boiling to thicken it and make coconut syrup. The syrup can then be evaporated further, dehydrated, and ground to make coconut sugar. These sugars have a low glycemic index and contain amino acids, minerals, and B vitamins. Certain brands of coconut sugar that are evaporated at low temperatures also contain live active enzymes. You will find a couple of recipes in this book using coconut sugar; it has a mild tropical flavor that is less sweet than maple sugar. You can use coconut nectar or coconut sugar in recipes that call for maple syrup or maple sugar. The production of coconut products is growing at a fast rate, so when purchasing coconut sugars, be sure they are produced by companies that are socially and environmentally responsible.

MAPLE SYRUP AND MAPLE SUGAR

Maple syrup, the boiled-down sap of the sugar maple tree, brings moisture and a binding quality to vegan baked goods, not to mention a gorgeous earthy, sweet flavor. Maple syrup contains zinc and manganese and trace amounts of amino acids. Grade A syrup is the most versatile, as its light color won't darken custards and creams, and the mild flavor enhances rather than overpowers other ingredients. Grade B is darker with a richer flavor; it's made from sap that was tapped later in the season. Maple sugar is great when you need a dry sweetener or when you want to replace regular sugar. One of the things I love most about maple products is that they can be purchased locally from small family producers here in New York. Be sure the maple syrup you buy is pure, as imitations contain high-fructose corn syrup.

MEDJOOL DATES

Also known as fresh dates or soft dates, Medjools are a variety originally from Morocco and now grown extensively in California. They are perfect for sweetening smoothies or nut milks, as their sweet, tender flesh adds body and a rich caramel-like flavor without being overpowering. I especially love the earthy sweetness they add to Vanilla Chia Pudding (page 111). For a quick sweet treat, try splitting one open, removing the pit, and filling it with almond butter—yum! Store dates in a cool pantry for a couple of months or in the refrigerator for six months or longer.

SOY MILK

Keeping a carton of soy milk in the pantry will save the day for last-minute baking and pancake making when you don't have freshly made almond milk on hand. The creamy texture of soy milk also tastes great in black tea or chai. I choose it over packaged almond milk because it's easier to find soy milk without questionable ingredients. Original Edensoy Organic Soymilk is my preferred brand, because it is made with kombu, filtered water, sea salt, and barley (for a subtle sweetness); it also comes unsweetened. As with all soy products, make sure you purchase organic, as anything non-organic is most likely genetically modified.

VANILLA BEANS AND EXTRACT

Vanilla beans are the fermented and cured pods of a hand-pollinated vanilla orchid. Good-quality pure vanilla extract is simply made by steeping vanilla beans in alcohol. Along with saffron, vanilla is the most expensive spice and one I wouldn't want to live without—the delicate floral aroma and unique flavor is by far my favorite for nut milks and desserts of all kinds. You can make vanilla extract yourself by scraping the seeds from a few vanilla beans, cutting the pod into inch-long pieces, combining them with a cup of rum or vodka, and sealing everything in a bottle for at least a month (shake it every now and then). Once it's been used, you can add more alcohol and steep it again. I also add leftover vanilla bean pods from making desserts to help keep it potent.

YAKON SYRUP

Yakon syrup is made from a tuberous root that's indigenous to the Andes Mountains. This low-glycemic sweetener contains minerals, potassium, amino acids, and prebiotic properties that encourage digestive health. With half the calories of sugar, it is perfect for avoiding spikes in blood sugar. The color and texture is reminiscent of caramel sauce but it's mildly sweet with a slight tropical flavor. It can be used in place of rice syrup or maple syrup. I use it in the Golden Amaranth Superfood Bars (page 347).

DRIED FRUITS

Dried fruits are a wonderful sweet source in cookies, bars, and granola. When purchasing them be sure to get organic and unsulfured. Sulfur dioxide is a preservative used on dried fruit to extend shelf life and retain the fruit's bright color. Sulfite use is banned on fresh produce but it is still used extensively on dried fruit, especially apricots and golden raisins, and other brightly colored dried fruits. Seek out organic dried fruit as pesticides also concentrate as the fruit dries.

BOTTLED AND CANNED ITEMS

While most meals made with all fresh ingredients are far superior, there are a few canned items that I like to keep in the pantry for adding interest to quick meals, snacks, and for making decadent desserts. Be sure that any canned food you buy is packaged in BPA-free cans (see page 53 for more information on plastic).

- **Coconut milk** is great for enriching soups, curries, and puddings such as Black Rice Breakfast Pudding (page 145). It's also excellent for creating thick, buttery vegan frostings like Citrus Frosting (page 339) and Chocolate Ganache (page 333).
- While freshly cooked **beans** are unbeatable, cans of chickpeas and black and white beans are good to have on hand for last-minute dips, spreads, sauces, and pâtés. Look for brands that have kombu or kelp in the ingredients, which improves digestibility and adds minerals and flavor to the beans. When using canned beans, drain and rinse them well to remove the tinny taste. Covering them with fresh water and simmering for 5 to 10 minutes then draining well greatly improves their flavor, which is especially helpful when using them in salads or Chickpea Mash (page 70).
- Whole and crushed bottled **tomatoes** are perfect for quick pasta sauces, soups, stews, and curries.
- Keep a bottle of pure **apple juice** around for marinades and desserts. Once opened, it will keep for at least a week in the fridge. Apple juice can be replaced with locally pressed cider when available, but it won't last as long.
- Bottled or canned plain **artichoke hearts** are a tasty addition to the White Bean Artichoke Aioli (page 214). I also keep a jar of roasted artichoke hearts in extra virgin olive oil for adding a special touch to everything from toast to snacks, salads, and cheese platters.

equipment

As I was moving around the world, exploring different cities, I cooked and ate very well with the one knife and pot that accompanied me on my travels. Since I've lived in New York, my kitchen has been fairly well stocked (thanks to my partner), but it wasn't until recently that I finally acquired my second knife—a Japanese vegetable knife, a bit smaller than my first. In terms of gadgets and appliances, I still prefer to keep things as simple as possible. The clutter of unused appliances or single-use gadgets takes up precious space both physically and mentally. I've found it best to slowly collect good-quality pots and kitchen things that I love, as the good ones will last a lifetime, often yield better results, and are worth carrying no matter where I may journey.

When I begin teaching or cooking for new clients, I work with them to make sure they have the items listed here so that they (and you!) will be able to cook any basic recipe without having to think too much. I have included what I consider to be two luxury items that I use almost daily: a pressure cooker and a Vitamix blender. I cannot recommend them enough—they will both change your life in the kitchen, giving you great results in a fraction of the time; however, they are not necessary for cooking any of the recipes in this book.

In the Resources section in the back of this book you'll find the brands I seek and use in my kitchen.

BAKING PANS

Although some pans and skillets I use taper at the bottom, most manufacturers measure the size across the top. To avoid any confusion, I have measured these pans the same way.

• A standard muffin pan for baking muffins and cupcakes. I line the cups with (unbleached recycled) cupcake liners, to protect the batter from aluminum and because vegan muffins can break easily when you're removing them from the pan.

• A 9-inch springform pan is perfect for cakes and tarts that have high sides or no sides at all; it is the most versatile size to have, although a couple of 8-inch cake pans come in handy for layer cakes.

• A 1-pound loaf pan for baking breads; mine is 9 × 4½ × 3 inches.

• A 9-inch (1 inch deep) fluted tart pan with removable bottom is used for most of the tarts in this book and is generally the most useful size; however, I prefer to make savory tarts larger and often use a 9½- to 10-inch (1¼ inches deep) fluted tart pan.

• Tartlet pans mean that each person at your table gets their own tart, sweet or savory. Good sizes are 4¾ and 3¾ inches, with ¾- to 1-inch sides, and it's best to get them with removable bottoms so the pastry shells can be removed easily.

CAST-IRON SKILLETS

A well-seasoned cast-iron skillet is naturally nonstick and perfect for everything from sautéing and caramelizing to cooking pancakes and toasting spices. It can go from stovetop to oven and gets better the more it's used. I have three ranging from 6 to 10 inches, although the 10-inch one certainly gets the most use. If you buy a new cast-iron skillet, follow the manufacturer's instructions for seasoning it and avoid using soap when washing it; simply clean it with hot water and a brush, dry, and rub occasionally with a little coconut oil, especially if any rust appears.

CERAMIC, GLASS, OR ENAMEL-COATED CAST-IRON BAKING DISHES

These dishes are used for making things like lasagna and bars and for roasting hard root vegetables. Since the sides are higher than those on sheet pans, they can easily be covered with parchment and foil to lock in steam and soften vegetables to speed cooking time. Good sizes to have are 8 × 12 inches, 8 × 8 inches, and 6½ × 10 inches.

CERAMIC VEGETABLE SLICER OR JAPANESE MANDOLINE

An excellent tool for quickly slicing vegetables into paper-thin slices. Slicers and mandolines are affordable, small, light, and super easy to clean and store. The ceramic blades stay sharp for ages and won't rust or corrode. Japanese mandolines come with a selection of removable and adjustable blades for different cutting styles and thicknesses.

CUTTING BOARDS

Well-used wooden cutting boards in a few sizes make a kitchen look and feel inviting and have many great uses apart from just being used for cutting. I often serve food on them in place of platters and plates and use them as trivets for hot pots when stove space is tight. When chopping vegetables, wood is a more enjoyable surface to cut on, and it's safe—your knives won't slip, and wooden cutting boards are naturally resistant to bacteria—so wood wins over plastic on all counts. For daily cleaning, scrub the surfaces with a vegetable brush (see my favorite later in this section) and very hot water, then let them dry thoroughly before storing. Spraying or wiping your boards with white vinegar is a great way to naturally disinfect them and keep them odorless. For stain removal and general freshening, sprinkle boards with coarse salt and rub vigorously with half a lemon, then rinse and dry. Mineral oil is often recommended for oiling wooden cutting boards, but since it's petroleum based, I prefer to use coconut oil, which is naturally resistant to bacteria.

ELECTRIC SPICE GRINDER

These grinders turn flax seeds into flax meal and spices into powder in seconds. To clean, just wipe them out with a dry cloth immediately after each use and wash only the lid. To remove oily residue from strongly flavored spices and general buildup in hard-to-reach places, fill the grinder with raw rice, grind until fine, and compost.

FLOUR SACK KITCHEN TOWELS

These thin, fast-drying towels are handy for so many things besides drying dishes: straining nut milks if you don't have a nut milk bag; covering sauerkraut to keep bugs away; straining labneh; drying salad greens—the list goes on ad infinitum. They're fairly inexpensive and are available in organic cotton.

FOOD PROCESSOR

A medium-size food processor with about an 11-cup capacity is necessary for everything from grinding nuts or tofu (for making cheese) to blending oats for tart crusts and cookies and whipping up smooth dips and pâtés. This size is small enough for grinding ingredients for one tart crust and large enough for blending frosting for a layer cake.

GLASS CONTAINERS

Clear glass containers in all shapes and sizes are great for storing cooked grains, beans, and any leftovers. Look for those that are heat- and coldproof, like Pyrex, so you can also reheat or freeze food in them.

GLASS JARS

Mason jars, Weck jars, and recycled jars from jams, pickles, nut butters, and so on are indispensable for storing soups, nut milks, cooked and raw grains and beans, toasted seeds, spices, salad dressings, leftover sauces and stews, and more. One can never have too many jars!

GRATERS

It is good to have two types of graters available: a box grater for grating vegetables and preparing quick salads like Carrot Parsley Salad (page 102); and a microplane for zesting citrus and grating hard cheeses, fresh turmeric and ginger, and nutmeg. A microplane is also perfect for grating garlic cloves directly into food, eliminating the need for a garlic press.

TAWASHI BRUSH (JAPANESE VEGETABLE BRUSH)

These lovely brushes make scrubbing vegetables a pleasure; because of their oval shape, they are perfect for root vegetables like carrots and burdock. Giving vegetables a good scrub with this type of brush not only gets dirt off but also cleans away a very thin layer of the outer skin, eliminating the need to peel and keeping important nutrients intact. These brushes last longer than any other vegetable brush I've found and are also perfect for cleaning cutting boards and cast iron pans.

KNIVES

One medium-size vegetable knife is all you really need for vegetarian cooking. I like Japanese knives, but plenty of other good brands are available. You'll need a serrated knife for bread, which can also be handy for slicing tomatoes when your regular knife isn't at its sharpest. Depending on how much you use your knives, it's a good idea to take them to a professional sharpener every year or so. For home sharpening, I prefer a MinoSharp—a ceramic water sharpener that's easy to use. Always wash and dry your knives by hand after using them to prevent wooden handles from warping.

MESH STRAINERS

I use a set of three (small, medium, and large) mesh strainers daily for various tasks like catching grains when washing them, sifting flour, draining seaweeds after soaking, and making nut milk. You can also sprout grains and beans in them (see page 79).

MIXING BOWLS

Small, medium, and large bowls can be used for just about everything: washing greens, mixing crusts and cake batters, soaking nuts, and tossing salads. If you buy nice-looking ceramic bowls, they can double as serving bowls.

NUT MILK BAG

These bags are made from strong, fine mesh cloth sewn into a bag and make straining the pulp from nut milks a breeze, resulting in a silky smooth texture. Just rinse them out and hang them to dry after each use. Fine mesh nut milk bags can also be used for straining blended vegetable juices, if you don't have a juicer.

PARCHMENT PAPER

Use this paper to line anything that is baked on aluminum or metal trays or pans so the food doesn't touch the surface. It also makes cleanup a breeze. Seek out unbleached and recycled parchment paper.

PEPPER GRINDER

Grinding pepper fresh, straight into food is the best and easiest way to use it. Peppercorns that are preground usually have a harsh and stale flavor. It's worth investing in a good quality, wooden pepper grinder as they can last generations.

POTS AND PANS

There are really only two kinds of pots worth buying: heavy-bottomed, high-quality stainless steel or enamel-coated cast iron. Both absorb and spread heat evenly, allowing food to cook long and slow without sticking to the bottom. Their tight-fitting lids trap flavor and steam, making them perfect for cooking grains and stews. Avoid any synthetically coated and nonstick pots; these materials release toxic gases when heated and also eventually peel off and end up in your food. Here is a list of pots that I reach for daily:

- A small, 1½- or 2-quart stainless steel pot for making oatmeal, cooking grains, and warming up soups and stews.
- A 2-quart enamel-coated cast-iron pot (also called a Dutch oven), which is the best choice for cooking 1 to 2 cups of brown rice and other grains.
- A medium (3½- to 4-quart) pot for making soups, stews, and larger pots of grains and congees.

- A large, 6-quart, heavy-bottomed, stainless steel pot with a steamer basket, which is perfect for reheating food and steaming greens. I also use this pot to make broths, soups, and stews and to cook noodles and pasta.
- A 10-inch sauté pan (or a wide skillet with a lid). The 2- to 3-inch-high sides make this skillet great for caramelizing large amounts of onions, sautéing greens, and cooking anything that needs to be covered at some point.

PRESSURE COOKER

A good quality pressure cooker is the secret to the most flavorful, perfectly cooked, and creamy beans ever! It can also be used to make vegetable soups and risottos in less than 10 minutes. The airtight seal around the lid causes pressure to increase and the internal temperature to rise, cooking food faster and locking in flavor. My best friend gave me a 5-quart pressure cooker sixteen years ago, and I still use it weekly. It's the perfect size for cooking 2 cups of dry beans and soups for up to four people. If you plan on making big pots of soup or beans, a 7-quart pot would be ideal. Many pressure cookers come with glass lids so they can be used as a regular medium or large pot as well. I don't recommend "jiggle top" cookers, as they are harder to regulate and potentially unsafe.

NOTE: Every recipe in this book was created and tested without a pressure cooker, so you don't need one; however, it really is a fantastic tool and will drastically change the way you approach cooking beans.

REUSABLE DRAWSTRING CLOTH BAGS

The less plastic you can use, the better, both for the planet and for your health. Drawstring cloth bags eliminate the need for plastic bags when shopping for bulk grains, nuts, seeds, and beans. They come in many different sizes, and are also great for storing washed greens and straining nut milks too. Thicker cloth bags can store produce and keep greens fresh for extended periods, helping to eliminate food waste as well as plastic use.

RIMMED BAKING SHEETS

Also called half sheet pans and jelly roll pans, these pans are usually 13 × 18 inches and fit in standard-size ovens. They're perfect for roasting vegetables, toasting nuts and seeds, and baking cookies and veggie burgers. Stainless steel baking sheets are difficult to find—most are made of aluminum, which is why I always suggest covering them with parchment paper. As with pots and skillets, avoid buying nonstick, as they let off toxic fumes when heated. I also like to keep a quarter sheet pan (13 × 9 inches) for baking brownies and bars.

ALUMINUM

Aluminum is a toxic metal that is released from aluminum cookware when it's scratched or when acidic foods come into contact with it. An accumulation of aluminum in the body has been linked to Alzheimer's disease. Scratching happens easily when food gets stuck to baking sheets or when metal utensils are used. Avoid this by covering aluminum baking sheets, cake pans, and loaf pans with parchment paper and lining aluminum muffin pans with unbleached muffin liners. This way, food doesn't come into contact with the metal and you avoid any possible scratching when the food is removed. When using aluminum foil, place a sheet of parchment paper between the food and the foil to avoid any contact. I suggest completely avoiding cooking and food preparation with aluminum pots and bowls, because acidic foods react to them, leaching metal into your food.

UPRIGHT BLENDER

A blender is indispensable for making everything from nut milks and smoothies to dressings and soups; and the more powerful your blender, the creamier and smoother the results will be. For the ultimate in texture and speed, a Vitamix truly is the best, and although expensive, it will last a lifetime. The only less expensive blender I recommend is a Waring Pro.

WATER FILTER

Clean water, like organic whole-food ingredients, is essential for creating healthy meals that have the potential to nourish and heal. As such, a good water filter is possibly the most valuable kitchen investment, as it rewards you daily with everything you eat and drink. Many water filters remove chlorine, but there are very few methods to remove fluoride (see page 51). Check with the manufacturer of any water filter you're considering to ensure that at least 95 percent of the fluoride is being removed, that beneficial trace minerals are being retained, and that no water is being wasted in the process. Reverse osmosis does remove 95 percent of fluoride, but other important trace minerals are lost in the process; more important, it wastes several gallons of water per gallon of filtered water it produces.

FILTERED WATER

Clean water is a vitally important ingredient in cooking meals that have a positive effect on your health and body. Unless your water is pure from a natural source, like an unpolluted spring, it most likely contains chemicals from pesticide runoff, is contaminated with heavy metals, and has had fluoride and chlorine added to it. Fluoride has been proven to have a negative effect on internal organs, and when consumed over time, it damages immune system function, increases the chances of degenerative diseases, speeds the aging process, and makes weight loss difficult. Adding fluoride to drinking water is now illegal in many European countries. Chlorine destroys intestinal flora and vitamin E in the body, and because of the way it combines with organic substances that may be present in your water, it can form chloroform, a cancer-causing chemical.

Installing a water filter is an investment that will reward you daily, not only for your peace of mind but also for drastically improved flavor in anything you cook or drink. Even if you seldom cook, a water filter means you will never have to buy bottled water again. Besides the severely damaging effects bottled water has on the environment (one of the biggest of our time), it is often just filtered tap water that has absorbed the toxic chemicals that leach from the plastic bottles.

OPTIONAL EQUIPMENT

FLAME DIFFUSER

I recommend these to people who don't have good control of how low a gas flame on their stove can go. It is a flat tin disc that is placed between the flame and the pot. It's especially good for cooking grains or other dishes that require long, slow cooking on very low heat.

GARLIC PRESS

Pressed garlic is paste-like, which makes it perfect for marinades and dressings or for when you don't want to dirty a cutting board. If you don't have a press, use a microplane zester or mince the garlic very fine with a pinch of salt and press it with the side of your knife until you get a paste.

OVEN THERMOMETER

Oven temperatures vary greatly. I recommend getting a thermometer to test your oven for accuracy so you can be sure to get good results when baking. Most thermometers cost only a few dollars and are really handy when cooking in unfamiliar kitchens.

SURIBACHI

A suribachi is a Japanese mortar and pestle. The mortar is made from ceramic with small grooves on the unglazed interior, which make it easy to crush ingredients like toasted sesame seeds for Black Sesame Gomasio (page 114). The pestle is made from wood rather than stone or ceramic. In Japan they are used to "puree" miso, tahini, and creamy tofu dressings and sauces.

SUSHI MAT

These mats are not only for making nori rolls; they're also great to use as covers for soaking beans, grains, and nuts. They also make ideal ventilated covers for cooling cooked food before storing it.

PLASTIC

There are many good reasons to avoid plastic as much as possible: the irreplaceable (and rapidly declining) natural resources used in its creation; the production process that releases carcinogenic dioxins into the environment; the toxic chemicals that leach into food from it; and the harmful effect it has on animals, nature, and our food chain over the thousand-plus years it takes to decompose.

Studies have shown that long-term exposure to bisphenol-A (BPA), a plastics chemical, and phthalates, a plastic softener, disrupts hormone regulators in the body and has been linked to cancer and damage to the reproductive system. These chemicals are especially harmful to infants and pregnant women.

Avoiding plastic is no easy task, but cutting down as much as possible is an important thing to do for your own health and that of the environment. Here are some ways to cut back on plastics in your kitchen:

• Eat a diet of fresh whole foods and shop at the farmers' market with reusable bags.

• Purchase bulk ingredients with reusable cloth bags.

• Install a water filter and carry a glass or stainless steel water bottle with you.

• Invest in reusable glass or stainless steel food storage containers instead of plastic containers and resealable plastic bags for storing leftovers and carrying lunch.

• Seek out alternatives to plastic wrap, such as beeswax-covered cloth and fabric bowl covers.

• Never store foods that are hot, contain oil, or are fermented in plastic, as they facilitate the transfer of plastic toxins.

• Purchase foods like peeled tomatoes and any prepared food in jars, and recycle them to store bulk food items at home.

• Purchase any canned beans from companies that use BPA-free lining.

• Retire any old plastic storage containers and use them to store nonfood items.

• Invest in reusable cloth produce bags to keep vegetables fresh.

Here are a few websites that provide even more ideas for cutting out plastic and helping the environment in other ways:

www.care2.com (care2 make a difference)

www.ewg.org (Environmental Working Group)

www.smallfootprintfamily.com (Small Footprint Family)

http://myplasticfreelife.com (My Plastic-Free Life)

cooking from the pantry

The recipes in this chapter are what I cook most often in my own kitchen. They are among the first dishes I teach to new students and what I turn to when I can't think about what to cook. They are the foundation of many great meals that can be built on endlessly, adapted easily, and often enjoyed over the course of a week.

Scanning the selection of grains, nuts, and beans on the shelves of my own pantry to choose what to soak for the following day is now an ingrained and pleasurable nightly ritual. This process is critical to sustaining healthy eating habits in our busy, fast-paced lives. It gives structure to meal planning and takes the guesswork out of healthy everyday food.

Perfectly cooked grains and beans are the blank canvas for delicious meals that can be enjoyed in every season. With the addition of flax oil, scallions, avocado, seeds, and something fermented (all from your stocked pantry), these basics become a meal in minutes. You can go a step further and make Roasted Vegetables (page 83), Arame with Carrots and Sesame (page 107), or Dijon Mustard–Marinated Tempeh (page 105). This simple eating is what sustains me in my daily life; it doesn't require hours in the kitchen or a special trip to the store—just a few minutes of advance planning.

Here you'll also find my staple breakfasts for summer and winter and a breakfast sprinkle that adds superfoods and substance to anything from fruit salads and yogurt to granola and muesli.

I have provided recipes for my favorite homemade condiments, including Curry Powder (page 112) for flavoring soups and curries; Harissa (page 112) for giving effortless zest to salads, marinades, simple vegetable dishes, and soups or stews; and Miso Mayonnaise (page 114) for slathering on sandwiches, toast, and crackers.

These recipes are the equipment for a lifetime of health-promoting, tasty meals, with endless variations and possibilities.

A WEEK OF MEALS IN MY KITCHEN

This weekly plan is fairly loose, as there is always a happy interruption—a meal out, an event, or dinner at a friend's. Since all these dishes can be kept for at least a few days, any leftovers are often the basis for spontaneous meals or snacks.

BREAKFASTS

In the cooler months, I soak ingredients for Superfood Oatmeal (page 87) every night as I make or clean up dinner. When the weather is warmer, I prepare three to four days' worth of Soaked Oats and Chia (page 88) at a time. I plan to start the week with a jar of fresh almond milk to add to whatever breakfast I eat. If I forget to soak ingredients for breakfast, I happily eat toast—either sprouted bread with almond butter or sourdough rye with avocado or tomato in summer.

LUNCHES AND DINNERS

SUNDAY: Scan my pantry for a grain or bean I'm in the mood for and soak it—I usually choose Brown and Sweet Rice (page 63) or an heirloom bean; this becomes the basis for Monday night dinner and lunch on Tuesday and Wednesday.

MONDAY: Wash and cook the soaked grain or bean. Then I steam vegetables, using whatever seasonal vegetables and greens are in the fridge, and serve them with either Black Sesame Flax Dressing (page 93) or just a drizzle of flax and tamari. Top the grains or beans with kraut or kimchi, and some avocado and sprouts if I have them on hand.

I may make some Quick Braised Tempeh (page 108) to go with the rice if I'm craving it and have time.

TUESDAY: In cooler months, I might make a pot of Simple Red Lentil Soup with Spinach, Lemon, and Pepper (page 91) or a curried variation leaving out the lemon; this can be dinner on Wednesday too. If it's midsummer—and I didn't eat rice for lunch—I'll toss last night's grain into a salad, adding chives, toasted seeds, avocado, and tamari, and whip up some Carrot Parsley Salad (page 102), serving it with a sheet of toasted nori.

WEDNESDAY: Eat leftover soup for dinner or make Whole-Wheat Fettuccini with Kale, Caramelized Onions, and Marinated Goat Cheese (page 98). Soak enough chickpeas for a few meals before bed.

THURSDAY: Lunch is leftover grains or beans from the previous days dressed up with toasted seeds, kraut, and so on. Cook the soaked chickpeas and either marinate them (page 70) or make Chickpea Mash (page 70) to have with a salad or steamed vegetables for dinner. Any leftovers can be warmed and spread over toast or crackers with sauerkraut for a light lunch or snack in the coming days. Soak quinoa (page 64) as the basis for dinner on Thursday and/or Friday.

FRIDAY: Steam kale to toss with leftover chickpeas and acocado for lunch. Cook the soaked quinoa. If it's cold, I may warm up the kitchen by roasting some vegetables (page 83) and make Zesty Flax Dressing for steamed broccoli (page 92). If it's warm, I'll top the quinoa with juicy cherry tomatoes, lots of chopped parsley, some fresh sprouts, and a crumble of goat milk feta or avocado—with flax oil, of course! If there's time, I'll make Marinated Beets (page 104) to have on the side and also to have on hand for adding to sandwiches or salads over the weekend.

WEEKENDS: With more time on my hands, I have the flexibility to make more involved recipes, whether just for my partner and me or for a dinner with friends. For most of the year, Saturday or Sunday trips to the farmers' market are a priority; this is when I shop for the majority of what I'll cook over the course of the week. Washing fresh greens and storing them for adding to soups, simple steamed vegetables, or salads during the week is a great way to lessen the steps for weeknight cooking.

PHYTIC ACID

Whole grains, beans, nuts, and seeds contain all the natural intelligence needed to grow into beautiful, healthy plants. This potential remains dormant until they are in the perfect environment in which to sprout. Phytic acid, present in the bran and hulls of these foods, preserves and protects them from sprouting in your pantry. This natural protective toxin also interferes with the absorption of zinc, magnesium, iron, and calcium, and it inhibits enzyme function. Soaking whole grains, beans, nuts, and seeds sparks the sprouting process, which neutralizes the phytic acid, making more minerals available and activating nutrients and the enzymes that aid in their digestion.

Phytic acid binds with minerals in the body, which can actually be therapeutic in some cases of disease, but when a diet is based on grains and beans, the body can become depleted over time. Besides soaking and sprouting, fermenting and toasting (to some degree) also remove phytic acid. In all traditional food cultures, grains and beans were prepared using these methods; it is only in more recent times that we have skipped these necessary steps. When cooking grains and beans, the addition of seaweed can assist in disabling phytic acid. Soaking grains can also help counteract sensitivities to wheat and other grains containing gluten. After soaking, it is important to discard the soaking water and thoroughly wash the grains, beans, nuts, or seeds to remove any phytic acid residue. Adding a small amount of acidic liquid to soaking grain is said to help activate phytase, which breaks down phytic acid—you can use vinegar, lemon juice, whey, or sauerkraut juice.

GRAINS

*Grains are my desert island food, and I could happily eat them at every meal;
they have been an important part of my daily cooking and eating my whole life. It's essential, for nutrition,
flavor, and texture, that grains be prepared properly. You'll find all the information you need
here, from the steps of washing, soaking, and cooking grains perfectly to what to do if your plans
change once you've soaked them. Although I could eat simple brown rice or quinoa every day, I have included some
variations to keep you interested throughout the seasons. Information on the nutritional
benefits of all the grains are in the "My Pantry Essentials" section, which starts on page 7.*

SOAKING GRAINS

Whole grains need to be soaked in water for 12 to 24 hours before being cooked in order to remove phytic acid (see page 58). This step enlivens the grain, activating nutrients as well as making them more digestible. Since quinoa sprouts faster than other grains, I find a 10- to 12-hour soak adequate, but longer is also fine. The soaking process also improves the texture and flavor, making my regular pot of whole grains even better.

At first, soaking grains will seem like another thing standing between you and eating well, another chore to cross off your list before going to bed at night or leaving the house in the morning, but the increased nutrients and improved flavor will reward you no end. The soaking habit is easy to get into: once the thought of dinner or food crosses your mind, go to the pantry and choose a grain and without thinking too much, place it in a 1½- to 2-quart pot (the one you'll cook it in), and add at least double the water. That's it! Ideally you wash the grain before soaking it (see below), but honestly, I usually leave that step until the following day. If you soak your grains before going to bed and cook them for lunch the following day, they'll have soaked for about 14 hours. If you cook them for dinner, it'll be closer to 20 hours.

If, like me, you live in a four-season climate, you can soak all grains outside of the fridge nine or ten months of the year; in the peak of summer or if your kitchen is particularly warm, put them in the fridge to soak. In warm temperatures or if they are left for more than a day, they can sometimes begin to bubble and ferment slightly, but not to worry, that just makes them even more digestible. (Although if they're left too long they will taste sour.) Just give them a couple of good washes and cook them as directed.

WASHING AND COOKING GRAINS

After grains have had a nice long soak, pour off the liquid, catching them in a strainer. Return the grains to the pot you soaked them in and fill it with fresh water. Swish them around with your fingers, let them settle, then pour the water off through a strainer. Repeat (preferably using filtered water for the last wash), drain, and cook as directed.

For the best results, cook grains in a heavy pot—2 quarts is a great size for 1½ cups of raw grain. It's important to cook them over very low heat so that they simmer gently. Once the water has come to a boil, cover the pot and turn the heat down low. You should see some movement during cooking, but it should not be boiling too rapidly. If you find that you can't lower the heat enough, get a flame diffuser (see page 52). Once the grain is cooked, set the pot aside and allow it to sit covered for 5 to 10 minutes before serving.

Adding a 1-inch piece of kombu to grains as they cook infuses them with minerals, helps further reduce phytic acid, and enhances flavor. You can eat the kombu or remove it before serving. For people on low-salt diets, kombu can replace salt in cooked grains.

WHAT TO DO IF YOUR PLANS CHANGE

You may think that before you soak anything you have to have a plan, a recipe in mind, and the ingredients to make it. You may worry that you'll waste the grain if your plans change. Don't sweat it! There are many ways to eat grains and things you can do if you can't attend to cooking them right away. Here are three suggestions to ensure you get the most out of your grains:

1. Strain off the soaking liquid and replace it with fresh water. Place it in the fridge if you're not sure when you'll get around to cooking it—it can stay there for two or three days. Left out of the fridge for a couple of days (less in warm weather), your soaking grain may start to bubble; this is the beginning of fermentation and will only help the grain become more digestible. Just wash it thoroughly a couple of times and cook it as usual.

2. Strain off the soaking liquid, rinse the grains, drain them in a strainer, and sprout them (see page 79 for directions). Quinoa will sprout and start growing through the strainer in less than 24 hours, which is exciting to see. Other grains take longer, but you can see a tiny sprout after a couple of days. Sprouted grains can be cooked as directed here and will result in a moister, stickier grain.

3. Cook it! Once cooked, you can set your grains aside to cool and eat them at room temperature in a few hours or refrigerate them to eat later. Cooked grains can last up to four days in the fridge and are the perfect basis for many quick and simple meals. See Parsley Brown Rice Salad with Seeds (page 97).

COOKING BASIC GRAINS

The following recipes are my favorite basic grains that are on constant rotation in my kitchen. If you forget to soak one of them, take it as an opportunity to cook whole-grain pasta or noodles or to make polenta instead. But just in case you have your heart set, you'll find liquid amounts for the times you forget to soak them.

BROWN AND SWEET RICE

This simple pot of brown rice is one of my weekly staples. Although I have cooked rice many different ways, the addition of sweet rice and an overnight soak is by far my favorite. The result is a satisfying combination of sweet and nutty, with the perfect amount of stickiness. Whenever I'm not sure what grain to soak and cook, I reach for brown rice. If you forget to soak your rice and can't wait to have a bowl, simply wash and drain it as directed on page 61, increase the cooking water to 2¾ cups, and cook for 60 minutes.

MAKES 4½ CUPS COOKED RICE

1 cup short-grain brown rice

½ cup sweet rice

2⅓ cups filtered water, plus more for soaking

Pinch sea salt

Wash and soak rice in at least 3 cups water for 12 to 24 hours. Drain and rinse rice. Place in a 2-quart pot and add filtered water and salt. Bring to a boil over high heat, cover pot, reduce heat to low, and cook for 50 minutes or until all the water is absorbed. To check if rice is done, insert a fork or spoon straight down through the center of the rice and feel the bottom of the pot—rice should be beginning to stick slightly, and you shouldn't see any water. If you do, continue cooking for 5 to 10 minutes longer. Remove from heat and set aside, covered, for 10 to 15 minutes before serving. Once cool, rice can be stored in the fridge for four days.

VARIATIONS

BROWN AND SWEET RICE WITH TEFF

Try adding a couple of tablespoons of teff to your rice for added protein. Since teff is a tiny seed that even gets through a fine mesh strainer, I don't soak or wash it when adding it to grains. Add teff after you have washed, soaked, and rinsed the brown and sweet rice, then cook as directed in the main recipe above.

BROWN AND SWEET RICE WITH CHESTNUTS

Rice and chestnuts are nothing short of a dreamy combination. The chestnuts enhance the naturally sweet flavor of the rice, complementing any savory foods you serve it with. Since fresh chestnuts have a very short season, I usually make this with dried chestnuts, but you could add roasted and peeled chestnuts (see page 171 for roasting instructions) to the soaked and washed rice and cook as directed here. (See the Resources section for ordering dried chestnuts.)

Add ⅓ cup (1¾ ounces) dried chestnuts to the pot with brown and sweet rice and wash and soak it in at least 4 cups water for 12 to 24 hours. Pick out chestnuts, removing any brown pieces of skin, and rinse. Break each chestnut up into 6 or 8 pieces and set aside. Rinse and drain rice, return it to the pot, and add chestnut pieces. Add 2½ cups filtered water and a pinch of salt; cook as directed in the main recipe above.

BROWN AND SWEET RICE STUDDED WITH RED OR BLACK QUINOA

I love how the dark dots of quinoa look against the background of beige rice, as well as the little burst of texture they provide.

Add 2 tablespoons red or black quinoa to brown and sweet rice before washing, then soak, rinse, and cook as directed.

BROWN RICE WITH AMARANTH

When using amaranth in combination with brown rice, I don't use sweet rice, because amaranth has a similar sweet, sticky quality. If you forget to soak your rice and amaranth ahead of time, increase the cooking water to 2¼ cups.

MAKES 3½ CUPS COOKED GRAINS

1 cup short-grain brown rice
¼ cup amaranth
2 cups filtered water, plus more for soaking
Pinch sea salt

Wash and soak the rice and amaranth in at least 3 cups water for 12 to 24 hours. Drain and rinse grains—you'll need a mesh strainer for this, as the amaranth seeds are tiny. Place in a 1- to 2-quart pot and add filtered water and salt. Bring to a boil over high heat, cover pot, reduce heat to low, and cook for 50 minutes or until all the water is absorbed. To check if grain is ready, insert a fork or spoon straight down through the center of the grain and feel the bottom of the pot. The grain should be beginning to stick slightly, and you shouldn't see any water. If you do, continue cooking for 5 to 10 minutes longer. Remove from heat and set aside, covered, for 10 to 15 minutes before serving. Once cool, the grain can be stored in the fridge for up to four days.

Try adding an umeboshi plum in place of salt when cooking rice. The flavor of the plum is dispersed into the grain, adding a mild salty, tangy flavor. Finding the soft flesh of the cooked plum is a nice surprise when you're eating the rice, but just remember to watch out for the pit.

SIMPLE QUINOA

Quinoa is another staple grain that I prepare weekly. Once it's soaked, it takes only 15 minutes to cook, making it perfect for busy weeknight cooking. Since quinoa is a complete protein, it's the perfect grain to reach for when you have neither beans nor another protein on hand. My favorite fast meal is a bowl of quinoa topped with flax oil, tamari, toasted black sesame seeds, avocado, chopped parsley, and kraut or kimchi. Be sure to wash quinoa thoroughly to remove the saponin, a naturally occurring, bitter protective coating. A handy thing to remember when cooking different or unmeasured amounts of soaked quinoa is that it's equal parts water to the amount of quinoa you soaked. The water should just cover the surface of presoaked grain. If you forget to soak quinoa, wash as directed on page 61, increase the water to 1¾ cups, and cook for 20 minutes.

NOTE: Quinoa comes in three colors: beige (sometimes called pearl), red, and black. They're all cooked using the same method, but the red and black quinoa (and some smaller beige varieties) have a seedlike, crunchy texture and don't open and fluff up the way the beige does.

MAKES 4 CUPS COOKED QUINOA

1 cup quinoa
1 cup filtered water, plus more for soaking
Pinch sea salt

Wash and soak the quinoa in at least 3 cups water for 8 to 24 hours. Drain and rinse quinoa. Place in a 2-quart pot and add filtered water and salt. Bring to a boil over high heat, cover pot, reduce heat to low, and cook for 15 minutes or until all the water is absorbed. Remove from heat and set aside, covered, for 5 to 10 minutes before fluffing with a fork and serving. Once cool, quinoa can be stored in the fridge for up to four days.

BUCKWHEAT WITH ONIONS

This buckwheat dish is a lovely addition to your grain rotation; although not technically a grain, it is prepared like one here. Served with a sprinkle of toasted sunflower seeds and a drizzle of tamari, it's a soothing, light dish with a decidedly earthy and savory flavor. The buckwheat will appear a little slimy after soaking; just rinse it well and allow it to drain thoroughly before cooking.

You may also use toasted buckwheat (kasha) in this recipe. It has a great nutty flavor and since it's pre-toasted it can be cooked without soaking.

NOTE: If you forget to soak buckwheat, wash and cook it as directed here (with onions), but increase the water to 2 cups.

MAKES 3 CUPS COOKED BUCKWHEAT

1 cup buckwheat groats

1 tablespoon extra virgin olive oil

1 medium onion, quartered and sliced

Pinch sea salt

1½ cups filtered water, plus more for soaking

Wash and soak the buckwheat in at least 2 cups of water for 12 to 24 hours. Drain and rinse buckwheat; set aside in a strainer to drain while you cook the onions. Warm oil in a 2-quart pot over medium heat. Add onions and sauté for 5 minutes, or until golden brown. Stir in a pinch of salt, the drained buckwheat, and filtered water, raise heat to high and bring to a boil. Cover pot, reduce heat to low, and cook for 20 minutes, or until all the water has absorbed. Remove from heat and set aside, covered, for 10 to 15 minutes before serving. Once cool, it can be stored in the fridge for up to four days.

SPELT BERRIES AND WHEAT BERRIES

Although these grains are not always part of my weekly routine, their earthy flavor and robust, chewy texture are wonderful as a base for salads. Wheat berries have a slightly rounder shape than spelt berries, and both taste great served as a simple side dish with olive oil, tamari, and chopped parsley. Unlike other grains in this section, these are cooked similarly to pasta—boiled in plenty of water and drained before using. Kamut, whole barley (also called hulled barley), and emmer can be cooked using this method as well. For great ways to use these grains, check out the Herbed Spelt Berry Salad with Peas and Feta (page 183) and Roasted Acorn and Delicata Squash Salad with Wheat Berries and Bitter Greens (page 195).

NOTE: You can cook any amount of spelt or wheat berries using this method, just be sure to increase the cooking water as necessary. I don't use salt here, because I've found the grains cook up tender in less time without it.

MAKES ABOUT 2¾ CUPS COOKED GRAINS

1 cup spelt or wheat berries

Wash and soak the grains in at least 3 cups water for 12 to 24 hours. Drain and rinse them. Place in a pot and cover with about 4 cups filtered water. Bring to a boil over high heat, cover the pot, reduce heat to low, and simmer for 1½ hours or until plump and tender. Add extra water as needed to keep grains submerged while simmering. Remove from heat and drain well. Once cool, spelt and wheat berries can be stored in the fridge for up to four days.

REHEATING GRAINS

The best way to reheat grains is in a steamer. Place as much as you are planning to eat directly into a steamer basket or add them to a heatproof container (like Pyrex) if you are heating smaller grains like quinoa that will fall through the holes in the basket. Cover and steam until heated through; this will take up to 5 minutes in a steamer, depending on how much you're reheating, and longer if in a heatproof container—in which case, stir it after a few minutes to ensure even heating. Storing grains in heatproof storage containers means they can go directly from the fridge to a steamer. Greens and other vegetables can be added to the steamer as the grains heat, giving you a one-pot meal.

BEANS

*Along with grains, beans are a mainstay of a whole-food, plant-based diet.
And as with grains, you needn't have a plan for beans before soaking them. Just soak a cup or two before
you go to bed and allow yourself to dream about their infinite possibilities. In fact, I usually
continue to conjure up ideas about what kind of dinner the beans will become over the course of the following day,
considering what I'm in the mood for, what vegetables I already have, or what I can pick up
on the way home. What ultimately becomes of the beans varies greatly depending on the season.*

*In warmer months, I crave large, creamy beans in tangy marinades.
I may add cherry tomatoes or marinated beets, along with lots of chopped parsley and chives, and eat them over a
bowl of greens drizzled with flax oil. Another great way to prepare beans, especially chickpeas, is to mash them
with a good, grassy olive oil and eat them with a grain or crackers or on garlic-rubbed toast.*

*In cool weather, bean soups and stews make up the majority of my meals. I find nothing
more warming or easier to prepare than a hearty bowl of soup or stew on a freezing night. Plant-based soups
and stews are made hearty and satisfying with the addition of beans and are a natural vehicle
for including more vegetables (both land and sea) into your diet.*

SOAKING BEANS

Beans, like grains, contain phytic acid (see page 58) and need to be soaked for at least 12 hours before cooking. Soaking not only removes the phytic acid and increases the availability of minerals, it also makes them easier to digest and faster to cook. The gas-causing enzymes present in beans are released into the soaking water, so it's important to discard it and wash them thoroughly before cooking.

Place beans in a medium to large pot or pressure cooker and briefly sort through them for any stones or lumps of dirt. Fill the pot with water, swish the beans around with your fingers, then pour off the water through a strainer. Add enough filtered water to cover the beans by at least 3 inches, and soak them for 12 to 24 hours. Place them in the fridge to soak if it's warm in your kitchen.

If your plans change and you can't cook the beans, drain off the soaking water, cover them with fresh filtered water, place them in the fridge, and cook them the following day. Soaked beans can also be sprouted (see page 79) and used in salads and sautés or cooked—cooking sprouted beans further increases their digestibility.

QUICK-SOAK METHOD

While it's best to soak beans for at least 12 hours, if you've forgotten to do so and you're set on cooking some, this method will serve in a pinch. Alternatively, you can embrace the occasion as a good opportunity to cook another protein like Simple Red Lentil Soup with Spinach, Lemon, and Pepper (page 91) or Quick Braised Tempeh (page 108).

Place the beans in a medium to large pot or pressure cooker and sort and wash them as already described. Add enough filtered water to cover them by at least 3 inches and bring to a boil over high heat; once they're boiling, cover the pot and take it off the heat. Set aside for one hour, then drain and rinse beans and cook as directed in the next section.

COOKING BEANS

The following are two methods for cooking beans; whichever you choose, it is important that the beans are thoroughly cooked. Even slightly undercooked beans are difficult to digest and won't absorb flavor well, whether they're in a marinade, soup, stew, or salad. Keep in mind that beans firm up when drained and cooled, so I recommend cooking them until they are completely soft. Sometimes they may begin to fall apart, but that's okay; the flavor of the final dish will be much better than if they're undercooked.

The amount of cooked beans you end up with varies greatly depending on the type; some beans almost triple in volume, some double. Since beans keep for up to four days in the fridge, I suggest cooking extra to have on hand.

Once the beans are cooked, add a pinch of salt and let them sit in their soaking liquid until you're ready to use them; the salt will add depth to their flavor.

Bean cooking liquid is a nourishing drink for the kidneys, especially if it's from black beans or adzuki beans. It's also infused with minerals from the kombu the beans are cooked with, and with a couple of drops of tamari added, the liquid makes a nice amuse-bouche for yourself or anyone else in the kitchen.

COOKING BEANS

COOKING BEANS IN A POT

The only tricky thing about using this method of cooking beans is that the cooking time can vary greatly, depending on the freshness of the bean. The challenge is that you can't tell if beans are old from looking at them, but older beans can take hours to cook. With this in mind, it's always a good idea to give yourself plenty of extra time.

1 to 2 cups dried beans, sorted and washed

2-inch piece kombu

Filtered water

Sea salt

Place the beans in a medium to large pot, add 4 to 6 cups filtered water, and soak them for 12 to 24 hours. Drain and rinse beans, and return them to the pot. Add kombu and water to cover beans by 3 inches. Bring to a rapid boil over high heat. Remove any foam that rises to the surface with a small strainer or slotted spoon. Cover pot, reduce heat to low, and simmer for 45 minutes. Every now and then, check that beans are actively simmering and still covered in plenty of water; if water evaporates, add more and return to a boil, then lower heat to a simmer again. If they boil over, crack the lid a little.

Taste a few beans—if they are soft and creamy all the way through and can be crushed easily, then they're ready. If not, continue cooking for 10 minutes more and check again. This can take up to 2 hours for some beans.

Once cooked, remove from heat, compost the kombu, and add a pinch of salt. Stir beans and set aside until you're ready to use them; at this point, they can be cooled and stored in the fridge—with or without their cooking liquid—for up to four days.

PRESSURE-COOKING BEANS

For consistently perfectly cooked and creamy beans, a pressure cooker is the way to go (see page 50). In as little as 25 minutes, your beans will be plump and happily sitting in a richly flavored cooking liquid. When using a pressure cooker, it doesn't seem to matter how old the beans are, but on the rare occasion that your beans are not cooked through, just put the lid back on, bring up the pressure again, and cook for 5 minutes longer.

Wash, soak, drain, and rinse beans (see instructions on page 67), and place them in a pressure cooker. Add kombu and filtered water to cover beans by 1½ to 2 inches. Keep in mind that you can only fill a pressure cooker two-thirds full; otherwise, the water will bubble up and out of the pressure valve and the pressure won't be able to build. Bring to a rapid boil over high heat. Remove any foam that rises to the surface with a small strainer or slotted spoon, then lock the pressure cooker lid in place and bring up to full pressure—two rings on the pressure gauge (located on the top of the lid). Lower heat and cook for 20 minutes for smaller beans, such as navy or black beans. Cook 25 minutes for chickpeas and 28 to 30 minutes for extra-large beans like scarlet runners or white bordals.

If the pressure gauge drops below the first ring during cooking, raise heat until it returns to high pressure, then lower heat again and continue cooking. There is no need to increase the cooking time, as the internal pressure remains very high.

Remove from heat and allow pressure to release naturally (this will take 5 to 10 minutes); the beans will continue cooking until the lid is removed. If you've lost track of time and worry you've overcooked them, you can speed up the pressure release by placing the pressure cooker under cold running water. Once the pressure gauge has completely released, it is safe to remove the lid. Do not remove the lid while the pressure gauge is still up, as it will cause very hot steam to escape, which can burn you.

VARIATION

COOKING BEANS FOR SOUPS AND STEWS

When cooking beans for soups and stews, I cook them with the intention of using the cooking liquid as the base. I add bay leaves and the herbs that I will be using in the stew or soup, treating the cooking liquid as a stock. As I'm prepping herbs for the dish, I'll often throw the stems into the bean pot. The bean cooking liquid adds much more flavor and body to a soup or stew than plain water, helping to create a creamy, satisfying dish. Be sure to keep the liquid amount high when cooking beans in a pot and fill a pressure cooker to the maximum amount (two-thirds full). Here are some of the ingredients I might add to the cooking liquid, depending on the desired flavor, that will end up as the base for my soup or stew: bay leaves, celery leaves, kombu, peeled garlic cloves, sun-dried tomatoes, and sprigs of herbs such as sage, parsley, thyme, rosemary, and oregano, wrapped in cheesecloth.

CHICKPEA MASH

Chickpea mash is a favorite side dish in my house. When made with freshly pressure-cooked chickpeas and served slightly warm, this mash is rich in flavor with a luxurious, almost fluffy texture. It's perfect for the sweltering heat of New York City summers when beans seem too heavy. I love serving the mash with juicy tomato and cucumber salads, as a side dish to simple grains, spread on toast, or with just about anything. Although it may sound reminiscent of hummus, because there's no lemon, garlic, or tahini, it's quite different—lighter and more versatile.

If you don't have a pressure cooker, I would advise using canned chickpeas here, as boiling them won't get them soft enough to mash them into creamy deliciousness. See page 45 for instructions on improving the flavor of canned beans, and use water instead of chickpea cooking liquid when mashing them.

MAKES ABOUT 3½ CUPS

6 cups cooked warm chickpeas,
 1 cup of cooking liquid reserved (see page 68)

3 tablespoons extra virgin olive oil

½ teaspoon sea salt, plus more to taste

TO SERVE:

Chopped parsley or chives

Cold-pressed flax oil or extra virgin olive oil

Add chickpeas and ½ cup cooking liquid to a medium pot over medium heat. Stir until heated through and remove from heat. Add olive oil and salt, and mash until creamy with a potato masher, adding more liquid as needed to get desired consistency. Season to taste, place in a bowl, and serve topped with parsley or chives and a drizzle of oil.

Any leftover mash will keep in the fridge for up to four days. It will become quite firm and needs to be warmed to soften it up before serving. Place it in a pot over medium heat with a splash of water, stir until smooth, and season to taste.

SIMPLE MARINATED BEANS

When marinating beans, I like to use larger varieties, as they are usually the creamiest, absorb flavors well, and stand up well to marinades. Try chickpeas or kidney beans or my favorite heirloom beans—scarlet runners or white bordals. For the best flavor, marinate them while they're warm. This recipe is a great base for a salad.

MAKES 2 CUPS

2 cups freshly cooked beans, drained well

1 tablespoon unpasteurized apple cider vinegar

1 teaspoon balsamic vinegar or red wine vinegar

2 tablespoons extra virgin olive oil

Sea salt to taste

Chopped parsley and scallions to serve

Place beans in a medium bowl and add vinegars, olive oil, and a good pinch of salt. Stir to combine and set aside to marinate, or serve immediately with scallions and lots of chopped parsley. Store in the fridge for up to four days and serve at room temperature, or gently warm them in a pot.

LEMONY MARINATED LENTILS

Lentils have an intriguing, earthy taste that goes perfectly with lemon. Cooked French lentils hold their shape well, making them perfect for marinating. They're lovely served slightly warm over some wilted greens with a poached egg in winter or at room temperature in summer. Add some roasted vegetables, arugula, and a crumble of goat cheese, and you have a hearty salad. Try using Meyer lemons when they are in season for a fragrant, sweeter flavor.

MAKES ABOUT 2¼ CUPS

1 cup French lentils, sorted and washed

3 cups filtered water, plus more for soaking

3 bay leaves

3 whole garlic cloves, peeled

2-inch piece kombu

Zest of 1 lemon

2 tablespoons fresh lemon juice

3 tablespoons extra virgin olive oil, plus more for serving

½ teaspoon salt, plus more to taste

Freshly ground black pepper

Chopped fresh parsley to garnish

Place the lentils in a medium pot, add at least 3 cups water, and soak for 12 to 24 hours. Drain and rinse lentils and return them to the pot. Add water, bay leaves, garlic, and kombu, and bring to a boil over high heat. Cover pot, reduce heat to low, and simmer for 20 minutes or until lentils are soft inside but not falling apart—this can take up to 30 minutes.

Remove from heat. Remove and compost the kombu and bay leaves. Thoroughly drain lentils and return to pot—the liquid can be discarded or saved to use as a stock for soup. Stir lemon zest, lemon juice, olive oil, salt, and a pinch of pepper into lentils, gently crushing the cooked garlic cloves as you stir. Season to taste and top with parsley and a drizzle of olive oil. Serve warm or at room temperature. Stored in the fridge, the lentils will last up to four days.

NUTS AND SEEDS

*Having a variety of nuts and seeds on hand is an essential
part of my pantry. Whether soaked and blended into luscious nut milks or toasted and sprinkled
over grains and vegetables, they add flavor, texture, protein, antioxidants, and
essential fatty acids to any meal of the day.*

SOAKING NUTS AND SEEDS

Raw nuts and seeds, like grains and beans, contain enzyme inhibitors and varying amounts of phytic acid (see page 58). Soaking is the ideal way of removing them while activating nutrients and increasing digestibility. Soaked nuts and seeds can be drained, rinsed, and stored in the fridge for up to four days or frozen for up to six months. Sprinkle them over dishes, eat them as a snack, or blend them into creamy nut milks. Soaked seeds can also be sprouted (nuts won't grow a sprout, so they are referred to as soaks); see page 79 for sprouting directions.

To soak, place nuts or seeds in a bowl or jar, cover with 2 to 3 inches of filtered water, and soak for 8 to 12 hours at room temperature. In very warm weather, place them in the fridge to soak. Adding a large pinch of sea salt to soaking nuts further deactivates enzyme inhibitors. Drain and rinse the nuts, and make nut milk or place them in the fridge to use later.

Cashews, pine nuts, hemp seeds, and macadamia nuts don't have skins containing enzyme inhibitors, so I soak them for just 2 to 6 hours, which helps soften them up to use in creamy desserts, nut cheeses, or nut milks. They can become slimy and lose flavor if you soak them longer than 8 hours.

If you own a dehydrator, soaked nuts and seeds can also be dehydrated until they're dry and crisp, about 12 to 24 hours. They taste great this way, like toasted nuts but with all their live active enzymes preserved.

FRESH NUT MILK

Almonds are my absolute favorite for making nut milk, especially with the addition of cinnamon and vanilla. Nut milk can also be made plain for a versatile, neutral-tasting milk. Occasionally I stray from almonds and use Brazil nuts, which make wonderfully rich, bright white milk. You can use any nut or combination (and add dried unsweetened coconut for a different flavor); all you need to remember is the ratio of **1 part nuts to 4 parts water.** You can also use sunflower, sesame, or hemp seeds in the same ratios.

Every week throughout the year, I make a batch of almond milk. In the cooler months, I warm it to pour over my daily bowl of Superfood Oatmeal (page 87); during the summer, I make Soaked Oats and Chia (page 88). It's also perfect for adding to smoothies. I prefer the more substantial texture and ease of unstrained almond milk when eating it for breakfast. For a silky smooth nut milk to drink straight or add to hot drinks, I strain it. There are many ways you can do this: through a thin kitchen towel (or flour sack), several layers of cheesecloth, or a nut milk bag (see the Equipment section). For a sweet treat, try adding a Medjool date or two before blending and straining. Nut milk foams up quite a bit while blending; if your blender isn't big enough to hold 6 cups, then make this recipe in two batches.

MAKES ABOUT 5 CUPS UNSTRAINED OR 4 CUPS STRAINED NUT MILK

1 cup whole raw nuts or seeds

4 cups filtered water, plus more for soaking

Tiny pinch sea salt

¼ teaspoon cinnamon

1 tablespoon vanilla extract

Place nuts in a bowl, add 2 cups filtered water, and soak for 6 to 12 hours, depending on what kind of nuts you're using. Drain and rinse nuts, place in an upright blender, add 4 cups filtered water, salt, cinnamon, and vanilla. Blend on high speed for at least a minute or until completely smooth and frothy. Pour into a glass jar or bottle and store in the fridge for up to five days. Shake before using.

VARIATION
SMOOTH NUT MILK

Line a large strainer with a nut milk bag, a clean, thin kitchen towel, or several layers of cheese cloth. Place it over a medium bowl. Pour almond milk through the lined strainer into the bowl. Gather up the edges of the nut milk bag or cloth and slowly squeeze out the nut milk, getting as much milk out as possible. Compost the leftover pulp or save it for another use (see sidebar below). Pour the milk into a clean glass jar or bottle with a lid, and store in the fridge. Shake before using.

Leftover pulp from straining nut milk can be added to oatmeal or other breakfast porridges. You can also stir some into pancake batters, breads, or other baked goods. If you make your nut milk plain (without cinnamon or vanilla), it can be added to savory dips, pâtés, or burgers. Nut pulp will keep for up to five days in the fridge and can also be frozen for six months.

TOASTING NUTS AND SEEDS

Toasting your own nuts and seeds not only makes them taste absolutely delicious, but also helps reduce phytic acid and makes them more digestible than when eaten raw (unless they are soaked first). Many store-bought toasted nuts and seeds are cooked with low-quality oils and refined salt; they also rarely taste fresh and just don't compare to toasting your own.

Toasting nuts and seeds perfectly can take some practice, but if you follow these directions (and your oven is accurate), they'll turn out great every time. Always use a timer, and keep in mind that they continue cooking after you remove them from the oven. Lining the baking sheets with parchment paper allows for quick removal from the tray if you overcook them and makes it easy to transfer them to jars; always save the parchment to use again. The cooking times may vary if you decide to toast a lot more or less than the amounts shown here. For even baking, make sure the nuts and seeds are spread out in a single layer on your baking sheet.

All nuts and seeds, toasted or raw, will keep better in the fridge, but if you don't have space, store them in a cool, dark place. Most will last longer than the times I have listed in the recipes, although they will begin to lose their fresh toasty flavor and irresistible fragrance. If you find that they have lost their crisp texture and flavor, just return them to a 300°F oven for 5 minutes and taste one. If they're still not crisp, continue cooking for another 2 to 3 minutes and check again.

In the recipes that follow, you'll see that I rinse seeds before toasting them; the resulting flavor is cleaner, maybe because they can collect dust and dirt, though I find that nuts don't need rinsing. Make sure you drain the seeds well. I like to do this while the oven is heating. Keep in mind that they take longer to toast than unrinsed seeds.

TOASTED ALMONDS

Toasted almonds have a rich, slightly sweet flavor and make a tasty and satisfying snack alone or combined with your favorite dried fruits. I always pack a small bag of them when traveling—they're the most convenient nutritious food to nibble on anywhere. They're also great to have on hand for adding interest to everything from salads and grain dishes to breakfasts and desserts.

2 cups whole raw almonds

Preheat oven to 300°F. Line a rimmed baking sheet with parchment paper. Add almonds and spread them out in a single layer. Place on middle rack of oven, toast for 10 minutes, stir, and continue toasting for 8 to 10 minutes or until fragrant. The inside should be light brown; if not, return to oven for another 2 minutes and check again. Remove from oven and allow to cool on tray. Transfer the nuts to a jar and store in the fridge for up to a month.

TOASTED SESAME SEEDS

Toasted black sesame seeds are an everyday condiment in my kitchen. Not only do they look gorgeous sprinkled over grains and vegetables, but they also have a higher mineral content than brown sesame seeds. Once you have a batch ready, try making Black Sesame Gomasio (page 114) or Black Sesame Rice Crackers (page 218). I use toasted unhulled sesame seeds to make Unhulled Tahini (page 115).

NOTE: If you want to toast a smaller amount of sesame seeds, simply put them in a skillet over low to medium heat and stir frequently for 8 to 10 minutes or until they crush easily between your fingers.

2 cups raw black or unhulled sesame seeds

Preheat oven to 300°F.
Place sesame seeds in a medium bowl and fill with water; swish seeds around and let them settle. Pour off water and catch seeds in a strainer; rinse under running water and then set aside to drain while the oven heats.

Line a rimmed baking sheet with parchment paper, add the drained seeds, and spread them out in a single layer. Place on middle rack of oven, toast for 10 minutes, stir, and continue toasting them for another 10 minutes. They are ready when they crush easily between your fingers and smell fragrant. Remove from oven and allow to cool on a tray. Transfer the seeds to a jar and store in the fridge for up to a month.

TOASTED PUMPKIN SEEDS AND SUNFLOWER SEEDS

Plain toasted pumpkin seeds are a favorite snack of mine. They taste great as a topping for grains or beans, or in the Amaranth Muesli (page 130). A sprinkle of toasted sunflower seeds is a lovely addition to any number of foods; their sweet taste and light texture are delicious over morning oatmeal and in salads. Try them in the Parsley Brown Rice Salad with Seeds (page 97) and the Sprout Salad with Toasted Sunflower Seeds and Umeboshi Vinaigrette (page 182).

2 cups raw pumpkin seeds or sunflower seeds

Preheat oven to 300°F.
Place seeds in a medium bowl and fill with water; swish seeds around and let them settle. Pour off water and catch seeds in a strainer; rinse under running water and then set aside to drain while the oven heats up.

Line a rimmed baking sheet with parchment paper, add the drained seeds, and spread them out in a single layer. Place on middle rack of oven and toast for 12 minutes. Stir and continue toasting for another 10 to 12 minutes or until puffed with a nice, toasty fragrance. Remove from oven and set aside to cool completely. Transfer the seeds to a jar and store in the fridge for up to three weeks.

VARIATIONS
SPICED PUMPKIN SEEDS

This zesty combination makes a lively snack or tasty addition to salads or grain dishes any time of year. This recipe can easily be doubled or tripled, depending on how much you want to make.

Rinse and drain 1 cup of pumpkin seeds as in the main recipe above. Toss with 4 teaspoons fresh lime or lemon juice, ¼ teaspoon cayenne pepper, and ½ teaspoon sea salt. Spread over a parchment-lined tray and toast as above. Let the seeds cool and then transfer them to a jar and store in the fridge for up to three weeks.

TAMARI-TOASTED SEEDS

These seeds make the perfect seasoning for brown rice or quinoa; they also make a satisfying salty snack. I usually use pumpkin or sunflower seeds, but you can also use sesame seeds or a combination.

Toast seeds as in the main recipe above; as soon as you remove them from the oven, tilt the parchment paper to gather the seeds in a mound. Drizzle with a teaspoon of tamari for each cup of seeds used and stir until combined. Spread out over the parchment in a single layer and allow to cool. Once seeds have cooled and dried, store in a jar in the fridge for two to three weeks.

TOASTED WALNUTS

Walnuts are a great way to add richness and interest to salads like the Roasted Winter Vegetables and Arugula Salad with Mustard Dressing (page 199). They add a buttery quality to many desserts and sweet treats and also make a tasty addition to trail mixes and topping for yogurt.

1 to 2 cups raw walnut halves or pieces

Preheat oven to 300°F. Line a rimmed baking sheet with parchment paper, add walnuts and spread them out in a single layer. Place on middle rack of oven, and toast for 4 to 5 minutes (for walnut pieces) or 6 minutes (for walnut halves). Taste one; if it's not crisp and fragrant, return to oven for another 2 minutes. Remove from oven and allow to cool on a tray. Rub walnuts between your fingers to remove the bitter, papery skin. Transfer to a jar and store in the fridge for up to a month.

TOASTED PECANS

Toasted pecans have a delicate, sweet, and buttery flavor and are easily substituted for walnuts in salads and sweet treats. Pecans always make me think of desserts, especially Cherry Pecan Cookies (page 350).

To toast pecans, follow the same directions as for walnut halves given previously. Pecans don't have a bitter skin, so there is no need to rub them after baking. Transfer the cooled nuts to a jar and store in the fridge for up to a month.

TOASTED HAZELNUTS

Toasted hazelnuts have a rich, assertive flavor and warm aroma that works beautifully in the Chocolate Hazelnut Layer Cake with Cherry Filling and Chocolate Ganache (page 333). They also stand up well in wintry salads like the Shaved Fennel Beet Salad with Blood Orange and Crushed Hazelnuts (page 196).

1 to 2 cups raw hazelnuts

Preheat oven to 300°F. Line a rimmed baking sheet with parchment paper, add hazelnuts and spread them out in a single layer. Place on middle rack of oven, toast for 10 minutes, stir, and continue toasting for another 4 minutes. Check that the inside is light brown; if not, return to oven for another 2 minutes and check again. Remove from oven and allow them to cool on a tray. Rub them between your fingers to remove their brown, papery skin. You won't be able to remove all of it, but most of it comes off easily. Transfer nuts to a jar and store in the fridge for up to a month.

TOASTED PISTACHIOS

Pistachios add a splash of vibrant color and interest to both sweet and savory dishes.

Try them sprinkled over Marinated Beets (page 104), with a crumble of goat feta and a few torn mint leaves for a quick and easy salad, or in Pistachio Pumpkin Seed Dukkah (page 216).

1 to 2 cups whole raw pistachios

Preheat oven to 300°F. Line a rimmed baking sheet with parchment paper, add pistachios and spread them out in a single layer. Place on middle rack of oven, and toast for 6 to 8 minutes or until fragrant and a shade darker. Remove from oven and allow to cool on a tray. Transfer nuts to a jar and store in the fridge for up to a month.

SPROUTING

Much of my history with sprouts has been the result of a happy accident from a neglected soaked grain or bean. Once a grain, bean, or seed is soaked, it can grow a sprout in a matter of days (nuts won't do this). Sprouting not only removes phytic acid (see page 58), but it also significantly increases the vitamin and enzyme content of grains, beans, and seeds, turning them into nutritional powerhouses. Sprouting grains transforms them into easily digested vegetables by converting starch into simple sugars and protein into amino acids. Sprouting can also reduce or eliminate an allergic reaction to common allergens such as wheat.

Sprouted grains and beans are most commonly thought of as foods to be eaten raw, but they can also be cooked, resulting in a softer, sweeter, and more digestible dish. Sprouts have a cooling, cleansing, and detoxifying effect on the body and therefore are generally better eaten in the warmest months, although cooking them will decrease the cooling effect.

Growing your own sprouts guarantees you have a nutritious minigarden in your kitchen year-round. After an overnight soak, sprouts are ready to eat in as little as two to three days, depending on what you grow. No special equipment is needed, just a jar and cheesecloth or a strainer.

1. Soak ½ to 1 cup whole grains, beans, or seeds in 2 cups filtered water for 10 to 12 hours at room temperature. Note that for small seeds such as alfalfa, broccoli, and mustard, you'll only need to soak a few tablespoons, as they produce much longer sprouts and therefore increase in volume.

2. Drain and rinse grains, beans, or seeds and either leave them in a strainer to drain over a bowl and cover with a cloth or place in a mason jar covered with a couple of layers of cheesecloth secured with a rubber band. Make sure the grains, beans, or seeds can drain well. If they're in a jar, tilt it on an angle and rest it in a bowl or on a dish rack. Place them somewhere in a ventilated area out of direct sunlight.

3. Rinse every morning and evening, and drain well. In very warm weather, rinse sprouts 3 to 4 times a day. Thorough rinsing and good drainage will give you a better, fresher tasting sprout.

4. Sprouts are ready when their tail is at least as long as the grain or bean. Some seeds, like alfalfa, will have a much longer tail. Sprouting can take as little as one to three days; some will take a day or two longer.

5. Once the sprouts are ready, don't rinse them again, as they store better when dry. Place them in a glass jar and store in the fridge for up to a week. If you sprouted them in a jar, make sure they are well drained before covering with a lid and placing in the fridge.

ROASTING VEGETABLES

*When I find myself in doubt in the kitchen and in need of something easy
and tasty, I turn to roasted vegetables. Before thinking too much, I heat the oven and gather
what I have—root vegetables; cauliflower or squash in fall and winter; asparagus,
radishes, over-ripe tomatoes, zucchini, and peppers in spring and summer. Almost any vegetable
tastes good when properly roasted, and I've found that people get surprisingly
excited about them. "Properly roasted" means they are roasted until they are deeply golden
brown, caramelized around the edges, and soft inside. Roasted vegetables
can be tossed into salads, stirred into stews, or eaten as finger food. They also last well
for three or four days in the fridge for impromptu meals and snacking.*

ROASTED VEGETABLES

RIMMED BAKING SHEET(S) LINED WITH PARCHMENT PAPER OR A DEEP BAKING DISH FOR FIRMER ROOT VEGETABLES

Seasonal vegetables

2 tablespoons melted extra virgin coconut oil (or ghee) or extra virgin olive oil per tray

Sea salt and freshly ground black pepper to taste

Fresh herbs (sage, rosemary, thyme), whole or minced, optional

WASH

Wash and drain vegetables before cutting them. Scrub root vegetables (thoroughly, with a vegetable brush) to remove any dirt and a very thin layer of outer skin; no need to peel them unless the skin is very wrinkly and old.

CUT AND SEASON

Roll cut sweet potatoes, zucchini, summer squash, and Asian eggplant into 1½-inch pieces (see page 172). Seed and cut winter squash into 1½-inch wedges. Carrots, Jerusalem artichokes, parsnips, and beets can be sliced on an angle in ½-inch pieces. Cut broccoli and cauliflower into medium-sized florets. Large tomatoes can be quartered, cherry tomatoes either halved or left whole. Asparagus can be left whole with their ends trimmed. Cut peppers in 1-inch triangles or strips.

Line a rimmed baking sheet with parchment paper. Add vegetables and spread them out in a single layer, drizzle with oil, a pinch of salt and pepper, and any herbs you want to use. Toss vegetables well and arrange evenly over tray in a single layer—overcrowding will prevent them from getting caramelized edges and cause softer vegetables to get soggy. Roast them in batches if you have too many. It's best to arrange them with the cut sides facing down so they will brown nicely—except for tomatoes, which roast better with the cut side up. To roast large pieces of harder vegetables like beets, Jerusalem artichokes, or onions, place them in a deep baking dish, season as directed, arrange in a single layer, and cover with parchment paper then foil.

ROAST

Preheat oven to 400°F. Place tray on middle rack of oven and roast for 20 minutes. Check thin asparagus at 15 minutes—it will most likely be ready; larger asparagus is usually ready after about 20 minutes. Remove from oven and turn each cut vegetable over (except tomatoes, as they'll fall apart), rotate tray, and return to oven for another 10 to 20 minutes or until vegetables are caramelized and brown on edges—cooking time varies, depending on the size and type of vegetables and how many trays you have in the oven at once. If you have more than one tray roasting at a time, change the positions of the trays after 20 minutes so vegetables brown evenly.

When roasting in a deep baking dish, roast for 20 to 30 minutes or until tender, then remove cover, turn the vegetables over, and continue cooking until brown around the edges.

SERVE OR STORE

Remove tray from oven, lift the corners of the parchment paper, and slide vegetables into a bowl or platter to serve. Once cool, vegetables can be stored in a jar in the fridge for up to four days.

ROASTING VEGETABLES ON A CONVECTION SETTING

Many ovens now come with a convection setting. The convection fan keeps the oven dry, so it's usually used for baking, but the setting is also great for speedy roasting and for vegetables with a higher water content, like tomatoes and zucchini. If you're using convection, set the oven at 370°F and be sure to check the vegetables after 15 minutes, as they can brown quickly. I also find, when using convection cooking, that it's better to cut hard vegetables a little thinner, as the insides can remain firm even as the edges brown. Stir or turn vegetables over and return to oven for another 10 to 15 minutes.

pantry recipes

SUPERFOOD OATMEAL
WITH GOJI BERRIES, CHIA, AND MULBERRIES

Eating a bowl of this oatmeal on a cold winter morning is like wrapping up in a cozy sweater. Without fail, I savor each and every mouthful every time I eat it. When I show my clients how quick and easy it is to make really good oatmeal packed with superfoods, they get hooked, too. If you warm your homemade, unstrained almond milk before pouring it over your oatmeal, you're in for a real treat!

The secret to making oatmeal efficiently is to soak everything the night before. Soaking rolled oats softens them, making the morning cooking time nice and quick; however, soaking rolled oats won't begin the sprouting process like with other whole grains, since they're presteamed. Soaking also allows the goji berries and mulberries to soften and melt, and the caramel flavor of the dried mulberries adds just the right amount of sweetness.

NOTE: If you forget to soak the oatmeal, just increase the cooking time by 5 minutes, stirring more often to prevent sticking.

SERVES 2

¾ cup regular rolled oats

¼ teaspoon cinnamon powder

2 tablespoons goji berries

1 to 2 tablespoons dried mulberries

2 cups filtered water

Small pinch sea salt

½ cup fresh or frozen blueberries

2 to 4 tablespoons soaked chia seeds (recipe follows)

TO SERVE:

Superfood Breakfast Sprinkle (page 117)

Homemade almond milk, unstrained (page 74)

Fresh raspberries, strawberries, or blueberries in season

In a small pot, combine the oats, cinnamon, goji berries, mulberries, water, and salt. Cover and soak overnight (or for 8 to 12 hours).

In the morning, bring oat mixture to a boil over high heat, stir, cover, reduce heat to low, and simmer for 10 minutes, stirring once or twice. Add blueberries and cook another minute or until heated through. Remove from heat and stir in soaked chia seeds.

Divide between two bowls, and top each bowl with 1 tablespoon Superfood Breakfast Sprinkle, a generous splash of almond milk, and fresh berries.

SOAKED CHIA SEEDS

Soaked chia seeds are a great item to have handy, not only for your oatmeal but also for adding an omega boost to smoothies. It takes seconds to put the mixture together and is ready to use in 10 minutes. If you make it with fresh almond milk, it can be kept in the fridge for five days; made with water, it will keep even longer.

MAKES 1¼ CUPS

¼ cup chia seeds

1 cup homemade almond milk, unstrained (page 74), or filtered water

Place chia seeds in a 2-cup jar or bowl and add almond milk. Stir well to make sure chia seeds are evenly distributed. Let sit 10 to 15 minutes, stir again, and use immediately, or cover and store in the fridge.

SOAKED OATS AND CHIA
WITH ALMOND MILK, FLAX, AND WHEAT GERM

Creamy, light, and satisfying, this has been my staple warm-weather breakfast for many years. Like my Superfood Oatmeal for fall and winter, this is my go-to breakfast once the weather heats up. It's just right for busy mornings, as it is best made ahead of time and travels well in a small jar. You can double or triple this recipe to have breakfast ready to go all week long. I recommend eating it at room temperature, so if you remove a portion from the fridge as soon as you get up, it'll be ready by the time your breakfast hour rolls around. If you have a gluten sensitivity, make sure to use gluten-free oats and replace the wheat germ with extra-ground flax or leave it out.

SERVES 2

¾ cup regular rolled oats

2 tablespoons chia seeds

1 tablespoon ground flax seeds

1 tablespoon wheat germ

¼ teaspoon cinnamon

2 cups homemade almond milk, unstrained (page 74)

TO SERVE:

Fresh berries

Homemade almond milk

Maca root powder, optional

Hemp seeds, optional

Combine the oats, chia, flax, wheat germ, and cinnamon in a bowl; mix well. Pour in almond milk and stir until everything is evenly combined. Set aside for 20 to 30 minutes at room temperature, or store in a jar and place in the fridge for 8 to 12 hours. The mixture will keep up to 4 days in the fridge. Serve topped with berries, a splash of almond milk, and a teaspoon of maca root powder and hemp seeds if you like.

SIMPLE RED LENTIL SOUP
WITH SPINACH, LEMON, AND PEPPER

The quality I like most about red lentils is their ability to dissolve and become a creamy pot of earthy goodness in very little time—for a legume, that is.

When I was in Istanbul, my friend Sila took me to a fantastic restaurant called Ciya Sofrasi on the Eastern side of the city, where I ate a memorable and incredibly simple red lentil soup. It was made with dried mint and served with a wedge of lemon, and I couldn't get over how nourishing it felt to eat. This recipe, although very different in flavor, has the same soothing effect, and I often make it when I'm in need of such a soup but have no desire to tackle chopping vegetables.

SERVES 4

2 tablespoons extra virgin olive oil

1 medium onion, finely chopped

5 garlic cloves, minced

2 cups red lentils washed and drained

6 cups filtered water, plus more to thin out soup as needed

1½ teaspoons sea salt, plus more to taste

¼ to ½ teaspoon freshly ground black pepper

4 cups (3½ ounces) baby spinach leaves

¼ cup freshly squeezed lemon juice, plus more to taste

TO SERVE:

Extra virgin olive oil

Freshly ground black pepper

Warm olive oil in a medium-large pot over medium heat. Add onions and sauté for 5 minutes or until golden. Stir in garlic and sauté for 2 to 3 minutes longer. Add lentils and water, and bring to a boil over high heat. Cover pot, reduce heat to low, and simmer for 30 to 35 minutes or until lentils are cooked and becoming creamy; stir pot every 10 minutes or so to make sure lentils aren't sticking. Remove lid, add salt and more water, if needed, to reach your desired consistency. Cover again and cook for 5 to 10 minutes longer or until lentils have completely dissolved and soup is creamy.

Stir in pepper and spinach, and cook for 1 minute or until spinach is wilted. Remove from heat and add lemon juice. Season to taste and serve with a drizzle of olive oil and black pepper.

MILLET CAULIFLOWER MASH

Deeply satisfying and warming, this mash is pure comfort food and extremely popular in my house. It's so easy and quick to make that I find myself cooking a pot anytime there's a chill in the air and cauliflower is available. It tastes great with a side of greens and a simple topping of flax oil and tamari. For a heartier meal, top it with a bean sauce or stew.

SERVES 4

1 cup millet, washed and soaked
    for 12 to 24 hours in 3 cups filtered water

1 medium cauliflower (2¼ pounds),
    cut into florets

2½ cups filtered water

1 teaspoon sea salt

TO SERVE:

Cold pressed flax oil

Tamari

Sliced scallions

Drain and rinse millet. Place in a medium pot and add cauliflower, water, and salt. Bring to a boil over high heat. Cover pot, reduce heat to low, and simmer for 25 minutes or until millet is soft and fluffy and all liquid is absorbed. Remove from heat and set aside for 5 minutes, then mash until creamy with a potato masher. Cover pot again for 5 minutes before serving. Spoon into bowls, drizzle with flax oil, and tamari, and top with scallions. Mash will thicken as it sits, and it becomes firm and hard when cool. Store any leftovers in the fridge for up to four days and reheat in a steamer basket.

NOTE: To cook mash in a pressure cooker, add ingredients and bring to a boil over high heat. Lock lid in place, bring up to high pressure, then reduce heat to low and cook for 10 minutes. Remove from heat and allow pressure to come down naturally, remove lid and mash until creamy.

STEAMED GREENS
WITH ZESTY FLAX DRESSING

For a quick, light, and healthy weeknight meal, this is what usually I turn to; there really isn't a faster, tastier way to eat steamed greens. I often vary the dressing by adding a splash of kimchi juice or a generous pinch of sauerkraut. You can also add toasted sesame seeds, hemp seeds, chopped scallions, or parsley. The measurements in this recipe are for steamed greens. If you're steaming other vegetables—squash, broccoli, baby turnips, or any other seasonal vegetable—steam enough for two servings and toss with the dressing.

SERVES 2

2 tablespoons cold pressed flax oil

1 teaspoon tamari

Small garlic clove, pressed

2 teaspoons freshly squeezed lemon juice

Pinch cayenne pepper

8 cups sliced (½-inch strips) collard greens,
    kale, chard, turnip greens, or a combination

Place flax oil, tamari, and garlic in a medium serving bowl, and stir to combine. Add lemon juice and cayenne, and stir again. Boil 1 inch filtered water in the bottom of a medium pot. Place steamer basket on top, add greens, cover pot, and steam for 2 minutes or until bright green and tender. Add greens to bowl with dressing, toss well to combine, and serve.

BLACK SESAME FLAX DRESSING

I created this tasty (and addictive) dressing for my clients to dress up simple grains and steamed vegetables, and it fast became a favorite. The dressing contains all the toppings I like to sprinkle over my everyday meals—flax oil, tamari, toasted black sesame, and scallions—in one convenient jar. The addition of brown rice vinegar wakes up the flavors and enlivens whatever you drizzle it over. Make the dressing ahead to have on hand; it keeps in the fridge for up to five days.

MAKES ABOUT ½ CUP

¼ cup cold pressed flax oil

4 teaspoons tamari

4 teaspoons brown rice vinegar

1 tablespoon toasted black sesame seeds (page 77)

2 scallions, thinly sliced

Place all ingredients in a small jar, screw lid on tight, and shake well to combine. Drizzle over grains or steamed vegetables, or store in the fridge for up to four days.

SIMPLE GREEN SALAD
WITH TANGY HEMP SEED DRESSING

The bright combination of apple cider vinegar, lemon, and flax oil is a favorite of mine and one I turn to most often when making salads of delicate seasonal lettuces and tender greens from the farmers' market. The addition of hemp seeds adds a nutritional boost of protein and omega fatty acids without being heavy or weighing the leaves down.

SERVES 2

1 tablespoon unpasteurized apple cider vinegar

1 teaspoon fresh lemon juice

Pinch sea salt

2 tablespoons cold pressed flax oil

1 tablespoon hemp seeds

8 cups (5 ounces) mixed greens (baby lettuces, mesclun, sprouts, or other seasonal greens)

Place apple cider vinegar, lemon juice, and salt in a medium serving bowl and whisk to combine. Add flax oil and whisk again. Stir in hemp seeds, add greens, and gently toss to combine; serve immediately.

PARSLEY BROWN RICE SALAD WITH SEEDS

I often forget just how good these simple ingredients taste together, especially the way the tangy, briny flavor of ume plum vinegar adds brightness and zing to the nutty brown rice and toasted seeds. It makes an ideal, light, and satisfying summertime meal and a tasty base for a variety of toppings. Try it with avocado or crumbled feta, and if you have cooked chickpeas on hand they make a great addition, too.

SERVES 4 TO 6

4½ cups cooked brown and sweet rice (page 63), cooled

2 teaspoons ume plum vinegar

2 tablespoons brown rice vinegar

1 teaspoon tamari, plus more to taste

1 tablespoon extra virgin olive oil or cold pressed flax oil

2 tablespoons toasted sunflower seeds (page 77)

2 tablespoons toasted unhulled sesame seeds (page 77)

1 cup chopped parsley, plus more to garnish

⅓ cup finely sliced scallions, white and green part, plus more to garnish

2 cups cherry tomatoes, halved

2 medium cucumbers, diced

Cold pressed flax oil to serve

Place cooled brown rice in a large bowl. Sprinkle ume plum vinegar, brown rice vinegar, tamari, and olive oil and stir to combine. Add toasted seeds, parsley, and scallions and mix again. Season to taste with extra tamari. Spoon into bowls and top with cherry tomatoes, cucumbers, chopped parsley, and scallions. Drizzle with flax oil and serve.

WHOLE-WHEAT FETTUCCINI WITH KALE, CARAMELIZED ONIONS, AND MARINATED GOAT CHEESE

There is a goat and sheep dairy farm in Victoria, Australia, called Meredith Dairy that makes the most amazing marinated cheese. It's like a soft goat cheese but richer from the sheep's milk, and it can transform pasta like no other cheese. You can find it in some gourmet shops and grocery stores in the United States, and for this culinary delight, I break my "local cheese" rule. If you spot it, you're in for a treat!

In this recipe, I use my own Marinated Goat Cheese (page 116), inspired by Meredith Dairy, with great results. If you have neither of these cheeses, it also works well with a good soft goat cheese.

I owe credit for this recipe to Melinda Dimitriades, a talented Australian food purveyor and chef, who arrived at my sister's tiny New York City apartment many years ago with a tub of the famous cheese. She made us a pasta dish that we all swooned over. We have been making variations of it ever since, and this one with kale has become a cold-weather favorite.

SERVES 4 TO 6

2 tablespoons extra virgin olive oil

3 medium to large red onions, thinly sliced

Sea salt

¾ pound whole-wheat fettuccini

10 cups sliced Lacinato kale (from about 1½ bunches)

8 ounces Marinated Goat Cheese (oil marinade reserved, page 116),
   at room temperature, divided

Freshly ground black pepper

Warm olive oil in a large skillet over medium heat and add onions. Sauté for 10 minutes or until beginning to brown. Add 1 teaspoon salt, lower heat slightly, and continue cooking for 15 to 20 minutes more or until onions are soft and caramelized. Meanwhile, bring a large pot of water to a boil and add a large pinch of salt. When onions are caramelized, add fettuccini to boiling water and cook for 10 to 12 minutes, or per package instructions, until al dente. Drain pasta and return to pot.

While pasta cooks, stir kale into onions, cover skillet, and cook for 6 to 8 minutes or until tender, stirring once or twice. Add onion and kale mixture, three quarters (6 ounces) of the marinated goat cheese, and lots of black pepper to pasta; toss well. Drizzle in a tablespoon or more of oil marinade and season to taste. Divide among bowls and top with a crumble of remaining goat cheese; serve immediately.

NOTE: I love using fettuccini and other ribbon-like pastas for this dish, but penne and other types of whole-grain pastas work well, too.

1. ARAME WITH CARROTS AND SESAME 2. GARLIC-TAMARI
BRAISED TOFU 3. MARINATED BEETS 4. CARROT PARSLEY
SALAD 5. MARINATED BEANS 6. DIJON MUSTARD—MARINATED
TEMPEH 7. CHICKPEA MASH 8. QUICK PICKLED RED CABBAGE

4

5

6

7

QUICK PICKLED RED CABBAGE

This cabbage comes together in minutes and can be used to add flavor, color, and texture to everything from simple grains and roasted veggies to bean dishes, curries, and tacos.

MAKES 2½ CUPS

4 cups thinly sliced red cabbage (about ¼ large cabbage)

½ teaspoon sea salt

2 tablespoons unpasteurized apple cider vinegar

Combine cabbage, sea salt, and vinegar in a bowl; use your hands to "massage" cabbage for a couple of minutes or until it begins to soften. Serve right away, or set aside to marinate for up to an hour before serving—cabbage will soften further and absorb marinade as it sits. Store any leftovers in a jar in the fridge for up to five days.

CARROT PARSLEY SALAD

This bright, tasty salad will liven up any meal at any time of year. It has often been a lifesaver for me when I'm throwing together quick lunches or dinners with nothing much on hand in the way of vegetables. I love it served with feta or avocado over quinoa or brown rice. It also makes an excellent sandwich filling and won't make the bread soggy (see The Pantry Sandwich, page 109). Cilantro works well in this salad too; feel free to use it instead of, or mixed with, parsley when you have it on hand.

MAKES 3 CUPS

4 medium-large carrots

1 cup chopped parsley

1 scallion, white and green parts finely sliced

2 tablespoons fresh lemon juice

1 tablespoon unpasteurized apple cider vinegar

3 to 4 tablespoons cold pressed flax oil or extra virgin olive oil

¼ teaspoon sea salt, plus more to taste

3 tablespoons toasted unhulled sesame seeds (page 77), optional

Grate carrots using largest hole of a box grater. Place in a medium bowl and add remaining ingredients. Mix well and season to taste. This salad tastes best when served immediately, but any leftovers can be stored in the fridge for a day or two.

MARINATED BEETS

Having marinated beets in the fridge means that a colorful and tasty meal is within easy reach. I like to add them to simple cooked grains, toss them with chickpeas, put them on a sandwich, purée and toss them with pasta and goat cheese, or eat them in a salad. For an excellent snack, pair them with Cashew Cheese (page 217) on rice cakes.

NOTE: When marinating golden or pink beets, substitute either unpasteurized apple cider vinegar or brown rice vinegar for the balsamic so the beets don't stain.

SERVES 4 TO 6 AS A SIDE DISH

3 medium trimmed red beets (about 1 pound)

1 tablespoon unpasteurized apple cider vinegar

1 tablespoon balsamic vinegar

1 tablespoon extra virgin olive oil

¼ teaspoon sea salt, plus more to taste

Place beets in a medium-large pot, cover with filtered water, and bring to a boil over high heat. Cover pot, reduce heat to low, and simmer for 40 to 50 minutes or until a toothpick or tip of a sharp knife is easily inserted into the center. Drain beets and slip off their skins under cold running water. Cut each beet in half, and cut each half into ½-inch wedges.

Place beets in a bowl and add remaining ingredients. Toss well to combine, season to taste, and serve immediately, or store in a jar in the fridge for up to five days.

DIJON MUSTARD–MARINATED TEMPEH

Tempeh can be a hard sell; people are often skeptical of the texture and flavor; but to me, it's delicious on all counts. If you're faced with personal uncertainty or other tempeh doubters, I suggest making this recipe. The combination of Dijon mustard, apple juice, and tamari complements the nuttiness of the tempeh well, and when baked until caramelized around the edges, it has a complex, savory flavor. This recipe is extremely versatile and a breeze to put together. You can eat it warm from the oven or let it cool and add it to sandwiches, salads, and nori rolls, or eat it for a satisfying and protein-packed snack. I often double this recipe so I will have tempeh on hand for a few days.

SERVES 2 TO 4

1 8-ounce package plain tempeh

½ cup apple juice or apple cider

1 tablespoon Dijon mustard

1 tablespoon tamari

2 tablespoons extra virgin olive oil

2 teaspoons unpasteurized apple cider vinegar

Lay tempeh flat on your cutting board and cut into four even rectangles. Slice each piece in half horizontally so you have eight thin rectangles, then restack and cut on the diagonal into sixteen triangles. Arrange tempeh in a baking dish in a snug, single layer—a 10 × 6½-inch dish works well.

Put the apple juice, Dijon mustard, tamari, oil, and vinegar in a bowl and whisk until emulsified. Pour over tempeh and set aside to marinate for 30 minutes to an hour. (If you don't want to cook it right away, you can cover the tempeh and store it in the fridge for up to three days.)

Preheat oven to 350°F. Bake tempeh for 35 to 40 minutes or until marinade has been absorbed, the top is golden brown, and the edges are dark and caramelized. Remove from oven and serve. Any leftover tempeh can be stored in the fridge for up to four days.

ARAME WITH CARROTS AND SESAME

Eating seaweed is a great way to boost overall health and vitality (see page 27). Although we may know that eating it daily is a good idea, it can often be a challenge to incorporate it into everyday foods. This tasty recipe is the perfect make-ahead dish that enables you to add a pinch of flavorful seaweed to meals over the course of a week. The mild sweet flavor of carrots, onion, and mirin complements the brininess of the arame, and it tastes great with the toasted sesame seeds. During the summer, I like to stir in steamed sweet corn kernels before serving.

MAKES 3 CUPS

1½ cups dried arame seaweed (1¼ ounces)

3⅓ cups filtered water, divided

1 tablespoon unrefined, untoasted sesame oil

1 medium onion, thinly sliced

2 medium carrots, cut in matchsticks (about 1½ cups)

¼ teaspoon sea salt

2 tablespoons mirin

2 teaspoons tamari, plus more to taste

2 tablespoons toasted unhulled sesame seeds (page 77)

Toasted sesame oil or hot pepper sesame oil to taste, optional

Place arame in a medium bowl and cover with 3 cups filtered water; soak for 15 minutes or until softened. Drain and set aside.

Warm sesame oil in a wide skillet over medium heat; add onion and sauté for 4 minutes or until golden. Stir in carrots and sea salt, and cook 2 minutes more. Add drained arame, remaining ⅓ cup water, mirin, and tamari and stir to combine. Increase heat and bring mixture to a simmer. Cover skillet, reduce heat to low, and cook for 10 minutes. Remove lid and cook a couple of minutes longer or until all liquid has evaporated.

Allow to cool completely before stirring in toasted sesame seeds. Sprinkle with a few drops of toasted sesame or spiced sesame oil and tamari to taste. Serve at room temperature or store in the fridge in a glass jar or container for up to four days.

CUTTING MATCHSTICKS

Medium to large carrots (or other long vegetables) work best when cutting matchsticks. Lay the carrot horizontally on your cutting board and slice it on a sharp diagonal into ⅛- to ¼-inch pieces. Stack five or six slices directly on top of each other and cut lengthwise into ⅛- to ¼-inch slices. Repeat with remaining slices.

QUICK BRAISED TEMPEH

I find myself cooking tempeh like this when I need a quick, high-protein snack or lunch. Prepared this way, it's best eaten right away, which is just as well as it's so fast and easy to make. Use it as a topping for grains, added to nori rolls, or on rice cakes with avocado. If you want tempeh on hand for a couple of days, I suggest cooking Dijon Mustard–Marinated Tempeh (page 105), as it keeps a little better.

SERVES 2 TO 4

1 tablespoon unrefined, untoasted sesame oil, extra virgin olive oil, or melted coconut oil

1 8-ounce package plain tempeh, cut crosswise in ¼-inch slices

1 tablespoon tamari

1 tablespoon mirin

½ cup filtered water

Warm oil in a wide cast-iron skillet over medium heat. Add tempeh in a single layer, and cook for 4 to 5 minutes or until golden brown. Turn the tempeh over, and cook for another 3 to 4 minutes or until golden brown. Reduce heat to low, sprinkle with tamari and mirin, then pour in water. Raise heat to medium, and simmer for about 5 minutes more or until water has evaporated and tempeh is beginning to caramelize. Turn tempeh over one more time and cook for a minute longer or until both sides are caramelized. Remove from heat and serve.

CURRIED QUINOA PILAF
WITH TOASTED CASHEWS

The first time I made this pilaf was when there was nothing much in my pantry except some basic vegetables and soaked quinoa that had begun to sprout and was begging to be used. In one pot, this fragrant and flavorful pilaf came together in less than half an hour and has become a weeknight staple ever since.

SERVES 4

1 cup quinoa, washed and soaked 12 to 24 hours in 2 cups filtered water

1 tablespoon extra virgin coconut oil or ghee

1 medium onion, diced

3 garlic cloves, chopped

1 tablespoon peeled and minced fresh ginger

¾ teaspoon sea salt

4 teaspoons homemade Curry Powder (page 112)

1 medium carrot, cut in ½-inch dice

¾ cup sweet corn kernels, fresh or frozen

½ cup raw cashews, pan toasted and roughly chopped (see note)

1¼ cup boiling filtered water

¾ cup frozen peas, defrosted

3 cups (2½ ounces) baby spinach leaves

TO SERVE:

Cold-pressed flax oil

Tamari

Drain and rinse quinoa; set aside in a strainer to drain thoroughly while preparing other ingredients.

Warm coconut oil or ghee in a medium pot over medium-high heat. Add onions and sauté for 3 minutes or until translucent. Add garlic, ginger, and salt, and cook 2 minutes more. Stir in curry powder and carrot, and cook another minute or two. Stir in quinoa, corn, toasted cashews, and boiling water; bring to a boil. Cover pot, reduce heat to low, and cook for 20 minutes or until all the water is absorbed. Remove from heat and spread peas then spinach over surface of quinoa. Cover the pot again quickly and let sit 5 to 7 minutes or until spinach is wilted. Stir gently to combine, cover, and set aside for 5 minutes longer before serving. Serve warm, topped with a drizzle of flax oil and tamari.

NOTE: To toast cashews quickly without turning on the oven, warm a skillet over medium heat, add cashews, and toast for 4 to 5 minutes or until fragrant and beginning to brown in spots; stir or shake pan every 30 seconds. Remove cashews from pan immediately and set aside to cool.

GARLIC TAMARI-BRAISED TOFU

Tamari was an ingredient that my father added to everything when I was growing up, and when I say everything, I mean everything! As a child, I remember him cooking this recipe frequently, and to this day, it's still my favorite way to eat tofu. Supersimple, requiring no special marinade, it's great if you need a quick, easy protein. I marinate tofu this way for grilling outdoors as well; just brush it with oil before placing it on the grill. Serve with Chimichurri Sauce (page 118) and grilled veggies for a great summer meal. It's also good in The Pantry Sandwich (recipe at right). For the best flavor, look for locally made tofu that's as fresh as possible.

SERVES 2 TO 4

1 15-ounce block plain, firm tofu

2 tablespoons tamari

2 garlic cloves, pressed

1 tablespoon extra virgin olive oil
 or unrefined, untoasted sesame oil

Rinse tofu and pat dry with a clean cloth. Slice into eight rectangles and lay in a baking dish or shallow bowl in a single layer. Sprinkle with tamari and rub with pressed garlic, turning slices over to coat evenly. Marinate for 20 minutes at room temperature, or cover and place in the fridge for up to three days.

Warm oil in a wide cast-iron skillet over medium heat, and add tofu in a single layer. Reduce heat to low, and cook for 5 to 6 minutes or until golden and starting to brown on the bottom. Use a flat spatula to flip tofu, and cook for 3 more minutes or until golden brown. Remove from heat and serve, or cool and store covered in the fridge for up to three days.

THE PANTRY SANDWICH

During the summer holidays, my family had a lunchtime tradition of epic sandwich making. My friends and I would run up from the river near my house, ravenous after spending hours swimming and playing. My parents would set out the fillings: marinated beets; braised tofu, mustard, and avocado; tomatoes, cucumbers, and lettuce from the garden; and a grated carrot salad. We would build our own sandwich creations on either rye or pita bread, piling them high and struggling to eat them as the beet juice stained our arms and dripped off our elbows. Before long, we were back at the river, washing it all off. If you've baked a loaf of the Spelt Brown Rice Bread with Sesame (page 134), make the sandwich on that!

MAKES 1 SANDWICH

2 slices of your favorite whole-grain bread
 (lightly toasted if desired)

1 tablespoon Miso Mayonnaise (page 114)

¼ of an avocado, sliced

2 teaspoons whole-grain Dijon mustard

2 slices Garlic Tamari-Braised Tofu (recipe at left),
 or 4 slices Quick Braised Tempeh (page 108)

¼ cup Carrot Parsley Salad (page 102)

6 pieces Marinated Beets (page 104)

Handful of greens, lettuce, or sprouts of your choice

Spread one piece of bread with Miso Mayonnaise and the other with avocado slices and mustard. Top avocado with tofu, and spread carrot salad evenly to cover. Lay beets on carrot salad, top with greens or sprouts, and cover with the other slice of bread. Cut in half and enjoy—outside, if possible.

VANILLA CHIA PUDDING

When chia seeds are added to liquid, they "bloom" and thicken the liquid, resulting in a tapioca-like consistency. When the chosen liquid is a luscious vanilla cashew milk sweetened with plump Medjool dates and enriched with coconut butter, like it is in this recipe, it makes for a delightful sweet treat that is loved by just about everyone. This pudding is the most requested dish among my clients, as they not only enjoy it as a light refreshing dessert or afternoon treat but also think it's pretty great for breakfast. If you want to serve it as a sweeter dessert, you can top each glass with a drizzle of maple syrup. It's always good topped with berries, but you can serve it in the cooler months with roasted plums (page 329), stewed apples, or a rhubarb compote. This pudding comes together in a flash without turning on the stove.

SERVES 6 TO 8

½ cup chia seeds

1 vanilla bean

1 cup raw cashews, soaked 2 to 6 hours in 2 cups filtered water

4 cups filtered water, divided

7 Medjool dates, pitted

Pinch sea salt

¼ teaspoon cinnamon

2 tablespoons coconut butter or extra virgin coconut oil

4 teaspoons vanilla extract

Fresh berries, to serve

Place chia seeds in a medium bowl. Split vanilla bean in half lengthwise, scrape out seeds with tip of a small knife, and add them to an upright blender. Place vanilla pod in bowl with chia seeds; set aside.

Drain and rinse cashews, and add to blender with 3 cups filtered water, dates, salt, cinnamon, coconut butter, and vanilla extract. Blend on highest speed until completely smooth, about 1 to 2 minutes. Pour into bowl with chia seeds along with remaining 1 cup water, and whisk thoroughly. (Alternatively, if you have a large blender with a 6-cup capacity, you can blend in all the water at once.) Let mixture sit for 10 minutes, whisking a couple of times to prevent chia seeds from clumping. Place in the fridge for 1½ to 2 hours or until completely chilled. Remove and compost the vanilla pod before serving. Divide into bowls, and serve chilled topped with berries. Store any leftover pudding in a jar in the fridge for up to five days.

VARIATION
CHOCOLATE CHIA PUDDING

Once pudding is chilled, remove the amount (in cups) you would like to flavor with chocolate and place it in a bowl. Sift in 4 teaspoons unsweetened cocoa powder for each cup. Stir well, and serve chilled topped with raspberries.

MAKE-AHEAD CONDIMENTS

HARISSA

Harissa is a spiced hot chili sauce that originated in Tunisia and is widely used in Morocco and Israel. You can find many variations: some are superspicy, some more fragrant, and others smoky. My variation is fragrant with a good kick from cayenne pepper. When I'm in the mood for something spicy and flavorful, I stir a little into lentil soups or bean stews; I love it best in Quinoa with Roasted Summer Vegetables and Harissa Marinade (page 187).

Harissa keeps well for up to two months in the fridge, or if you leave out the lemon juice, it will keep almost indefinitely—just bring it up to room temperature and stir the lemon juice in when you're ready to use it.

MAKES ABOUT ⅓ CUP

1 tablespoon cumin seeds

1 tablespoon coriander seeds

1 tablespoon caraway seeds

2 teaspoons ground paprika

½ teaspoon cayenne pepper, or more to taste

1 garlic clove, pressed

⅛ teaspoon sea salt

¼ cup extra virgin olive oil

1 tablespoon fresh lemon juice

Warm a small to medium skillet over medium heat. Add cumin, coriander, and caraway seeds; toast seeds, stirring continuously, for 2 minutes or until fragrant. Transfer to an electric spice grinder and grind until fine. Place ground spices in a bowl; add paprika, cayenne, garlic, salt, olive oil, and lemon juice. Stir until smooth. Store in a sealed glass jar in the fridge for up to two months, or as mentioned above, leave out the lemon for storing indefinitely.

CURRY POWDER

When I begin cooking for a new client, one of the first things I do is make a jar of this fragrant powder to have handy for quick curried soups and stews. I know, you've heard it before—once you make your own curry powder, you'll never consider buying it in a jar again, but it's true! The flavor and smell of the freshly toasted and ground spices is nothing short of intoxicating, and it stores well for a few months.

MAKES ABOUT ½ CUP

1-inch piece cinnamon stick, broken up into several pieces

¼ cup coriander seeds

1 tablespoon cumin seeds

1 teaspoon fenugreek

6 whole cloves

6 cardamom pods

1 teaspoon black peppercorns

2 tablespoons ground turmeric

2 tablespoons ginger powder

¼ teaspoon cayenne pepper, optional

Warm a medium skillet over medium heat. Add cinnamon stick, coriander, cumin, fenugreek, cloves, and cardamom; toast spices, stirring continuously, for 2 to 3 minutes or until fragrant. Remove from skillet immediately and place in an electric spice grinder along with peppercorns; grind until fine. Transfer to a bowl and add turmeric, ginger, and cayenne if using; mix well. Store in a sealed glass jar; use within three months.

1. UNHULLED TAHINI 2. CURRY POWDER 3. HARISSA 4. MARINATED GOAT CHEESE 5. BLACK SESAME GOMASIO 6. MISO MAYONNAISE 7. TOASTED ALMOND BUTTER 8. SUPERFOOD BREAKFAST SPRINKLE

MISO MAYONNAISE

When I was experimenting with this recipe, my goal was to achieve mayonnaise with that thick, whipped consistency, a potential challenge without eggs or tofu. To my delight, it worked the first time, and I immediately slathered it on toast with slices of juicy tomato. This is still my favorite way to enjoy it. Tangy, salty, and silky, this spread will elevate the flavor of anything it touches, from a simple snack of avocado on rice crackers to a hearty meal like Tempeh Portobello Burgers (page 255).

NOTE: I have made this mayonnaise in many different kitchens and found that, when using a larger blender, the recipe must be doubled for it to blend properly.

MAKES 1 CUP

3 tablespoons unpasteurized sweet white miso

3 tablespoons brown rice vinegar

3 tablespoons fresh lemon juice

1 teaspoon tamari

1 teaspoon mirin

1 tablespoon finely chopped scallions, white part only

¼ clove of garlic

½ cup extra virgin olive oil

Place all ingredients except olive oil in an upright blender, and blend on high speed for 1 minute or until completely smooth. Remove lid and scrape down the sides. With the blender running on the lowest speed, slowly pour in the olive oil and blend until thick and smooth, about 30 seconds. Mayonnaise will thicken further after it's refrigerated. For best texture results, refrigerate overnight or for at least 2 hours before serving. Store in a jar in the fridge for up to three weeks.

NOTE: Sometimes the mayonnaise will separate over time; just sit it on the counter for 5 minutes and give it a good stir before serving. Also note that it will melt as it comes to room temperature, so for the best results, keep it cool.

BLACK SESAME GOMASIO

Gomasio is a Japanese sesame condiment made by grinding toasted sesame seeds with sea salt. Its nutty flavor can turn a simple bowl of brown rice into a heavenly experience. Black sesame seeds are particularly beneficial to the kidneys and also high in calcium, iron, and vitamins A and B. This recipe can be made with toasted, unhulled sesame seeds with the same great flavor.

In Japan, gomasio is traditionally made with a suribachi, a mortar and pestle–like tool with ridges on the inside that make it easy to crush the seeds. In its place, you can use a regular mortar and pestle or pulse the seeds a couple of times in a spice grinder. A food processor can be used instead, but unless it's small, you'll need to double or triple the recipe so there are enough seeds to be crushed by the blades.

MAKES ABOUT ½ CUP

½ cup toasted black sesame seeds (page 77)

¼ teaspoon sea salt

Place toasted sesame seeds and salt in a suribachi or mortar; crush the seeds, using a circular motion with the pestle, until coarsely ground. Place in a sealed glass jar and store in the fridge. For best flavor, use within a month.

UNHULLED TAHINI

Health-food stores in Australia and Europe stock both regular (hulled) and unhulled tahini, and it's a mystery to me why it's not common here in the United States. Unhulled tahini is made from sesame seeds that still have the hull intact, which means you get all the benefits from the whole seed, including iron, calcium, minerals, and the fiber you need to help digest the fats the seeds contain. It also means that it has a more robust flavor and heartier texture than tahini made from hulled sesame seeds. Always seek out unhulled tahini made from roasted sesame seeds, or make your own, as the roasting helps remove the phytic acid present in the hulls (see page 58 for more information).

Whenever friends visit from Australia or Holland, they bring me jars of unhulled tahini. Last time I ran out, I decided to try making my own. It isn't as smooth as commercially ground tahini (or sesame butter, as it's sometimes called), but I like the slight crunch and extremely fresh taste. The salt is optional, but it really brings out the deep, toasty flavor of the seeds. Use tahini to make a tasty sauce for roasted vegetables and grains, as in the next recipe, or slather it over rice cakes with avocado and a smear of miso for a snack.

MAKES ABOUT 1 CUP

2 cups unhulled toasted sesame seeds (page 77)

Scant ½ teaspoon sea salt

4 to 6 tablespoons unrefined, untoasted sesame oil

Place sesame seeds in a food processor with sea salt and blend for 1 minute. Scrape down sides with a rubber spatula and blend again. With the motor running, slowly add 4 tablespoons oil and continue blending for another few seconds. Add more oil as needed to get desired consistency and blend until smooth, about a minute, scraping sides as necessary. Transfer to a glass jar and store in the fridge for up to three months.

TAHINI SAUCE

This is a great sauce to whip up when you want to make a meal out of simple steamed or roasted veggies. It is particularly good with roasted sweet potatoes and can be made in about 2 minutes flat. I always make this with unhulled tahini (see the preceding recipe), not only for the health benefits that are preserved when the seeds are ground whole, but also because of the big, nutty flavor.

The variations on this simple recipe are endless; try adding some finely grated ginger, a pinch of cayenne, or lemon juice in place of the orange juice. If you're using an unsalted tahini, you'll likely want to add a pinch of sea salt or a dash of tamari to bring out the flavors.

MAKES ABOUT ½ CUP

¼ cup unhulled tahini

2 tablespoons filtered water

1 teaspoon whole-grain Dijon mustard

1 teaspoon unpasteurized sweet white miso

1 small garlic clove, pressed

3 tablespoon fresh orange juice

Place tahini in a small bowl, add water, and stir to combine. Add mustard, miso, garlic, and orange juice; stir until smooth. Serve immediately, or store in a jar for two to three days in the fridge.

MARINATED GOAT CHEESE

When I was growing up, there was a time when my mother was really into making marinated feta cheese. As was the way with many things she undertook in the kitchen, this was done on a large scale. She filled gallon-sized jars with cubes of feta; covered the cheese with olive oil, herbs from the garden, red chilies, and garlic; and placed the glistening jars on a big dresser in the kitchen where they tempted me daily. When she wasn't around, my friends and I would climb up, unscrew the lids, and devour a couple of oil-soaked cheese morsels.

It wasn't until living in New York that I started marinating my own cheese, mainly because I missed Meredith Dairy's divine marinated goat and sheep's milk cheese in Australia (you can find out more about my love for it and one of my favorite recipes that includes it on page 98) and my mother's big kitchen productions. Here I use a local fresh goat cheese that I buy at the Union Square Greenmarket from a woman named Lynn Fleming, who runs a goat dairy called Lynnhaven in Pine Bush, New York. Her cheese tastes fresh and light, with no trace of the strong "goaty" flavor you get from packaged goat cheese. Since soft goat cheese can crumble easily, I recommend thoroughly chilling it before slicing it into rounds.

1 8-ounce fresh goat cheese log, sliced into ½-inch rounds

½ cup extra virgin olive oil

8 sprigs fresh thyme

½ teaspoon whole peppercorns

3 garlic cloves, halved lengthwise

4 bay leaves

Lay goat cheese in a single layer on the bottom of a dry, wide-mouth, 10- to 12-ounce jar. Pour in enough olive oil to cover cheese. Add a couple sprigs of thyme, a few peppercorns, 2 pieces garlic, and a bay leaf. Continue layering the remaining cheese, oil, and seasonings until you have used up all ingredients. Lightly press the last layer of cheese down to make sure it's completely submerged in oil. Seal jar and place in the fridge to marinate for one week before using. Cheese will keep for at least two months. Bring to room temperature before serving.

The oil is luscious drizzled over toast or pasta, with or without the cheese, or you can use it in salad dressings. Keep any leftover oil in the fridge until ready to use.

NOTE: The cheese will spoil if it isn't covered by oil at all times. If you remove a few pieces, make sure the remaining cheese is covered, adding more oil in as needed, before closing the lid.

TOASTED ALMOND BUTTER

Slathered over sprouted English muffins for breakfast, paired with Medjool dates as a snack, or just straight off a spoon, I find toasted almond butter irresistible. When made fresh it tastes so incredibly good that you'll always want to have some in the fridge.

MAKES ABOUT 1 CUP

2 cups whole raw almonds, toasted (page 77)

Place freshly toasted and cooled almonds in a food processor and blend for 30 seconds. Scrape down sides, and continue blending until smooth. This takes a few minutes. If a ball forms, break it up into a few pieces and continue blending and scraping down the sides until the almond butter is completely smooth with a slight sheen. Store in a jar in the fridge and use within one month.

SUPERFOOD BREAKFAST SPRINKLE

I spent years sprinkling the components of this recipe individually over my morning oatmeal before I finally combined them. I love the flavor of all these nutritional ingredients and use 1 to 2 tablespoons on my breakfast to make sure I get a good dose of each; however, if these ingredients are new to you, you may want to start with less and add more as you become familiar with the flavors. Soon you'll find your breakfast isn't complete without this sprinkle. It's delicious not only on Superfood Oatmeal (page 87) and Amaranth Muesli (page 130) but also added to yogurt and fruit salad when summer is at its peak.

MAKES JUST OVER 1 CUP

½ cup freshly ground flax seeds

½ cup wheat germ, raw or toasted

¼ cup maca root powder

Place all ingredients in a wide-mouth glass jar and stir to combine. Seal lid and store in the fridge for up to three months.

The flavor of freshly ground flax seeds is far superior to what you can buy preground and packaged. To grind your own, place up to ½ a cup in a spice grinder and grind until fine, about 5 seconds. Place in a sealed glass jar and store in the fridge for up to three months.

CHIMICHURRI SAUCE

No matter where I am, the bright, herbaceous flavor of chimichurri sauce instantly reminds me of long summer evenings cooking and eating outdoors. Originally from Argentina, chimichurri was traditionally made with parsley, olive oil, garlic, and vinegar and served with grilled meats, but these days, you can find it made with many different herb and vinegar combinations. Its tangy flavor is truly a revelation and successfully livens up anything you put it on—simple grilled tofu and grilled veggies—or as a sauce for beans and grains. Chimichurri can be made by blending all the ingredients in a food processor, but I like the rustic texture of the sauce when everything is chopped by hand; it also means you can prepare it outdoors by the grill in summer.

MAKES ABOUT 1¼ CUPS

¾ cup chopped cilantro

¾ cup chopped flat-leaf parsley

¼ cup chopped mint leaves

1 tablespoon chopped oregano

4 garlic cloves, minced

¾ teaspoon ground cumin

½ teaspoon red chili flakes

¼ cup red wine vinegar

¾ teaspoon sea salt, plus more to taste

¾ cup mild extra virgin olive oil

In a medium bowl, combine all chopped herbs, garlic, cumin, and chili flakes. Add red wine vinegar and salt, then whisk in olive oil. Season to taste and serve, or store in a jar in the fridge for a few days. Bring up to room temperature before serving.

MY FAVORITE FERMENTS

I was introduced to the magical world of fermented foods by Sandor Katz, the famous fermentation fetishist, who has written two of my most treasured books: The Art of Fermentation *and* Wild Fermentation. *After an inspiring five-day workshop with him, I dreamt about moving to a house in the country with a big kitchen and lots of room to fill crocks with all sorts of bubbling ferments. Not only did I learn how to make the following two ferments from Sandor, but the workshop also opened up a whole world of exciting culinary possibilities for me.*

Sandor's philosophy includes the mandate that everyone everywhere can pickle and ferment any vegetables they happen to have on hand in whatever empty vessel happens to be around. On the first day of our workshop, to make his point, he brought a small bucket containing his latest fermentation experiment, which was a mixture of cabbage and weeds he had found on his journey to the workshop from his home in Tennessee.

Lactobacillus acidophilus, found in fermented foods, is beneficial in restoring healthy intestinal flora, a key factor to assimilating nutrients in the digestion process, and helpful to the body's production of natural antibiotics (that support the immune system) and anticarcinogenic compounds (that help fight cancer). Some form of fermentation was used in all traditional food cultures as a means to preserve crops and make food more nutritious and interesting. Many of the foods we eat today are fermented—sourdough bread, miso, cheese, chocolate, wine, and coffee, to name a few. Since the advent of refrigeration, we haven't had to rely on natural fermentation to preserve our food as our ancestors did. Wild yeasts present in the air make each fermented food unique to its location. As food ferments, the flavors become more layered and complex. Variants in climate and temperature affect the way it tastes; a batch of sauerkraut made in New York will taste different from one made in another part of the country.

These two recipes are great building blocks for your fermentation experiments. Experiment with vegetables you have in abundance, adding any flavorings you like, and follow the tips I've provided on the following page.

- Cabbage is a great vegetable to base your first fermentation experiments on. Its low sugar content and sturdy leaves produce good results with little effort.

- Make sure your hands and equipment are clean (no need to sterilize) and that no form of metal comes into contact with the vegetables as they ferment, as salt and acids from fermentation will corrode metal.

- When experimenting with different ferments, a good rule of thumb for salting is to taste your vegetables before packing them into jars or crocks—they should taste a little saltier than you want your end result to be.

- When packing your vegetables into jars or crocks, it is important to get out as much air as possible. You can use your fist, a flat-ended rolling pin, or a wooden cocktail muddler. Packing them tightly helps encourage the liquid to rise to the top and removes any air pockets, where mold can potentially grow.

- Vegetables create their own brine when salt is added. Be sure the vegetables are completely covered with brine at all times. If the vegetables you use don't release enough of their own liquid when massaged with salt and packed into your vessel, then you'll need to add some brine. Make it by combining 2 cups of water with 2 teaspoons of sea salt, and add it to the vegetables until the surface is well covered. Placing a weight (like a jar full of water) on the surface of the vegetables allows the liquid to rise and prevents the vegetables from floating up.

- These recipes can be made in wide Weck or Mason jars or in crocks. When using jars, I like to use smaller, narrower jars or bottles filled with water as weights. When using a crock, I use a plate that can fit directly on the vegetables and then place a weight on top of the plate.

- The temperature of your kitchen will affect the speed at which your vegetables ferment. A cool place (about 65°F) enables them to ferment slowly and develop a complex flavor. Check them more frequently in summer by removing a little and tasting. Once they reach your desired level of tanginess and pungency, they are ready to eat and can be stored in the fridge to slow further fermentation. Once the flavor and texture is to my liking, I find that they improve further after a couple of days in the fridge.

- Discard any vegetables that may have floated to the top and lift off any mold that may have formed. Fear not—as long as there is no mold among the vegetables themselves, then they are perfectly safe to eat. You can drink the brine, add it to salad dressings, or use it in your next fermentation experiment.

PINK KRAUT

Sauerkraut's literal translation from German is "sour cabbage," and it is traditionally flavored with juniper berries. Here the combination of mostly light green cabbage with a little red cabbage results in a pretty pink sauerkraut. If red cabbage isn't available, use all green; you can also add some spices, like caraway seeds, sliced jalapeños, garlic, mustard seeds, fennel, or anything else you fancy.

MAKES ABOUT 3 CUPS

1 medium green cabbage, cored and thinly sliced (about 10 cups)

¼ small-to-medium red cabbage, cored and thinly sliced (about 2 cups)

2–3 teaspoons sea salt

Place cabbages and salt in a large bowl; use your hands to "massage" it for a few minutes until the cabbage becomes juicy and starts to soften. If you're adding any spices, mix them in now. At this point, I always taste a little to make sure it's a little saltier than I want the end result to be; if I'm adding any spices, I make sure I like the flavor of those as well.

Add a handful of cabbage to a crock or two wide-mouth jars and pound the cabbage down to release any air pockets. Repeat with remaining cabbage, adding a handful at a time, then divide in any remaining liquid from the bowl between the jars or pour it into the crock. The surface should be covered with liquid; if not, continue pushing the surface down until liquid rises (see the preceding tips if you need to add brine). Press down any pieces of cabbage from the sides of the crock or jars so they are submerged as well. If you're using two jars, fill 2 smaller jars or bottles with water and place them on the surface of the cabbage as a weight to keep it below the liquid. If you're using a crock, use a small plate to hold the cabbage down and place a weight on top of the plate. Cover with a cloth to keep dust and bugs out and place in a well-ventilated, cool area. Ferment for five to ten days.

Taste the kraut after five days and then every day until the flavor is to your liking, then cover jar with a lid or transfer from crock into jars and store it in the fridge. It will keep months, and the flavor will continue to develop and strengthen over time.

KIMCHI

Kimchi is a pungent Korean condiment made from cabbage fermented with radishes, carrots, chili, garlic, ginger, scallions, and sometimes dried fish. I add a lot of chili, as I love the red color, but you can adjust to suit your taste. When you have fresh chilies available, use a few to taste in place of the dried. Although the smell of kimchi fermenting in your kitchen can be quite funky, it has a uniquely tangy and layered flavor that perks up any simple meal or snack in an instant.

MAKES ABOUT 4 CUPS

1 medium Napa cabbage (1¾ pounds), outer leaves removed

2 medium carrots, thinly sliced on a diagonal

6 radishes, thinly sliced

½ cup thinly scallions (about 7 scallions)

2½ teaspoons sea salt

3-inch piece ginger, roughly chopped

8 large garlic cloves

¼ cup dried red chili flakes

Quarter and core cabbage. Slice each quarter into 1-inch strips; place in a large bowl and add carrots, radishes, scallions, and salt. Toss to combine and set aside.

Place ginger, garlic, and chili flakes in a food processor and blend until finely ground. Scrape sides and blend again. Add to bowl of vegetables and use your hands to mix thoroughly. Continue mixing and massaging vegetables for a few minutes until they become juicy and start to soften. (At this point, I always taste a little to make sure it's just a little saltier than I want the end result to be.)

Add a handful of vegetables to two wide-mouth jars or a crock, and pound down firmly with your fist to release any air pockets. Repeat with remaining vegetables, a handful at a time, then divide any remaining liquid from the bowl between jars, or pour it into the crock. The surface should be covered with liquid; if not, continue pushing the vegetables down until liquid rises (see the tips on page 121 if you need to add brine). Press any pieces of cabbage down from the sides of the crock or jars so they are submerged as well. If you're using two jars, fill two smaller jars or bottles with water and place them on the surface of the vegetables as a weight to keep them below the liquid. If you're using a crock, use a small plate to hold the vegetables down and place a weight on top of the plate. Cover with a cloth to keep dust and bugs out and place in a well-ventilated, cool area. Ferment for five to seven days or for up to ten days or longer.

Taste the kimchi after five days and then every day until the flavor is to your liking, then cover jars with a lid or transfer from crock into jars and store in the fridge. It will keep for months, and the flavor will continue to develop and strengthen over time, and the vegetables will soften.

the recipes

breakfast

The morning hours have always been a time of great creativity for me, which is lucky because for the many years I worked in restaurants my days began at 5 a.m. Most of the menu decisions were made by 7 a.m., and by 8:00 I was pulling cakes from the oven and tasting the soup of the day. Though it was hard work, I loved the camaraderie between the early morning crew and the farmers that arrived as the sun was rising.

As a child, the clatter of my mother beating egg whites with a whisk was the sound I awoke to early many winter mornings. Those egg whites were to be folded into her beloved milk-millet pudding. She served this decadent soufflé-like breakfast pudding with stewed apples and a drizzle of heavy cream! We would huddle around the old combustion stove eating warm bowls of it before school.

I still love getting up early. The peace and stillness of New York City at dawn is my most treasured time to cook—sometimes I can feel myself being drawn up and out of bed by all the possibility that awaits me in the kitchen while the rest of the city sleeps.

Though I love cooking and baking in the morning, I have a few easy "go to" breakfasts that I'm happy to eat for an entire season—altered slightly depending on what's available. These breakfast staples can be found in the pantry section of this book. The recipes on the following pages are what I turn to when I want to embrace what's just come into season, when I have a little more time, or when I am eating breakfast with friends or houseguests.

Here you'll find seasonal inspiration to take you through the whole year, from the light protein packed Amaranth Muesli (page 130), which is perfect with berries and summer fruits when the mornings are warm, to the tasty and savory Millet, Squash, and Sweet Corn Pilaf (page 138) and Quinoa Congee (page 146) when you need warmth and sustenance.

The fragrance of My Mother's Spelt Almond Waffles (page 131) is sure to bring everyone into the kitchen, as are any of the muffin recipes you'll find here. If I plan ahead, I make a batch of Cherry Coconut Granola with extra virgin olive oil (page 151), or a loaf of Spelt Brown Rice Bread with Sesame (page 134), which can be part of a breakfast spread. Whether you're eating breakfast alone or sharing it with a group, it will always taste better with a good pot of tea.

AMARANTH MUESLI WITH TOASTED SEEDS

In midsummer, when the heat of the season seeps into the early morning, you'll be glad to have this refreshingly light and nourishing breakfast on hand. The popped amaranth is crisp and full of protein, and its toasty flavor goes perfectly topped with juicy summer fruits, fresh berries, and homemade almond milk (page 74). If black currants are in season, they make a lovely addition and striking color contrast.

Once you get the timing down, popping amaranth is easy, and you'll want to make extra to add to your other favorite breakfast cereals. If you have toasted nuts and seeds on hand, this muesli comes together in a flash. I like to leave the sweetness to the summer fruit I serve with it, but you could add dried fruits like cherries, dates, mulberries, or apricots instead for a sweeter result at any time of year.

MAKES ABOUT 4 CUPS
SERVES 4 TO 6

2 cups regular rolled oats, divided

1 cup puffed amaranth (see sidebar)

½ cup toasted almonds (page 77), roughly chopped

½ cup toasted pumpkin seeds (page 77)

½ cup toasted sunflower seeds (page 77)

3 tablespoons hemp seeds

TO SERVE:

Fresh berries

Sliced peaches, nectarines, or apricots

Homemade almond milk (page 74) or yogurt

Superfood Breakfast Sprinkle (page 117), optional

Warm a wide skillet over medium heat for 1 minute, then add 1 cup oats. Toast oats for 5 minutes, or until golden and fragrant, stirring every 30 seconds or so to ensure even toasting. Transfer to a medium bowl to cool and repeat with remaining oats.

Add puffed amaranth, almonds, pumpkin seeds, sunflower seeds, and hemp seeds to oats; toss to combine. Serve with berries, fruits, and almond milk, and top with breakfast sprinkle if desired. Since this recipe contains hemp seeds, store leftover muesli in a jar in the fridge and use within two weeks.

PUFFED AMARANTH

Amaranth is a high-protein seed that was once the sacred food of the Aztecs. It's also high in calcium and amino acids and has a sweet, nutty flavor.

Popping amaranth seems a little challenging at first, so if you burn the first batch, don't worry; once you get the hang of it, it's easy and fun. Popping happens superfast (in about 15 seconds!), and you need to remove the popped grain from the pot immediately to avoid burning.

Puffed amaranth can be sprinkled over fruit or vegetable salads for a light, crunchy texture and protein boost. It can also be used in the Golden Amaranth Superfood Bars (page 347).

MAKES ABOUT 1 CUP

¼ cup amaranth

Warm a small heavy-bottomed pot with a lid over high heat for 2 minutes. Add 1 tablespoon amaranth and cover pot immediately. Count 5 seconds and shake pan; you will hear the grain popping rapidly. Repeat twice or until all the grains are popped. Quickly transfer to a bowl. Repeat with remaining amaranth, 1 tablespoon at a time. Once cool, store puffed amaranth in a jar and use within two weeks.

MY MOTHER'S SPELT ALMOND WAFFLES

A trip back to Australia would not be complete without a long summer morning eating these tender, fragrant waffles on my mother's verandah. She tops them with big, juicy blackberries from her garden, slivers of mango, the thickest biodynamic yogurt I have ever eaten, and a drizzle of maple syrup. It's a heavenly experience, especially surrounded by the thick Australian bush and a constant bustle of wildlife to entertain you.

NOTE: I find that most whole-grain waffles need to be cooked a minute or two longer than the instructions on waffle irons suggest.

MAKES 8 MEDIUM WAFFLES
EQUIPMENT: WAFFLE IRON

1¼ cup sprouted spelt flour or whole spelt flour

½ teaspoon aluminum-free baking powder

¾ cup almond meal

2 eggs, yolks and whites separated

¼ cup extra virgin olive oil or melted extra virgin coconut oil

Zest of 1 orange

½ cup fresh orange juice

¾ cup homemade almond milk (page 74) or plain soy milk

3 tablespoons brown rice syrup

Extra virgin coconut oil or melted butter for brushing the waffle iron

TO SERVE:

Thick, whole-milk yogurt

Fresh berries and seasonal fruit

Maple syrup

Preheat waffle iron. Sift spelt flour and baking powder into a medium mixing bowl. Add almond meal and stir well to break up any lumps; set aside.

In a separate bowl, whisk egg yolks, olive oil, orange zest, orange juice, and almond milk until combined. Stir into dry mixture; drizzle rice syrup over batter and stir again. In a clean bowl, beat egg whites into stiff peaks and gently fold into batter.

Brush preheated waffle iron with melted butter or oil. Ladle in about ½ cup batter per waffle, close lid, and cook for about 4 minutes or until golden brown. Repeat with remaining batter; serve warm topped with yogurt, berries, fruit, and a drizzle of maple syrup. Leftover waffles can be frozen in an airtight container for up to three months, simply reheat in a toaster or oven.

BLACKBERRY CORNMEAL MUFFINS

I love baking a batch of these muffins when I have people coming over for breakfast or morning tea. The delicate, sweet scent of coconut oil, orange, and maple mingled with nutty whole-grain flour is irresistible to anyone who walks through the door. Jam-packed with berries, slightly sweet. and full of grainy goodness, these are everything I want in a muffin.

When I'm baking a batch for coconut lovers (or I don't have corn grits in my pantry), I replace the corn grits with a ½ cup of dried, unsweetened, shredded coconut—pulsing it a few times in an electric spice grinder the same way I grind the corn grits. This results in a super moist and fragrant muffin.

This extremely versatile recipe can form the base for many different kinds of muffins, depending on the season. In spring, try replacing the blackberries with diced rhubarb and sliced strawberries. In summer, try peaches and raspberries, and in fall, the wonderful combination of pears with cornmeal. Make them any time of year with frozen berries, apple juice in place of orange, and extra virgin olive oil in place of coconut oil—although the coconut oil will do a better job of keeping the muffins moist for a day or two.

NOTE: I prefer grinding corn grits in a spice grinder rather than using store-bought cornmeal, because unless it's freshly ground, it often has a stale and slightly bitter flavor. I also love the brighter yellow color of corn grits. If you use cornmeal frequently and have it on hand, you can substitute it in equal parts for the corn grits if you like.

MAKES 10 MUFFINS

2 tablespoons chia seeds

½ cup homemade almond milk (page 74) or plain soy milk

⅓ cup yellow corn grits

1½ cups sprouted spelt flour or whole spelt flour

1 tablespoon aluminum-free baking powder

½ cup almond meal

Zest of 1 orange

½ cup fresh orange juice (from 1 juicy orange)

⅓ cup melted extra virgin coconut oil

⅓ cup maple syrup

1 tablespoon vanilla extract

¼ teaspoon sea salt

2 cups blackberries

Preheat oven to 350°F. Line a standard muffin pan with 10 cupcake liners and set aside.

Whisk chia seeds and almond milk together in a medium bowl; set aside for at least 10 minutes to thicken. Grind corn grits in a spice grinder for 30 seconds or until they're the consistency of a coarse flour, and place in a medium bowl. Sift spelt flour and baking powder into bowl with grits. Add almond meal and whisk to combine, breaking up any small lumps.

Add orange zest, orange juice, coconut oil, maple syrup, vanilla, and salt to chia seed mixture; whisk to combine. Add dry ingredients and use a rubber spatula to stir until almost combined; add blackberries and stir briefly.

Spoon batter into lined muffin cups, filling all the way to the top, and bake for 30 to 35 minutes or until a toothpick inserted in the center comes out clean. Remove from oven, and allow the muffins to sit for 5 minutes before serving or transferring to a wire rack to cool. These are best the day they're made, but any leftovers can be stored in an airtight container for a day or two.

SPELT BROWN RICE BREAD WITH SESAME

Every Saturday in Amsterdam's Jordaan district, there is a small, bustling organic farmers' market called the Boerenmarkt. When I called that city home, I was lucky enough to live just blocks away and would spend the morning buying flowers and vegetables before meeting friends for hot apple pie at the café on the corner. It was at that market that I discovered my forever-favorite bread—whole-grain sourdough with brown rice. Since sourdough isn't part of my regular routine, I thought I'd try making the bread based on Jim Lahey's famous no-knead method. To my delight, it worked, and I now enjoy this moist, wholesome bread any time I'm missing Amsterdam.

NOTE: The dough needs to ferment at room temperature for 14 hours. I like to make the mixture at 5 p.m., then continue the process at 7 a.m., and enjoy the bread by 10 a.m. The recipe is pretty forgiving, so don't worry if you're slightly off with the timing.

MAKES ONE 9-INCH LOAF

2½ cups sprouted spelt flour or whole spelt flour

½ cup cornmeal (see note on page 133)

½ teaspoon instant yeast

1½ teaspoons sea salt

1½ cups warm filtered water

1 teaspoon unrefined sesame oil or extra virgin olive oil, for oiling bread pan

2 cups cooked brown and sweet rice (page 63)

¼ cup unhulled sesame seeds, divided

Combine spelt flour, cornmeal, yeast, and salt in a medium bowl. Add water and mix until combined; dough will be sticky and quite wet. Cover bowl with a plastic bag secured with a rubber band, or plastic wrap, and allow to sit at room temperature (70°F) for 14 hours. Batter will look slightly puffy and bubbly.

Brush loaf pan with oil. Remove plastic from bowl (save it for covering bread again), and add brown rice and half the sesame seeds to the dough. Use your hands to mix until rice and seeds are evenly distributed. Place dough in the oiled pan and press lightly to distribute evenly. Sprinkle top with remaining sesame seeds and cover with reserved plastic wrap. Place in a draft-free place to rise for 1 hour.

Preheat oven to 350°F. Bake bread for 1 hour and 15 minutes or until crust has formed and bread sounds hollow when tapped. Remove bread from pan and allow to cool for at least 20 minutes before slicing. Once cool, store the bread in an airtight container for a couple of days; in summer, store it in the fridge. It can also be sliced and frozen for up to three months.

The fermentation that occurs in sourdough bread removes the phytic acid present in the flour, making it more digestible and nutritious (see page 58 for more information). Since this bread isn't made using a sourdough method, I make it with sprouted flour, because the sprouting process also removes phytic acid. The recipe works with regular whole-grain flour as well.

PEACH CHIA BREAKFAST SHAKE

The peak of summer is the only time I ever want to drink a cool smoothie for breakfast. According to traditional Chinese and Ayurvedic medicine (and also macrobiotic principles), everything we eat or drink should be either at room temperature or warm; otherwise, our qi (or prana) is weakened, and our ability to digest food diminishes. But when the humidity is high this cool shake really hits the spot. When I do make smoothies, I usually add all sorts of superfoods to the mix, which can be great, but they often end up overpowering the delicate flavor of the fruit unless sweeteners are added. I've left this shake simple so the nectar-like flavors of fresh summer peaches can really shine, though it's also terrific made with blueberries when peaches aren't available. Instead of adding ice or frozen banana as a thickener, the chia seeds create a luscious consistency and provide abundant omega fatty acids and steady endurance for the day ahead. If you want to sneak in an extra superfood, go for blending in a little maca root powder or a sprinkle of bee pollen on top.

NOTE: For the best results, it's essential to make this recipe with homemade almond milk and ripe local peaches. Honey can be a nice addition, depending on the sweetness of your peaches and your preference, so it's optional here.

SERVES 2

2 tablespoons chia seeds

1½ cups strained homemade almond milk (page 74)

3 large peaches (1¼ pounds), pitted and quartered

1 tablespoon coconut butter or extra virgin coconut oil

1 teaspoon vanilla extract

⅛ teaspoon cinnamon

2 to 3 teaspoons raw honey, optional

Place chia seeds in a clean, dry, 1-quart jar with a tight-fitting lid and set aside.

Put almond milk, peaches, coconut butter, vanilla, cinnamon, and honey (if using) in an upright blender. Blend on high speed for at least 1 minute or until completely smooth. Pour half of mixture into jar with chia seeds, tighten lid, and shake well, making sure that no chia seeds stick to the bottom. Add remaining peach mixture, tighten lid, and shake until chia seeds are evenly distributed.

Place in the fridge and chill for 2 hours or overnight. It's ready when mixture has thickened and the shake is thoroughly chilled.

VARIATION
PEACH CHIA PUDDING

This shake transforms beautifully into a peach-flavored chia pudding that makes a lovely, light summer dessert. Simply increase the chia seeds to ¼ cup and serve with sliced peaches on top.

MILLET, SQUASH, AND SWEET CORN PILAF
WITH TAMARI-TOASTED PUMPKIN SEEDS

When the air is fresh and crisp and there is no mistaking the transition of summer into fall, I make this for breakfast. This pilaf is perfectly good for lunch or dinner, but I love the way a savory breakfast sustains you throughout the day. The flavor combination of sweet squash and earthy millet is a comforting way to begin the morning, and the addition of turmeric lends healing and detoxifying properties. Turmeric is a true superfood; a natural anti-inflammatory, it is the best source of beta-carotene of any food and helps cleanse and tone the liver while strengthening the immune system. I also like how it adds a lovely golden hue to the millet.

Kabocha, red kuri, or buttercup squash all work well here. You can also use frozen corn if no fresh sweet corn is available.

SERVES 6

1 cup millet, washed and soaked 12 to 24 hours in 2 cups filtered water

1 medium onion, diced

3 cups winter squash, peeled, and cut in 1-inch dice

1 cup sweet corn kernels

¼ teaspoon turmeric

½ teaspoon sea salt

2½ cups filtered water

1 teaspoon tamari, plus more to serve

TO SERVE:

Cold pressed flax oil

Thinly sliced scallions

Tamari-Toasted Pumpkin Seeds (page 77)

Drain and rinse millet; place in a medium pot with a tight-fitting lid. Add onion, squash, corn, turmeric, salt, and water. Stir and bring to a boil over high heat. Cover pot, reduce heat to low, and cook for 30 minutes or until all liquid has been absorbed. Remove from heat and sprinkle with tamari; replace lid and let sit for 5 to 10 minutes before stirring gently. Serve topped with a drizzle of flax oil, scallions, tamari-toasted pumpkin seeds, and tamari to taste.

NOTE: To cook pilaf in a pressure cooker, add the ingredients and bring it to a boil over high heat. Lock the lid in place and bring it up to high pressure, then reduce heat to low and cook for 10 minutes. Remove from heat and allow the pressure to release naturally. Remove the lid, sprinkle with tamari, gently stir, and serve. Store any leftovers in the fridge for up to four days, and steam in a steamer basket to reheat.

Millet is the only grain that has alkalizing properties; it soothes the stomach, spleen, and pancreas; helps strengthen the kidneys; and is a rich source of B vitamins and iron. Note that millet needs to be washed very well, as it has a bitter coating that will alter its flavor if not thoroughly removed.

PUMPKIN BREAD WITH TOASTED WALNUT CINNAMON SWIRL

On chilly fall mornings, nothing beats sitting in a warm kitchen filled with the aroma of cinnamon, maple, and pumpkin. Since this bread is made with sprouted flour, it doesn't feel too decadent to enjoy for breakfast and is perfect for morning tea. If you steam the squash and get your ingredients ready the night before, it comes together quickly. Any leftover bread is very good sliced and toasted the following day. I suggest storing it in an airtight container—and keep it in the fridge if you want to keep it for a few days.

NOTE: You can use any winter squash, but I find the dense-fleshed ones like kabocha and red kuri squash work the best because of their lower water content.

MAKES ONE 9-INCH LOAF

CINNAMON WALNUT SWIRL:

1 cup toasted walnut halves (page 78), chopped

2 teaspoons ground cinnamon

2 tablespoons maple sugar

2 tablespoons maple syrup

PUMPKIN BATTER:

½ medium kabocha squash, peeled, seeded, and cut in ½-inch dice (about 3½ cups)

2 cups sprouted spelt flour or whole spelt flour

2 teaspoons aluminum-free baking powder

¼ cup plus 2 tablespoons extra virgin olive oil

½ cup maple syrup

2 tablespoons almond milk or plain soy milk

½ teaspoon sea salt

2 teaspoons vanilla extract

1 egg, beaten

MAKE THE CINNAMON WALNUT SWIRL:

Place walnuts, cinnamon, maple sugar, and maple syrup in a bowl; mix to combine and set aside.

MAKE THE PUMPKIN BATTER:

Steam squash for 10 to 12 minutes or until soft. Place in a medium bowl and mash with a fork. Measure out 1½ cups and set aside.

Preheat oven to 350°F. Lightly oil a loaf pan and line bottom and two longer sides with a sheet of parchment paper; set aside.

Sift spelt flour and baking powder into a medium bowl and stir to combine. Add olive oil, maple syrup, almond milk, salt, vanilla, and egg to the mashed squash; whisk until smooth. Using a rubber spatula, fold flour mixture into squash mixture until just combined. Spread half of batter over bottom of loaf pan. Layer cinnamon-walnut mixture evenly over batter and top with remaining batter. To create a swirl, use a small rubber spatula or butter knife to zigzag back and forth through the batter (across pan) and one stroke straight through the center of the loaf (lengthwise).

Place in oven, and bake for 45 to 50 minutes or until a toothpick inserted in the center comes out clean. Remove from oven and allow loaf to sit 5 minutes before turning out and placing on a wire rack. Slice and serve warm.

VARIATION

BANANA BREAD WITH TOASTED WALNUT CINNAMON SWIRL

When squash isn't available, replace it with mashed banana for a scrumptious banana bread—you'll need about 4 large bananas in place of the squash. Since bananas are much sweeter than squash, you can opt to halve the maple sugar and maple syrup in the swirl or leave it out completely.

PLUM MILLET MUFFINS

These muffins are tender, fragrant, and surprisingly light. They make a great healthy breakfast treat that's mildly sweet yet feels decadent when you bite into the large pieces of juicy cooked plums. The millet sprinkled over the top adds a nice crunchy contrast to the soft fruit. If you prepare the millet ahead of time, these muffins are a snap to make. You can also use quinoa in place of the millet; you'll need 1 cup cooked, plus a couple of tablespoons to sprinkle over the top (see page 64 for instructions on cooking quinoa).

NOTE: If you're using particularly juicy plums, place them in a strainer over a bowl for 5 minutes to drain off any excess juice. You may also need to bake the muffins for a few minutes longer. If you forget to soak the millet, increase the cooking liquid by 2 tablespoons.

MAKES 10 MUFFINS

MILLET:

¼ cup millet, washed and soaked 12 to 24 hours in 1 cup filtered water

½ cup filtered water

Pinch sea salt

MUFFINS:

1½ cups sprouted spelt flour or whole spelt flour

1 tablespoon aluminum-free baking powder

Zest of 1 orange

Zest of 1 lemon

½ cup fresh orange juice

¼ cup plus 2 tablespoons maple syrup

¼ cup plus 2 tablespoons extra virgin olive oil or melted extra virgin coconut oil

¼ cup almond milk or plain soy milk

1 tablespoon vanilla extract

¼ teaspoon sea salt

4 medium red plums (12 ounces), pitted and cut into ½-inch slices

¼ teaspoon cinnamon

COOK THE MILLET:

Drain and rinse millet. Place in a small pot, add ½ cup water and salt. Bring to a boil over high heat; cover pot, reduce heat to low, and simmer for 20 minutes. Remove from heat; let sit at least 10 minutes before removing lid and fluffing with a fork. You should have 1 cup plus 2 tablespoons cooked millet.

MAKE THE MUFFINS:

Preheat oven to 350°F. Line a standard muffin pan with 10 paper liners.

Sift flour and baking powder into a medium bowl; whisk to combine and set aside. In another bowl, combine orange zest, lemon zest, orange juice, maple syrup, olive oil, almond milk, vanilla, and sea salt; whisk until emulsified. Add flour mixture, and using a rubber spatula, gently stir mixture until almost combined. Fold in plums and 1 cup cooked millet, stirring until just combined—don't overmix.

Divide batter into muffin cups, filling them all the way to the top. Sprinkle cinnamon and the remaining millet over the tops and bake for 30 to 35 minutes. Muffins are cooked when a toothpick inserted in the center comes out clean. Remove from oven and leave muffins in pan for 5 to 10 minutes before transferring to a wire rack to cool.

These muffins are best the day they're made.

BLACK RICE BREAKFAST PUDDING
WITH COCONUT AND BANANA

The first time I ate black rice pudding for breakfast, I was a young girl and my family was visiting Bali. We ate it topped with yogurt, tropical fruit, and palm sugar in the small cafés that lined the bustling streets. The nutty, sweet flavor and pretty purple color of black rice intrigued me. It wasn't until I visited again more recently that I remembered how much I loved it and started making black rice pudding at home. The unmistakable tropical flavors of coconut and banana combined with black rice instantly send me back to the sounds and scents of Bali in the early morning.

This pudding takes longer to cook than some other porridges, but a batch can last up to four days in the fridge, so it's worth the extra time it saves later. It will thicken a lot as it cools, so when you want to eat some, just remove a portion and add a little water or almond or coconut milk to get the desired consistency. It can be eaten cool or warmed up in a pot.

Like rice pudding, this can be enjoyed as dessert too—if you cook it for this purpose, I recommend using the optional sweetener.

SERVES 4 TO 6

1 cup forbidden black rice, washed and soaked 12 to 24 hours in 4 cups filtered water

¾ cup unsweetened full-fat coconut milk

1½ cups homemade almond or Brazil nut milk (page 74), plus more to get desired consistency, either strained or unstrained

2 cups filtered water

Pinch sea salt

¼ cup maple syrup or coconut nectar, optional

TO SERVE:

Sliced banana

½ cup toasted coconut flakes (see sidebar)

Homemade almond or Brazil nut milk

Maple syrup, coconut nectar, or coconut sugar to taste

Drain and rinse black rice. Place in a heavy-bottomed medium pot and add coconut milk, almond milk, water, and salt. Bring to a boil over high heat. Cover pot, reduce heat to low, and simmer for 1 hour. Stir porridge every 15 minutes, then more frequently toward the end of cooking to prevent sticking. Add more almond milk or water to get desired consistency, and stir in sweetener if using. Spoon into bowls, top with sliced banana, toasted coconut, a drizzle of almond milk, and sweetener of your choice.

NOTE: To cook a pudding in a pressure cooker, add ingredients and bring to a boil over high heat. Lock lid in place and bring up to high pressure, then reduce heat to low and cook for 20 minutes. Remove from heat and allow pressure to release naturally. Remove lid, stir well, and continue cooking uncovered for 5 minutes or until you get the desired consistency, adding more almond milk or water as needed.

To toast coconut, heat a wide skillet over medium heat; add coconut flakes and stir constantly for about 3 to 4 minutes or until golden brown and fragrant. Remove from heat and place in a bowl to cool.

QUINOA CONGEE

Congee is a healing, Chinese soup-like dish that is most often made with rice, although any grain can be used. This congee is a little thicker and resembles a porridge, but you can add more water to create a soupier consistency if you like. Either way, it has a deeply soothing and warming effect, making it perfect for times when you feel under the weather.

As with all grains, I love to eat a bowl of this congee topped with a drizzle of flax oil, tamari, avocado, toasted seeds, and something fermented. It makes a tasty, satisfying breakfast in winter and is great served for dinner too. Here, I add kombu and shiitakes for added minerals and nutrients and a savory flavor. If you're in the mood for a sweet breakfast, leave them out and try topping it with toasted seeds and nuts and a drizzle of maple syrup, yakon syrup, or honey instead.

SERVES 4

1 cup quinoa, washed and soaked 12 to 24 hours in 4 cups filtered water

2 dried shiitake mushrooms

2-inch piece kombu

5 cups filtered water

½ teaspoon sea salt

TO SERVE (OPTIONAL):

Cold pressed flax oil

Tamari

Kimchi or sauerkraut

Thinly sliced scallions

Sliced avocado

Chopped parsley

Toasted black sesame seeds (page 77) or Black Sesame Gomasio (page 114)

Hemp seeds

Drain and rinse quinoa, and place in a heavy-bottomed medium pot. Wrap shiitake mushrooms and kombu in a piece of cheesecloth; add to quinoa along with water and salt. Bring to a boil over high heat and stir. Cover pot, reduce heat to low, and simmer for 1½ hours, or until the mixture is thick and creamy, stirring every 30 minutes. Remove from heat; compost kombu and shiitakes, or slice shiitakes and return to pot.

Divide among bowls and add toppings of your choice. Any leftover congee can be cooled and stored in an airtight container in the fridge for up to four days.

COCONUT AND QUINOA PANCAKES

I got so excited when I first made these pancakes. Not only do they contain two much-loved ingredients (coconut and quinoa), but they are also completely flour- and gluten-free and still remain tender and tasty. They're a great whole-grain breakfast option to add to your repertoire.

These pancakes go great with fresh berries or sliced nectarines in summer, as well as with cooked fruit compote in winter. You will need to soak the quinoa overnight (or for 12 to 24 hours) for this recipe, but in the morning, you'll realize they're the fastest pancakes you've ever made—no sifting or egg beating required.

The inspiration for these pancakes came from a recipe for Overnight Millet, Buckwheat, and Coconut Waffles in Rebecca Wood's excellent book, *The Splendid Grain*. Like her delicious waffles, these pancakes have plenty of texture and body.

NOTE: For a vegan version, replace the egg with a chia or flax "egg" (see page 38).

MAKES TEN 4-INCH PANCAKES

½ cup quinoa, washed and soaked 12 to 24 hours in 1 cup filtered water

½ cup regular rolled oats

¾ cup dried, unsweetened, shredded coconut, divided

1 cup homemade strained or unstrained almond milk (page 74)

1 egg

2 tablespoons melted extra virgin coconut oil, plus more for cooking pancakes

2 teaspoons vanilla extract

1 teaspoon aluminum-free baking powder

½ teaspoon cinnamon

Zest of 1 large lemon

TO SERVE:

Seasonal fruit and berries

Maple syrup or honey, optional

Lemon wedges, optional

Drain and rinse quinoa, and place it in an upright blender. Add oats, ¼ cup coconut, almond milk, egg, coconut oil, vanilla, baking powder, and cinnamon. Blend on high speed for about 40 seconds or until completely smooth, scraping down sides as necessary. Add remaining coconut and lemon zest and stir with a rubber spatula to combine.

Warm a wide cast iron skillet over medium heat; add about 1 teaspoon coconut oil and spoon in ¼ cup batter for each pancake. Spread the batter out a little with the back of a spoon to make a 4-inch pancake. Cook for about 3 minutes or until surface is covered with bubbles and bottom is golden and beginning to brown. Flip and cook for another 2 minutes or until golden brown. Remove from skillet and repeat with remaining batter.

These pancakes are best hot off the pan, but they can also be kept warm in a 200°F oven as you cook the whole batch. Serve warm with fruit, berries, maple syrup, and a squeeze of lemon.

CHERRY COCONUT GRANOLA WITH EXTRA VIRGIN OLIVE OIL

My mother always made huge batches of granola—or toasted muesli, as she called it—whenever we went on camping trips or went to stay with friends or extended family. Today, I find myself carrying on the tradition. The addition of rice syrup in this recipe was inspired by a granola my cousin Jessica made for a family reunion on Stradbroke Island in Queensland, Australia. I loved the subtle, malty sweetness and rich sheen the rice syrup provided so much that I've been making granola with it ever since.

This is a deluxe granola, one that I make for special occasions and holiday gifts. It looks gorgeous packaged in jars or cellophane bags tied with ribbon. Most people I know enjoy it with the full amount of maple syrup, but if you're looking to cut down on sweeteners, you can reduce or omit the maple syrup completely. I have also made this with coconut nectar in place of the maple syrup, which results in a less sweet-tasting granola. Either way, it's sublime served with tangy yogurt, berries, and figs when they're in season.

NOTE: You can replace the extra virgin olive oil with coconut oil for a richer, coconuty flavor, or you can use unrefined sesame oil for a nutty, less sweet taste.

MAKES 12 CUPS

½ cup raw pumpkin seeds

½ cup raw sunflower seeds

½ cup raw unhulled sesame seeds

5 cups regular rolled oats

1 cup whole raw almonds, roughly chopped

2½ cups dried, unsweetened coconut flakes

1 teaspoon ground cinnamon

½ cup brown rice syrup

¼ to ½ cup maple syrup

½ teaspoon sea salt

½ cup extra virgin olive oil

1 tablespoon vanilla extract

⅓ cup thinly sliced unsulfured dried apricots

⅓ cup unsulfured golden raisins

1 cup unsweetened dried cherries

Preheat oven to 300°F. Line two rimmed baking sheets with parchment paper and set aside. Place pumpkin, sunflower, and sesame seeds in a medium bowl and fill it with water. Swish the seeds around and let them settle. Pour off the water and catch the seeds in a strainer. Rinse under running water and set aside to drain while you prepare the other ingredients.

Place oats, almonds, coconut, and cinnamon in a large bowl; toss to combine and set aside.

Warm rice syrup, maple syrup, and salt in a small saucepan over medium heat. Stir until mixture begins to simmer, then remove from heat and stir in olive oil and vanilla; set aside. Stir the drained seeds into the oat mixture. Pour in the olive oil mixture and stir until evenly combined.

Divide between baking sheets and bake for 15 minutes. Stir, rotate baking sheets, and bake another 15 minutes. Stir again and return to oven for an additional 5 to 10 minutes or until granola is golden and toasty.

Place warm granola in a bowl, add dried fruit, and toss gently. Cool completely before storing in jars. Granola will keep well for four to six weeks.

HERBED BLACK QUINOA MUFFINS
WITH SWEET POTATO AND CARAMELIZED ONIONS

The first time I tested this muffin recipe and ate one warm from the oven, I couldn't believe how much I enjoyed it. The mashed sweet potato in the batter adds a pleasantly moist and sweet background to the onions, herbs, and delicate crunch of black quinoa.

For a variation, try substituting winter squash for the sweet potato and adding rosemary in place of thyme. You can also use ½ cup of any leftover cooked grain in place of the black quinoa. Toasted pecans or walnuts are a tasty addition to the mix too. Whatever you use, your kitchen will smell inviting, and you'll end up with a delectable savory treat.

NOTE: If you forget to soak the quinoa, increase the water by 2 tablespoons and cook for 20 minutes.

MAKES 10 MUFFINS

BLACK QUINOA:

¼ cup black quinoa,
   washed and soaked 12 to 24 hours
   in 1 cup filtered water

¼ cup filtered water

Pinch sea salt

MUFFINS:

2 tablespoons ground flax seeds

¼ cup plain soy milk or plain nut milk

¼ cup plus 1 tablespoon
   extra virgin olive oil, divided

1 medium onion, diced

2 tablespoons chopped sage leaves

2 teaspoons chopped thyme,
   plus thyme sprigs to garnish

1 teaspoon sea salt, divided

1½ cups sprouted spelt flour
   or sprouted whole-wheat flour

1 tablespoon aluminum-free
   baking powder

¼ teaspoon baking soda

1 cup mashed sweet potato (see sidebar)

¾ cup filtered water

2 teaspoons unpasteurized
   apple cider vinegar

1 teaspoon tamari

COOK THE BLACK QUINOA:

Drain and rinse quinoa. Place in a small pot, add water, and bring to a boil over high heat. Reduce heat to low, cover pot, and simmer for 15 minutes or until all water is absorbed. Remove from heat and allow to sit, covered, for 10 minutes; fluff with a fork. Measure out ½ cup and set aside. Save the remaining couple of tablespoons of quinoa to sprinkle over muffins.

MAKE THE MUFFINS:

Preheat oven to 350°F. Line a regular muffin pan with 10 paper liners.

Place flax and soy milk in a medium bowl and whisk to combine. Set aside to thicken while you cook the onion.

Warm 1 tablespoon olive oil in a skillet over medium heat. Add onion, and sauté for 5 minutes or until golden brown. Add sage, thyme, and ½ teaspoon salt; reduce heat to low and continue cooking for another 5 minutes or until caramelized. Remove from heat and set aside.

Sift flour, baking powder, and baking soda into another medium bowl. Whisk to combine and set aside.

Add sweet potato, water, vinegar, tamari, and remaining ½ teaspoon salt to the flax-soy milk mixture and whisk until smooth. Add remaining ¼ cup olive oil; whisk again and add flour mixture. Use a rubber spatula to stir mixture gently until almost combined, then fold in cooked quinoa and onions.

Divide batter between lined muffin cups, filling them all the way to the top. Garnish each muffin with a thyme sprig and a sprinkle of remaining cooked quinoa. Bake 45 to 50 minutes or until a toothpick inserted in the center comes out clean. Remove from oven; leave muffins in the pan for 5 minutes before transferring them to a wire rack to cool slightly before serving. Once cool, any leftover muffins can be stored in an airtight container in the fridge for up to two days.

For 1 cup mashed sweet potato, peel 1 medium sweet potato (14 ounces) and cut it into rough ½-inch dice (about 2 cups). Place in a steamer basket over boiling water, and steam for 5 minutes or until soft. Remove from heat, transfer to a bowl, mash with a fork, and measure out 1 cup.

soups

With its ability to simultaneously soothe, warm, and elevate your mood, nothing compares to a bowl of homemade soup. As soon as the crisp air sneaks into late summer days, I find myself drawn into the kitchen to put a pot on to cook. Soups are a great means of articulating the spirit of the season, and at the same time, they are a cure-all for any weather condition. In the cold months, look to the Hearty Winter Miso Soup with Adzuki Beans, Squash, and Ginger (page 174) to fortify and nourish you; on scorching summer days, Gazpacho with Heirloom Tomatoes (page 163) will satisfy and tame your thirst—and you don't even have to turn on the stove to make it.

Soups can come together simply with two or three ingredients puréed into creamy lusciousness or over time with more complexity by layering flavors derived from stocks and broths. They are a tolerant and forgiving medium, allowing you to swap out one vegetable for another and use up any past-its-prime produce. I encourage you to adapt these recipes to your own pantry and mood—add vegetables you have on hand to the French Lentil Soup with Rosemary, Squash, and Rainbow Chard (page 167); asparagus or broccoli make a great substitution for zucchini in the Pea Zucchini Soup with Dill (page 159); the celery root in the Creamy Cauliflower and Celery Root Soup with Roasted Shiitakes (page 168) can be replaced with parsnips; and, of course, any combination of dense-fleshed squash can used in the Kabocha Chestnut Soup with Nori Sesame "Leaves" (page 171).

Whichever recipe you choose to cook, soup is also the perfect dish to share or to eat over the course of a few days. Knowing you have a jar of soup in the fridge is reassuring; it means a comforting and nutritious dish is at the ready. Serve it with greens on the side or stirred in at the last minute, along with garlic-rubbed toast or a tartine, for a satisfying and complete meal.

SPRING MISO SOUP WITH LEMON

Miso soup and many other Japanese dishes begin with dashi, a stock made by simmering kombu seaweed and often dried shiitake mushrooms. Not only does the dashi add depth of flavor to your soup, but the kombu enriches it with minerals, and the shiitakes provide a host of healing benefits—from abundant antioxidants and cancer-fighting properties to lowering cholesterol and boosting immunity. If you soak the kombu and shiitakes in the water overnight before making this soup, you get a richer tasting dashi and will need to simmer it for only 10 minutes.

I use white miso here for its light, sweet flavor, but you could also use chickpea miso, mellow white miso, or a combination of your favorites. Make sure any miso you purchase is naturally fermented and unpasteurized (see page 36 for more information) so you get all the benefits of the live active enzymes it contains. And be careful not to boil miso, as you will lose the enzymes and many of its nutrients; warm gently and remove from heat just before the soup begins to simmer.

This soup is a pretty way to celebrate the delicate flavors and colors of spring vegetables, and it is ideal for cooler spring days when you're craving something warm and light.

SERVES 4

DASHI:

6 cups filtered water

4-inch piece kombu

3 dried shiitake mushrooms

SOUP:

8 asparagus spears, trimmed
    and cut diagonally in ¼-inch slices

1 cup sugar snap peas, strings removed
    and sliced in half lengthwise

3 medium radishes, thinly sliced

6 tablespoons unpasteurized
    sweet white miso

Zest of 1 lemon, cut in long strips

1 tablespoon fresh lemon juice

1 small bunch watercress, trimmed
    (about 2 cups)

¼ cup thinly sliced scallions or chives

MAKE THE DASHI:

Add kombu, shiitakes, and filtered water to a medium pot, and bring up to a boil over high heat. Cover pot, reduce heat to low, and simmer for 20 minutes. Remove kombu and shiitakes; you can slice the shiitakes and return them to the soup with the other vegetables if you like, or save for adding to other vegetable soups or sautés. Compost the kombu.

MAKE THE SOUP:

Bring the dashi up to a simmer over high heat. Add asparagus and sugar snap peas, and cook for 30 seconds. Add radishes and cook for another 30 seconds, then remove all vegetables immediately using a strainer or slotted spoon. Spread vegetables out on a large plate and set aside to cool.

Reduce heat to low. Add the miso to a medium strainer and place over the pot of dashi so the miso sits in the broth; stir to dissolve miso. You may be left with some hulls from the miso; they can be added to the soup or left out for a smoother result. Add blanched vegetables and watercress; warm gently over low heat for a minute or until watercress is wilted. Be careful not to boil the soup. Remove from heat and stir in lemon zest and juice. Divide scallions between bowls and add soup. Serve immediately.

NOTE: If you want to make this soup ahead of time, leave out the miso and keep the blanched vegetables and dashi separate. Reheat together; then add miso, lemon zest, and juice.

PEA ZUCCHINI SOUP WITH DILL

The luscious, creamy texture and sweet pea flavor of this soup make it ideal for rainy spring days—providing just the right amount of warmth while keeping its verdant spring flavor. Once the weather heats up, it can be served chilled; just thin it out with a little water and season to taste after it's completely cool.

If ramps (wild leeks) grow in your area, use a bunch of them instead of the leek. Once spring is in full swing, I love to make use of the abundance of garlic scapes at the farmers' market by replacing the garlic cloves with ½ cup of chopped scapes. Fresh shelling peas don't arrive at my local farmers' market until well into June, so I often use frozen peas (see note) when making this soup with excellent results.

SERVES 4

2 tablespoons extra virgin olive oil

1 medium onion, diced

6 garlic cloves, chopped

1 teaspoon sea salt

1 medium leek
  (top 4 inches of greens removed),
  cut in ½-inch slices

5 medium zucchini (1¾ pounds),
  cut in ¾-inch dice

1½ pounds fresh English peas, shelled
  (1½ cups shelled peas), or frozen peas

3½ cups filtered water

½ cup chopped fresh dill

Freshly ground black pepper

Pea shoots to garnish

Warm olive oil in a medium pot over medium heat. Add onions, and sauté for 5 minutes or until golden. Stir in garlic and salt, and cook for another minute; add leek and continue cooking for 2 minutes more. Add zucchini, peas, and water; bring to a boil over high heat. Cover pot, reduce heat to low, and simmer for 6 minutes or until zucchini is tender and peas are cooked.

Remove from the heat. Stir in dill and set aside, uncovered, for 10 minutes before blending. Blend soup in batches in an upright blender on highest speed for 1 to 2 minutes, or until completely smooth and velvety. Add a little more water if needed to get desired consistency. Season to taste with salt and black pepper. Serve warm, garnished with pea shoots.

NOTE: When using frozen peas, leave them out to thaw while making the soup; add them after simmering the zucchini for 6 minutes, cover, and cook 1 minute before removing from heat and proceeding with recipe.

UME SHISO BROTH WITH SOBA NOODLES

I'm in love with this delicate, floral, and clean-tasting broth. It clears your head without the use of ginger, wasabi, or miso, yet it has a distinct Japanese flavor from the shiso and umeboshi paste. The dish is inspired by a broth I ate in a Japanese restaurant many years ago; the vegetables were cut in squares (as here), which I think makes it look special, but it's not necessary.

In New York, you can find bunches of red and green shiso at the farmers' market from spring through early fall. Use both the leaves and the stems in the broth for a rich, heady flavor. Other times of the year, shiso leaves can be found at Japanese markets, though these are expensive, and since they don't usually come with stems, you'll need more leaves to create a tasty broth. For these reasons, I suggest making this soup when you can find fresh bunches of shiso.

NOTE: If you can't find tatsoi, use bok choy, watercress, or spinach instead.

SERVES 4

BROTH:

8 cups filtered water

3 stalks celery with leaves, chopped

2 large carrots, chopped

1 medium onion, chopped

4-inch piece kombu

4 dried shiitake mushrooms

2 cups packed shiso leaves and stems (about 3 bunches)

1 teaspoon coriander seeds

SOUP:

½ package 100 percent buckwheat soba noodles (4 ounces)

8-inch piece daikon, at least 1½ inches in diameter, peeled

2 large carrots, about 1½ inches in diameter

½ teaspoon sea salt, plus more to taste

2½ teaspoons umeboshi paste

1 small head tatsoi (4 ounces), trimmed

TO SERVE:

Coriander seeds

Thinly sliced scallions

Nanami togarashi (Japanese hot pepper–sesame condiment), optional

Add water, celery, carrots, onion, kombu, shiitakes, shiso leaves and stems, and coriander seeds to a large pot; bring to a boil over high heat. Cover pot, reduce heat to low, and cook for 40 minutes. Remove from heat, strain broth, and compost vegetables. You should have about 7 cups broth. Return broth to pot and set aside.

Cook soba noodles according to package directions or until tender. Drain and rinse thoroughly with cold water; set aside to drain until ready to serve.

Cut sides off daikon to create a rectangular shape (save scraps to eat as a snack), then cut into ½-inch-thick squares. Cut carrot the same way.

Bring broth to a simmer over high heat and add carrots, daikon, and salt. Cover pot, reduce heat to low, and simmer for 6 to 7 minutes or until vegetables are tender. Ladle a small amount of broth into a cup, add umeboshi paste, mix until dissolved, then stir it back into broth. Add tatsoi; cook 30 seconds or until bright green and tender. Season to taste, then remove from heat.

To serve, divide noodles among four bowls. Ladle broth and vegetables into each bowl and top with a few coriander seeds and sliced scallions. Serve with Nanami togarashi on the side.

When cooking with soba noodles, always make sure to purchase 100 percent buckwheat soba; otherwise, they are made with half or more refined wheat. They are more delicate than regular soba noodles and can quickly become mushy, so keep an eye on them while cooking and be gentle when rinsing. In this recipe, you can use whole-wheat udon noodles instead, if you prefer.

GAZPACHO WITH HEIRLOOM TOMATOES

As soon as tomatoes hit the stands at the farmers' market, the weather is hot enough to crave gazpacho. Sometimes, sipping a cup of this tangy herbal goodness is the only remedy for summer in the city. Having a jar of it in the fridge is a good idea any time the temperature is soaring, and you'll love not having to heat up your kitchen to make it—all you need is a blender. Light and refreshing, gazpacho is a perfect make-ahead starter for a summer dinner party. I love to garnish the bowls with an array of colored tomatoes, but you can also add cucumbers, more herbs, and even a little crumbled feta to dress it up.

SERVES 4 TO 6

9 medium-large ripe tomatoes (3½ pounds), roughly chopped

1 garlic clove, or more to taste

1 medium jalapeño, seeded

3 tablespoons extra virgin olive oil, divided

3 tablespoons red wine vinegar, divided

Sea salt

3 tablespoons minced red onion

¼ cup chopped cilantro leaves

¼ cup finely sliced basil (about 10 leaves)

TO GARNISH:

3 to 4 mixed heirloom tomatoes, sliced in thin wedges

½ cup colored cherry tomatoes, halved

Cilantro leaves

Extra virgin olive oil

Place about a third of the tomatoes in an upright blender; add minced garlic, jalapeño, 1 tablespoon olive oil, 1 tablespoon vinegar, and a pinch of salt. Blend on highest speed for 1 to 2 minutes or until completely smooth. Pour into a large bowl and repeat with remaining tomatoes, olive oil, and vinegar in two more batches. Add to bowl and taste for heat, returning 1 cup soup to blender if you want to blend in more jalapeño. Stir in onion, cilantro, and basil, and season to taste. Place in the fridge for 1 to 2 hours or until cool. Gazpacho is best the day it's made, but anything left over can be kept in the fridge for a couple of days.

To serve, divide gazpacho between bowls, jars, or glasses, and top with a couple of wedges of colored heirloom tomatoes, a few cherry tomato halves, cilantro leaves, and a drizzle of olive oil.

NOTE: Since the heat of jalapeños varies so much, try adding a little at a time while blending the soup. If it's still not spicy enough, add some of the seeds.

SWEET CORN SOUP
WITH BLACK SESAME GOMASIO AND CHIVES

Silky, sweet, and golden, this soup effortlessly captures the essence of summer in a bowl; it's so flavorful that it seems to vanish each time I make it. Although it's perfect eaten plain, the salty, toasty flavor of the Black Sesame Gomasio is a nice contrast in taste and color.

For a more refined soup, or to serve this as a starter for a multicourse dinner, you can strain it through a fine mesh strainer, resulting in a lighter and supersmooth consistency.

SERVES 4

2 tablespoons extra virgin olive oil

1 medium onion, diced

4 garlic cloves, chopped

1 teaspoon sea salt, plus more to taste

5 cups sweet corn kernels (from about 6 large ears),
  3 cobs reserved for cooking soup

4 bay leaves

5 cups filtered water

TO GARNISH:

Black Sesame Gomasio (page 114)

Chopped chives

Warm olive oil in a large pot over medium heat. Add onion, and sauté for 5 minutes or until golden. Stir in garlic and salt, and cook for 2 minutes more. Add corn kernels, bay leaves, and water. Break or cut reserved cobs in half and add to pot. Raise heat and bring to a boil. Cover pot, reduce heat to low, and simmer for 20 minutes or until corn is bright yellow and cooked.

Remove and compost corn cobs and bay leaves. Puree soup in batches in an upright blender on highest speed for 1 to 2 minutes or until completely smooth and velvety. Season to taste, and serve warm topped with gomasio and chives.

FRENCH LENTIL SOUP
WITH ROSEMARY, SQUASH, AND RAINBOW CHARD

French lentils are perfect for soups, as they manage to create a creamy texture while still maintaining their pretty pebble-like shape. I love their earthy flavor, which is a great complement to fragrant rosemary and sweet butternut squash—it's exactly what I crave in fall and winter. If you don't have Swiss chard on hand, you can use spinach or kale instead, just note that kale is a heartier green and will take a bit longer to cook.

SERVES 4 TO 6

1½ cups French lentils, sorted and soaked 12 to 24 hours in 4 cups filtered water

2-inch piece kombu

6 bay leaves

7 cups filtered water

2 tablespoons extra virgin olive oil

1 medium onion, diced

1 teaspoon sea salt, plus more to taste

6 garlic cloves, minced

3 tablespoons minced fresh rosemary

½ medium butternut squash, peeled, seeded, and cut into ¾-inch pieces (about 4 cups)

3 cups sliced rainbow chard (about half a bunch), plus more to garnish

2 teaspoons tamari

2 teaspoons balsamic vinegar

Freshly ground black pepper

TO SERVE:

Cold pressed flax oil or extra virgin olive oil

Drain and rinse lentils; place in a large pot with kombu, bay leaves, and water. Bring to a boil over high heat. Scoop off any foam that rises to the surface with a small strainer or slotted spoon. Cover pot, reduce heat to low, and simmer for 20 minutes or until the lentils are cooked. Remove and compost kombu and bay leaves. Drain lentils and reserve cooking liquid—you should have about 4½ cups; if not, add a little water.

Warm olive oil in a large pot over medium heat. Add onions and salt; sauté until golden, about 5 minutes. Stir in garlic and rosemary, and cook 2 minutes longer. Add squash and reserved lentil cooking liquid, raise heat and bring to a boil. Cover the pot, reduce heat to low, and simmer for 6 to 8 minutes or until squash is tender. Stir in drained lentils, and simmer covered for 10 minutes, remove the lid and simmer another 10 minutes or until soup has thickened and lentils are beginning to melt. Add chard and continue cooking for a few minutes longer until the leaves are wilted and tender. Stir in tamari and balsamic vinegar, and season with salt and pepper to taste; remove from heat. Serve each bowl with a drizzle of flax or olive oil and a pinch of thinly sliced chard.

Unlike red lentils, which are peeled, French lentils need to be soaked to remove phytic acid (see page 58). If you forget to soak them ahead of time, you can still make this soup, just increase the lentil cooking time to 30 minutes.

CREAMY CAULIFLOWER AND CELERY ROOT SOUP
WITH ROASTED SHIITAKES

I make creamy cauliflower soups throughout fall and winter and even into spring, adding different vegetables to the cauliflower to vary the flavors. My clients adore them! The addition of celery root and roasted shiitakes was inspired by a soup I saw in *Gourmet* magazine when I was working at Angelica Kitchen in New York City. I put this vegan version on a special five-course Thanksgiving menu and served it drizzled with a bright green chive oil. It was so popular that it immediately became part of our regular soup rotation.

Roasting the garlic for this soup is an extra step, but the celery root needs the contrast of the deep mellow flavor, since there is no dairy to tame its strength. The garlic can be roasted up to three days ahead of making this soup, and roasting some extra garlic to have on hand is a good idea, as it's a great flavor to add to dips (see White Bean Artichoke Aioli, page 214) or smear on bread.

SERVES 4 TO 6

2 large garlic bulbs

2 tablespoons plus 2 teaspoons extra virgin olive oil, divided

Sea salt

1 medium onion, diced

1 medium-large head cauliflower (2½ pounds), cut in 1½-inch chunks

1 medium celery root (1 pound), peeled and cut in ½-inch dice

6 cups filtered water

1 teaspoon tamari

Freshly ground black pepper

Roasted shiitakes to garnish (recipe follows)

Preheat oven to 400°F.

Slice ¼-inch off top of each garlic bulb, drizzle tops with 1 teaspoon olive oil each, and sprinkle with a pinch of salt. Wrap bulbs in a piece of parchment paper, then in foil, and seal tightly. Place in oven and roast for 1 hour or until cloves are soft and golden brown. Set aside to cool.

In a large pot, warm remaining 2 tablespoons olive oil over medium heat. Add onion and 1½ teaspoons salt, and sauté for 5 minutes, or until golden. Add cauliflower, celery root, and water. Stir, raise heat, and bring to a boil. Cover pot, reduce heat to low, and simmer for 15 to 20 minutes or until vegetables are soft but not falling apart. Add tamari and remove from heat.

Squeeze garlic cloves out of their skins and add to soup. Purée soup in batches in an upright blender on the highest speed until completely smooth and velvety. Season to taste with freshly ground black pepper and salt. Serve garnished with roasted shiitakes.

ROASTED SHIITAKES

These mushrooms are crisp and slightly chewy, making them a tasty addition to many dishes. Try them in leafy green salads or sprinkled over your favorite whole grains. They are also an irresistible snack straight out of the oven—you may want to double the recipe, as they have a way of disappearing fast!

NOTE: Be sure to serve the roasted shiitakes within a few hours of making them, as they tend to soften over time and don't store well in the fridge.

MAKES 1½ CUPS

¾ pound fresh shiitakes

3 tablespoons extra virgin olive oil

½ teaspoon sea salt

Freshly ground black pepper

Preheat oven to 400°F. Line a large rimmed baking sheet with parchment paper and set aside.

Cut stems off shiitakes and save them for making a stock. Thinly slice mushrooms and place on baking sheet. Drizzle with olive oil, sprinkle with salt and pepper, toss well to combine. Spread out in a single layer over baking sheet.

Roast for 15 minutes, stir, and roast for another 5 minutes or until beginning to brown. Remove from oven and allow to cool, or serve immediately.

KABOCHA CHESTNUT SOUP WITH NORI SESAME "LEAVES"

Winter squash and chestnuts are a heavenly combination—the chestnuts add a buttery, earthy element to the sweet squash, resulting in a flavorful and richly smooth soup. I have made this soup with excellent results using chestnuts in all forms: dried chestnuts (see the Resources section), precooked chestnuts (sold in jars in most gourmet food shops), and when in season, fresh chestnuts. Good fresh chestnuts can be a challenge to find, as they often sit around unrefrigerated at the market, and become moldy because of their high water, low oil content. I recommend purchasing some as soon as they appear at your local shop or farmers' market, usually between October and December. Check for any signs of mold on their shells and store them in a breathable bag in the fridge for no longer than two weeks.

SERVES 6

2 tablespoons extra virgin olive oil

1 medium onion, diced

4 garlic cloves, chopped

1 teaspoon sea salt, plus more to taste

1 medium kabocha squash (3¼ pounds), peeled, seeded, and cut into ¾-inch dice

2 cups (10¼ ounces) cooked, peeled chestnuts

7 cups filtered water

1 large sprig sage

3 bay leaves

2 teaspoons tamari, plus more to taste

Nori "leaves" to garnish (see sidebar)

Warm olive oil in a large pot over medium heat. Add onion, and cook for 5 minutes or until golden. Stir in garlic and salt, and continue cooking for another 2 to 3 minutes. Add kabocha, chestnuts, water, sage, and bay leaves; bring to a boil over high heat. Cover pot, reduce heat to low, and simmer for 20 minutes or until squash is soft. Remove and compost bay leaves and sage. Stir in tamari, and remove from heat. Blend soup in batches in an upright blender on highest speed for 1 to 2 minutes, or until completely smooth and velvety. Season to taste with tamari and salt, and serve topped with nori sesame "leaves."

TO COOK FRESH CHESTNUTS:

1 pound chestnuts

Preheat oven to 425°F.

Rinse chestnuts and place flat-side down on a cutting board. Use a serrated knife to cut a slit in the shell across the top. Place in a saucepan, cover with filtered water, and bring to a boil. Once water has come to a boil, remove from heat and drain chestnuts. Transfer to a roasting pan or rimmed baking sheet, and bake for 15 minutes or until the shells have split open. If they haven't opened, return to the oven for another 5 minutes. Remove from the oven, cover with a towel, and set aside for 15 minutes to steam. Pop them out of their skins and measure out 2 cups.

TO COOK DRY CHESTNUTS:

1 rounded cup dry chestnuts (6 ounces)

Soak chestnuts in 3 cups filtered water overnight or for 8 to 12 hours. Drain, rinse, and peel off any brown skin. Place chestnuts in a pot with 4 cups filtered water; bring to a boil. Cover pot, reduce heat to low, and simmer for 1 hour or until chestnuts are soft when pierced with a knife. Drain and use in the recipe as instructed.

NORI SESAME "LEAVES"

I call these leaves because they curl up around the edges like autumn leaves. The flavor of tamari and nori goes brilliantly with kabocha and chestnut, but these tasty little morsels are also a great snack on their own, so feel free to make extra—they can be kept in an airtight container for a couple of days.

MAKES ABOUT 3 CUPS LEAVES

2 teaspoons mirin

2 teaspoons extra virgin olive oil or unrefined, untoasted sesame oil

1 teaspoon toasted sesame oil

4 sheets toasted nori

¼ cup toasted unhulled sesame seeds (page 77)

Preheat oven to 300°F. Line 2 rimmed baking sheets with parchment paper and set aside.

Combine mirin, olive oil, and toasted sesame oil in a small bowl. Use a pastry brush to brush each nori sheet liberally with mirin-oil mixture. Tear sheets into irregular triangles or rectangular bite-size pieces, and arrange on baking sheets. Sprinkle generously with sesame seeds; bake 4 minutes, rotate trays, and continue baking for another 4 minutes or until leaves are curling at edges and crisp. Remove from oven and set aside to cool.

FALL VEGETABLE BROTH WITH TURNIP GREENS

Whenever I return home from traveling, I always crave clean, restorative food to reset my body after eating so many meals out. I developed this recipe to do just that and find myself returning to it whenever I need something warming and fortifying. The earthy flavors of burdock and Jerusalem artichoke work wonderfully with the sweetness of dense fall squash and turnips.

I love Japanese turnips for their sweet, crisp texture and tender greens; if you can't get them, use a couple of regular turnips and cut them in half or quarters before slicing. You can also replace turnip greens with spinach, bok choy, tatsoi, watercress, or Swiss chard.

NOTE: The squash skin can be left on for both the broth and the soup. Only peel it for the soup if the skin is rough.

SERVES 4 TO 6

STOCK:

8 cups filtered water

3 dried shiitake mushrooms

4 garlic cloves, peeled

2-inch piece ginger, sliced

2 medium carrots, chopped

2 stalks celery with leaves, chopped

6-inch piece burdock root, chopped

¼ medium kabocha or red kuri squash, cubed (about 3 cups); seeds reserved to add to stock

2 sprigs rosemary

4 sprigs oregano

8 sage leaves

8 sprigs parsley

5 bay leaves

2-inch piece of kombu

SOUP:

2 tablespoons extra virgin olive oil

1 medium onion, sliced

4 garlic cloves, thinly sliced

1 teaspoon sea salt, plus more to taste

2½ cups kabocha or red kuri squash, cut into ¾-inch triangles

1 medium parsnip, roll cut in ¾-inch pieces (see sidebar)

1 medium carrot, roll cut in ½-inch pieces (see sidebar)

6 medium Japanese turnips (10 ounces), quartered; leaves reserved and chopped (about 2 cups)

4 ounces Jerusalem artichokes, sliced in ¼-inch pieces (about ¾ cup)

MAKE THE STOCK:

Place all stock ingredients in a large pot, and bring to a boil over high heat. Cover pot, reduce heat to low, and simmer for 2 hours. Remove from heat and strain. You should be left with just over 6 cups broth.

MAKE THE SOUP:

Warm olive oil in a large pot over medium heat. Add onions, and sauté for 3 minutes or until translucent. Stir in garlic and salt, and continue cooking for 2 minutes more. Add squash, parsnip, carrot, turnips (except leaves), and artichokes; stir to combine. Slowly pour in stock, raise heat to high, and bring to a boil. Cover pot, reduce heat to low, and cook for 15 minutes or until vegetables are cooked through. Stir in turnip leaves, and cook for another minute. Season with sea salt to taste before serving.

A roll cut, also called an oblique cut, is an easy and pretty way to cut any long vegetable, thick or thin. I use it for everything from carrots, sweet potatoes, and parsnips to zucchini and Asian eggplant. The slices can be as small or as large as you like. Lay the vegetable horizontally on your cutting board and slice off a piece at a 45-degree angle. (If the vegetable tapers, start at the tapered end.) Roll the vegetable 90 degrees (a quarter turn) and slice at an angle again; roll and repeat. For tapered vegetables, increase the angle as the vegetable's diameter increases so the pieces are even.

HEARTY WINTER MISO SOUP
WITH ADZUKI BEANS, SQUASH, AND GINGER

Layers of earthy, sweet, salty, and pungent flavors come together harmoniously in this soup to create a deeply nourishing meal. Much more substantial than a traditional "brothy" miso soup, and perfect for times when you're feeling chilled, run-down, or just in need of something warming on a cold winter night; this soup will work wonders.

Adzuki beans and squash are a classic combination in macrobiotic cooking; the beans help strengthen the kidneys, and squash supports spleen and pancreas function. They also taste great together.

As with the Spring Miso Soup with Lemon (page 158), any combination of your favorite misos will work here, but darker, stronger varieties are traditionally used in winter, as they're more strengthening and warming.

SERVES 4 TO 6

½ cup adzuki beans, sorted and soaked 12 to 24 hours in 2 cups filtered water

8 cups filtered water

3 dried shiitake mushrooms

2-inch piece kombu

1 tablespoon unrefined, untoasted sesame oil

1 medium onion, quartered and thinly sliced

1 medium carrot, halved lengthwise and thinly sliced on a diagonal

2 cups winter squash cut in ½-inch dice

1 cup thinly sliced kale leaves, preferably Lacinato

2 tablespoons (¼ ounce) dried wakame, either instant or soaked and drained (see note)

3 tablespoons plus 2 teaspoons dark miso, either barley or brown rice miso

3 tablespoons chickpea miso or mellow white miso

4 teaspoons fresh ginger juice (see sidebar)

Thinly sliced scallions, to garnish

Drain and rinse adzuki beans. Place in a medium-large pot; add water, shiitakes, and kombu; and bring to a boil over high heat. Cover pot, reduce heat to low, and simmer for 30 to 35 minutes or until beans are soft and creamy inside. Remove from heat and set aside; remove and compost kombu. Take out shiitakes and set aside; once they're cool enough to handle, cut off stems and compost them, slice the caps as thinly as possible, and return to pot with beans.

Warm sesame oil in another large pot over medium heat; add onions, and sauté for 3 minutes or until translucent. Stir in carrots and squash, and cook for a minute more. Add adzuki beans and their cooking liquid; bring to a boil over high heat. Cover pot, reduce heat to low, and simmer for 10 minutes or until vegetables are cooked. Stir in kale and wakame, and simmer for 1 minute. Add misos to a medium strainer and place over pot so the bottom sits in the soup; stir to dissolve miso. You will be left with some hulls from the miso; they can be added to the soup or left out for a smoother broth. Stir in ginger juice, and remove from heat. Ladle soup into bowls, top with scallions, and serve.

NOTE: Instant dried wakame comes in bite-size pieces with the tough stems removed, ready to add directly to soups. Other dried wakame needs to be soaked: place it in a bowl, cover with filtered water, and soak 5 to 10 minutes or until tender. Drain, slice off any tough stems, roughly chop, and add to soup.

To make ginger juice, finely grate fresh, unpeeled ginger root and place it in your palm. Squeeze over a cup or small bowl to extract juice. To get 4 teaspoons, you will need about a 2½-inch piece of fresh ginger root.

KITCHARI

Kitchari is a healing Ayurvedic dish with a risotto-like consistency. It's often made with white basmati rice and lentils, but here I use brown basmati rice and mung beans and soak them overnight. The result is a creamy and nourishing dish that is perfect any time you need something comforting and restorative to eat. I use ghee when I'm in the mood for a decidedly richer Indian flavor; otherwise, coconut oil does the trick. Either way, it makes for an aromatic and warming meal.

NOTE: If you can't find curry leaves, just leave them out; you'll still have plenty of flavor from the other ingredients. If you do spot them, they keep in the fridge for a week or two and can be frozen for up to six months. They'll lose their green color in the freezer but not their aromatic flavor.

SERVES 4 TO 6

1 cup brown basmati rice

½ cup mung beans

1 tablespoon ghee
    or extra virgin coconut oil

1 teaspoon black mustard seeds

1 tablespoon peeled and minced ginger

1 teaspoon cumin seeds

¼ cup fresh curry leaves

½ cinnamon stick

1 teaspoon ground turmeric

2-inch piece kombu

6 cups boiling filtered water, divided

2 teaspoons tamari, plus more to serve

1 teaspoon sea salt, plus more to taste

TO SERVE:

Cold pressed flax oil

Chopped cilantro

Sliced red chilies, optional

Place rice and mung beans in a medium pot. To wash, fill pot with water, swish rice and beans around with your hands, and let them settle. Pour off the water, repeat, and drain. Cover with 4 cups filtered water and soak 12 to 24 hours. Rinse and drain rice and beans; set aside.

Warm ghee or coconut oil in a large pot over medium heat. Add mustard seeds, ginger, cumin seeds, and curry leaves; sauté for 3 minutes. Stir in drained rice and beans, cinnamon stick, and turmeric. Add kombu and 4 cups boiling water. Bring mixture to a boil over high heat, stir, cover pot, reduce heat to low, and simmer for 1 hour. Remove and compost kombu, cinnamon stick, and curry leaves. Add remaining 2 cups boiling water, tamari, and sea salt; continue simmering for another 30 minutes, stirring every 10 minutes to prevent sticking. Remove from heat and set aside, covered, for 10 minutes before serving.

Spoon into bowls. Serve drizzled with flax oil and tamari and topped with chopped fresh cilantro and chilies, if using.

SPICY CARROT SOUP WITH KAFFIR LIME LEAVES AND COCONUT

Making a pot of this invigorating soup in the middle of winter is the perfect antidote to cold, gray days. The lively flavors of ginger and chili are tempered by a good splash of coconut milk, creating a gorgeous texture and bright orange color. The Kaffir lime and lemongrass give the soup a nice lift, but if you don't have them on hand, don't worry. I have made this dish many times without them with delicious results.

NOTE: In cold weather, coconut milk is solid at room temperature. To melt it, place the can in a bowl of hot water for a few minutes, then shake well before opening.

SERVES 6

2 stalks lemongrass, halved lengthwise and chopped in 2-inch pieces

6 Kaffir lime leaves

2 tablespoons extra virgin coconut oil

2 medium onions, diced

6 garlic cloves, chopped

2 tablespoons peeled and minced fresh ginger

1 serrano chili, seeded and minced

1½ teaspoons sea salt, plus more to taste

2 teaspoons homemade Curry Powder (page 112)

1 teaspoon turmeric

3 tablespoons minced cilantro stems, leaves reserved for garnish

10 medium-large carrots (2½ pounds), cut in ¾-inch dice (about 8 cups)

6 cups filtered water

1 13.5–fluid ounce can unsweetened full-fat coconut milk, stirred and divided

⅛ to ¼ teaspoon cayenne pepper, optional

TO SERVE:

Cilantro leaves

Sliced red chilies

Wrap lemongrass and Kaffir lime leaves in a piece of cheesecloth and tie it tightly; set aside.

Warm coconut oil in a large pot over medium heat. Add onions, and sauté for 5 minutes or until golden. Add garlic, ginger, serrano chili, and salt; cook for 2 to 3 minutes more, lowering heat if mixture begins to stick. Stir in curry powder, turmeric, and cilantro stems. Add carrots, water, 1¼ cups coconut milk, and lemongrass-lime leaf bundle. Raise heat to high and bring to a boil. Cover pot, reduce heat to low, and simmer for 20 minutes or until carrots are tender. Remove from heat and remove lemongrass-lime leaf bundle and compost.

Blend soup in batches in an upright blender on highest speed for 1 to 2 minutes, until completely smooth and velvety; return to pot and season to taste. Stir in the cayenne pepper if using. Ladle the soup into bowls and garnish each bowl with a drizzle of reserved coconut milk, cilantro leaves, and sliced chilies.

salads

sprout salad with toasted sunflower seeds and umeboshi vinaigrette / 182

herbed spelt berry salad with peas and feta / 183

shaved zucchini salad with purslane and pine nut lemon dressing / 184

quinoa with roasted summer vegetables and harissa marinade / 187

whole-wheat udon noodle salad with sautéed peppers, sweet corn, and sesame marinade / 188

quinoa beet salad with feta, chili, garlic, and sautéed beet greens / 191

kale slaw with creamy mustard dressing / 192

roasted acorn and delicata squash salad with wheat berries and bitter greens / 195

shaved fennel beet salad with blood orange and crushed hazelnuts / 196

roasted winter vegetables and arugula salad with mustard dressing / 199

simple pressed salad / 200

Whether it's a whisper of spring greens beneath a delicate dressing, a salad bursting with summer produce, or the contrasting autumnal flavors of sweet roasted squash with bitter greens, a salad can be the perfect way to reflect the seasons. Depending on where you live, salads can be close to 100 percent, if not completely local—fluently echoing your walk through the farmers' market or a wander around your garden, plucking what's ready for harvest.

Typically, salads are thought to be raw, leafy, and light and are habitually used as a way to refresh your palate and take a pause during a meal. In this chapter, you'll find a few that fulfill that purpose, but many more can function as a satisfying light meal or as the dish to map your lunch or dinner around. Quinoa with Roasted Summer Vegetables and Harissa Marinade (page 187) becomes a perfect summer meal when served with White Bean Artichoke Aioli (page 214) or Chickpea Mash (page 70) with a few leafy greens on the side. For a tasty meal to welcome spring, try the same approach with the Herbed Spelt Berry Salad with Peas and Feta (page 183). The Whole-Wheat Udon Salad with Sautéed Peppers, Sweet Corn, and Sesame Marinade (page 188) can become a satisfying meal with the addition of Quick Braised Tempeh (page 108). Many of the salads you'll find here last well for a few days and make the perfect meal to go for either workday lunches or leisurely picnics. Most of all, the salads, dressings, and marinades in this chapter are flavorful, versatile, and forgiving, and I urge you to use them as the basis for whatever is growing abundantly in your locale.

SPROUT SALAD
WITH TOASTED SUNFLOWER SEEDS AND UMEBOSHI VINAIGRETTE

I find myself turning to this salad when I need a light and refreshing course to begin a meal; it's especially good served before a curry or other Asian meal, as its delicate flavor won't overpower your palate. The light pink, purple, and green sprouts are so pretty that presentation is effortless, and the plate requires no garnish. In New York, I'm lucky to be able to get an exciting variety of sprouts and microgreens year-round from Windfall Farms at the Union Square Greenmarket. If you don't have access to sprouts use a combination of watercress, microgreens, or baby lettuces.

Either way, you'll love the dressing for its bright flavor, which comes from ume plum vinegar. The vinegar is the brine from umeboshi plums—a pickled Japanese plum with a strong tangy and salty flavor that's perfect for salad dressings. (For more about umeboshi plums and ume plum vinegar, see pages 26 and 25.)

SERVES 4 TO 6

DRESSING:

2 tablespoons unpasteurized apple cider vinegar

2 teaspoons ume plum vinegar

Pinch sea salt

2 tablespoons extra virgin olive oil

2 tablespoons cold pressed flax oil

SALAD:

8 ounces mixed sprouts: radish sprouts, sunflower sprouts, pea shoots, and/or buckwheat sprouts (about 8 cups)

6 radishes, trimmed and thinly sliced

2 scallions, thinly sliced

2 tablespoons toasted sunflower seeds (page 77)

MAKE THE DRESSING:

Add apple cider vinegar, ume plum vinegar, and salt to a small bowl; mix well to combine. Add oils and whisk until emulsified; set aside.

MAKE THE SALAD:

Place sprouts, radishes, scallions, and sunflower seeds in a medium to large salad bowl. Toss gently to combine, being careful not to damage the delicate sprouts. Drizzle dressing over salad, toss gently again, and serve immediately.

HERBED SPELT BERRY SALAD WITH PEAS AND FETA

Pink pickled radishes, green peas, herbs, and crumbled white feta make this salad look like a pretty spring dress. The flavors and textures are an excellent combination and always put me in the mood to celebrate spring.

The pickled radishes in this salad can be made several days in advance; their lovely pink color deepens over time. I recommend preparing them when you soak the spelt berries the day before; they take seconds to make with a Japanese mandoline. If you have extra radishes on hand, make a double batch to use as a topping for simple grains or to serve with cheese. Frozen English peas work well when fresh peas are not available.

SERVES 4 TO 6

PICKLED RADISHES:

5 radishes, very thinly sliced

2 teaspoons ume plum vinegar

2 teaspoons unpasteurized apple cider vinegar

SALAD:

1¼ cups spelt berries, washed and soaked 12 to 24 hours
    in 3 cups filtered water

3 tablespoons extra virgin olive oil, divided

1 large garlic clove, minced

2 cups English peas, fresh or frozen

Sea salt

Freshly ground black pepper

½ cup chopped flat-leaf parsley

¼ cup chopped fresh dill

5 ounces goat milk feta, drained and crumbled

Place radishes in a bowl and add vinegars; toss well. Marinate for at least 6 hours and up to four days in the refrigerator.

Drain and rinse spelt berries. Place in a pot and cover with about 4 cups filtered water. Bring to a boil, cover, reduce heat to low, and simmer for 1½ hours or until tender. Add extra water as needed to keep spelt berries covered while simmering. Remove from heat, drain well, and set aside to cool.

If using fresh peas, bring a small pot of water to a boil. Add peas, and cook 2 minutes or until tender. Remove from heat, drain, and set aside to cool. If using frozen peas, skip this blanching step.

Warm 2 tablespoons olive oil in a skillet over medium heat. Add garlic, and sauté for 1 to 2 minutes or until golden. Stir in peas, add a pinch of salt and pepper, and cook 2 minutes longer or until heated through. Remove from heat and set aside to cool.

Place spelt berries, radishes and pickling liquid, remaining olive oil, peas, parsley, dill, and feta in a large bowl; toss to combine. Season to taste with salt and pepper, and serve immediately.

SHAVED ZUCCHINI SALAD
WITH PURSLANE AND PINE NUT LEMON DRESSING

Yes, this salad dressing requires a blender, but don't write it off—it's worth the effort! Not only is it rich and creamy from the pine nuts, with a lovely, light, lemony flavor, but it's also very versatile. If you like, double the recipe, chill it, and keep it on hand to use as a mayonnaise-like spread for sandwiches or crackers or as a dressing for your favorite slaw. Since some domestic blenders are larger that others, you may need to double the recipe in order for the dressing to blend properly.

I definitely recommend using small, tender zucchinis here, as their flesh is buttery and sweeter than large zucchinis. You'll find an abundance of different colors at the farmers' market that all look beautiful shaved and tossed with red or golden cherry tomatoes. If you can't find purslane, you can add a big handful of chopped flat-leaf parsley, and it'll still taste great.

SERVES 4

DRESSING:

¼ cup pine nuts, plus
    2 tablespoons for salad

1 garlic clove

1 scallion, white part only,
    roughly chopped

2 tablespoons
    fresh lemon juice

2 teaspoons
    white balsamic vinegar

¼ teaspoon sea salt

Freshly ground black pepper

¼ cup plus 2 tablespoons
    extra virgin olive oil

SALAD:

8 small zucchinis (1 pound),
    mixed gold and green

1 cup cherry tomatoes,
    halved

2 cups trimmed purslane
    sprigs (see sidebar)

¼ cup chopped chives

MAKE THE DRESSING:

Warm a small skillet over medium heat. Add pine nuts and toast, stirring constantly, for about 2 minutes or until golden and fragrant. Remove from heat and transfer to a bowl. Roughly chop 2 tablespoons and set aside for salad. Place remaining ¼ cup pine nuts in an upright blender along with garlic, scallion, lemon juice, balsamic vinegar, salt, and a pinch of black pepper. Blend on high speed for 1 minute, scrape sides using a rubber spatula, and blend again. While blender is running, slowly add olive oil and continue blending until thick and creamy. Transfer to a jar and set aside until ready to serve salad. Dressing can be refrigerated for up to three days, but allow to come to room temperature and mix well before using.

MAKE THE SALAD:

Wash and trim ends of zucchini. Cut any zucchini that are longer than 5 inches in half. Using a mandoline or vegetable peeler, shave the zucchini into long, thin strips. Place in a salad bowl along with cherry tomatoes, purslane, and reserved crushed pine nuts; toss to combine and sprinkle with chives. If dressing has separated, shake well and drizzle over salad, lightly toss and serve immediately.

Purslane is a succulent weed that can be found throughout the summer, growing everywhere from the cracks in sidewalks to the side of the road. It is one of the best sources of omega-3 fatty acids, containing higher amounts than some fish oils. It's also high in iron, calcium, and vitamin C. It has a lovely, lemony flavor when eaten raw and can also be cooked. After plucking off the tender sprigs, any leftover stems can be chopped and added to sautéed vegetables, soups, or stews.

QUINOA WITH ROASTED SUMMER VEGETABLES
AND HARISSA MARINADE

I have prepared this salad for parties, picnics, and my clients for many years; it's always enjoyed with great enthusiasm. The fragrant, spicy flavor of Harissa complements the succulent roasted vegetables and salty feta perfectly, while quinoa provides the ideal protein-rich background. If you want to make it heartier, stir in some cooked chickpeas or eat it with humus or Chickpea Mash (page 70) on the side. Serve it over baby spinach leaves or arugula for a perfect summer meal. You can easily double or even triple the recipe if you're feeding a crowd; use other summer vegetables, like summer squash or eggplant, in place of or in addition to those listed here.

SERVES 4 TO 6

2 medium zucchini, roll cut into 1-inch pieces (see page 172)

2 medium red bell peppers, seeded and cut into 1-inch pieces

2 cups cherry tomatoes, large ones cut in half

5 tablespoons extra virgin olive oil, divided

Sea salt

1 medium red onion, cut into ½-inch wedges

4 cups cooked quinoa (page 64), cooled

⅓ cup homemade Harissa (page 112)

1 cup chopped flat-leaf parsley

5 ounces goat milk feta, drained and crumbled

Olives, to garnish

Preheat oven to 400°F. Line 2 baking sheets with parchment paper. Place zucchini, peppers, and cherry tomatoes in a bowl and toss with 3 tablespoons olive oil and ½ teaspoon salt. Divide vegetables between baking sheets and spread out into a single layer. Roast for 25 minutes. Gently stir vegetables, rotate trays, and roast 10 minutes more or until browning. Remove from oven and set aside to cool.

Warm remaining 2 tablespoons olive oil in a skillet over medium heat. Add red onion and sauté for 5 minutes. Lower heat a little and cook for 15 minutes longer, stirring every minute or so, until soft and caramelized. Stir in a pinch of salt, remove from heat, and set aside to cool.

Transfer quinoa to a large bowl, fluff with a fork, add Harissa, and mix well. Add roasted vegetables, caramelized onions, and parsley; toss gently to combine and season to taste with additional salt. Crumble feta over top, and serve garnished with olives.

WHOLE-WHEAT UDON NOODLE SALAD WITH SAUTÉED PEPPERS, SWEET CORN, AND SESAME MARINADE

Cilantro, sweet corn, brightly colored peppers, and a tasty sesame marinade is a winning combination that stands up to the heartiness of whole-wheat noodles. Refreshing and satisfying, this salad makes the perfect meal in hot, humid weather. Quick Braised Tempeh (page 108) is the ideal accompaniment on the side or cut and tossed into the salad; it pairs well with the flavors and gives some added protein. This salad also looks and tastes great when made with buckwheat noodles in place of udon noodles.

SERVES 4 TO 6

SALAD:

½ cup dried arame seaweed (⅜ ounce)

2 ears sweet corn, shucked

1 8-ounce package
    whole-wheat udon noodles

2 tablespoons unrefined, untoasted
    sesame oil or extra virgin olive oil

1 medium red bell pepper,
    seeded and thinly sliced

1 medium orange bell pepper,
    seeded and thinly sliced

1 medium yellow bell pepper,
    seeded and thinly sliced

½ teaspoon sea salt, plus more to taste

1 teaspoon dried red chili flakes

MARINADE:

1 clove garlic, pressed

2 tablespoons tamari, plus more to taste

¼ cup brown rice vinegar

3 tablespoons
    toasted black sesame seeds
    (page 77), plus more to garnish

¼ cup plus 1 tablespoon
    toasted sesame oil

½ cup finely sliced scallions

1 cup chopped cilantro

MAKE THE SALAD:

Cover arame with 2 cups filtered water, and soak for 15 minutes or until tender. Drain and set aside.

Boil a large pot of water. Add corn and cook for 2 minutes, then remove from pot, reserving water; set corn aside to cool. Use a strainer to remove any stray corn silk from the boiling water. Add udon noodles and cook according to directions on package or until tender. Drain and rinse noodles under cold running water; set aside to drain well.

Warm oil in wide skillet (with a lid) over medium heat. Add peppers and sauté for 10 minutes; stir in salt, reduce heat to low, cover skillet, and cook for 5 minutes. Remove lid; raise heat to medium; and cook, stirring constantly, for 5 minutes more or until peppers are cooked through and beginning to brown. Stir in chili flakes, and set aside to cool.

MAKE THE MARINADE:

Add garlic, tamari, rice vinegar, and sesame seeds to a salad bowl, and whisk to combine. Drizzle in sesame oil and whisk again. Add noodles; toss until evenly coated with marinade. Cut corn off cobs and add to noodles along with scallions, cilantro, and arame. Mix well to combine, then gently stir in peppers. Season to taste with extra tamari or sea salt. Sprinkle with black sesame seeds and serve at room temperature.

QUINOA BEET SALAD
WITH FETA, CHILI, GARLIC, AND SAUTÉED BEET GREENS

Here, marinated red beets are tossed with plain cooked quinoa; I love the way they add vibrant, rich color and blood-building nutrients to plain cooked grains and find myself adding them to brown rice and millet too. I have used this beet-stained quinoa base for many different salad variations, adding cooked chickpeas, chopped dill, or parsley and roasting vegetables I have on hand like sliced carrots, sweet potatoes, or other root vegetables and tossing them in too. It's a terrific make-ahead salad; just bring to room temperature and top with feta, garlic-chili mixture, and beet greens right before serving. Speaking of beet greens, this salad is a great way to use up any you may have left from buying beets by the bunch. If they're not available, you can use Swiss chard or another dark, leafy green, or simply serve the salad without greens.

SERVES 4 TO 6

BEETS:

2 medium-large red beets (1 pound),
    leaves reserved

2 tablespoons extra virgin olive oil

2 tablespoons
    unpasteurized apple cider vinegar

1 tablespoon balsamic vinegar

¾ teaspoon sea salt

SALAD:

4 cups cooked quinoa (page 64), cooled

2 tablespoons extra virgin olive oil,
    divided

4 shallots, sliced

Sea salt

2 fresh red long chilies, thinly sliced

4 large garlic cloves, thinly sliced

GARNISH:

Beet greens from 2 bunches beets,
    large stems trimmed (6 cups packed)

6 ounces goat milk feta,
    drained and crumbled

PREPARE THE BEETS:

Place the beets in a medium pot and add enough water to cover. Bring to a boil over high heat, cover, reduce heat to low, and simmer for about 40 to 45 minutes, or until tender. Test them by inserting a toothpick or tip of a sharp knife into beet; it should glide in easily. Drain beets and slip off skins under cold, running water. Cut beets in half, thinly slice, and place in a medium bowl. Add olive oil, apple cider vinegar, balsamic vinegar, and salt. Toss gently to combine; set aside.

MAKE THE SALAD:

Transfer cooled quinoa to a large bowl and fluff with a fork. Add marinated beets, mixing until completely combined. Set aside.

Warm 1 tablespoon olive oil in a medium skillet over medium heat. Add shallots and a pinch of salt; sauté for 6 to 8 minutes or until golden brown. Remove from pan and toss with beets and quinoa. Season with salt to taste, and set aside. Wipe out skillet, and warm remaining 1 tablespoon olive oil over medium heat. Add chilies, garlic, and a pinch of salt. Sauté for 2 minutes or until garlic is golden. Remove from heat, transfer to a small bowl, and set aside.

MAKE THE BEET GREEN GARNISH:

Place same skillet, retaining any oil residue, over medium heat. Add beet greens and a splash of water; stir until greens begin to wilt. Cover pan, and cook for 1 minute. Remove lid and continue cooking until tender. Remove from heat and set aside.

TO SERVE:

Spoon quinoa-beet mixture into bowls. Crumble feta over each portion and top with garlic-chili mixture. Garnish with beet greens.

KALE SLAW WITH CREAMY MUSTARD DRESSING

This mustard dressing is undeniably delicious—the cashew butter makes it rich and creamy, while the vinegars and whole-grain mustard add just the right amount of bright, tangy flavor. I often make extra and serve it as a dip for fresh, crunchy vegetables. If you're used to a dairy-based dressing on your slaw, then you'll enjoy this as a change. Although any kale will work, here Lacinato kale is the easiest to slice and looks the best.

SERVES 4 TO 6

DRESSING:

2 tablespoons raw cashew butter

2 tablespoons filtered water

1 small garlic clove, pressed

1 tablespoon unpasteurized apple cider vinegar

1 teaspoon ume plum vinegar

2 tablespoons whole-grain Dijon mustard

Sea salt, to taste

Freshly ground black pepper

3 tablespoons extra virgin olive oil

SALAD:

5 cups thinly sliced kale (from about 1 medium bunch)

2 cups thinly sliced red cabbage
 (from about ¼ small-medium red cabbage)

1 medium carrot, cut in matchsticks

1 small bulb fennel, trimmed and thinly sliced

2 thinly sliced scallions

2 tablespoons toasted sunflower seeds (page 77)

MAKE THE DRESSING:

Place cashew butter and water in a small bowl, and mix until smooth. Stir in garlic, vinegars, mustard, and a pinch of salt and pepper. Add olive oil, mix again until smooth and creamy, season to taste, and set aside.

MAKE THE SALAD:

Place kale, red cabbage, carrot, fennel, scallions, and sunflower seeds in a large salad bowl; toss to combine. Drizzle with dressing; toss until slaw is evenly coated and serve.

ROASTED ACORN AND DELICATA SQUASH SALAD
WITH WHEAT BERRIES AND BITTER GREENS

Here's a salad with all my favorite elements: tangy dressing; sweet, roasted squash; nutty aged goat cheese; spiced seeds; and a scattering of plump whole grains combined with sturdy fall greens. I'm not sure it gets better than this! Any aged goat cheese will work in this salad, but I suggest a smooth cheese, aged around six months. The wheat berries can easily be replaced with other large whole grains like spelt berries or kamut. If you can find small mustard leaves, they won't be as bitter and can be left whole; if not, tear the larger leaves into bite-size pieces and remove tough stems.

NOTE: If you cook the full amount of wheat berries on page 65, you will be left with extra; use them to add texture to soups and stews or other salads.

SERVES 4 TO 6

ROASTED SQUASH:

1 medium acorn squash (1½ pounds), seeded, quartered lengthwise, and cut in ⅓-inch slices

1 medium delicata squash (1 pound), halved lengthwise, seeded, and cut in ⅓-inch slices

2 tablespoons extra virgin olive oil

Sea salt

Freshly ground black pepper

DRESSING:

4 teaspoons unpasteurized apple cider vinegar

¼ cup extra virgin olive oil

¼ teaspoon sea salt

Freshly ground black pepper

½ cup cooked wheat berries, drained and cooled (page 65)

SALAD:

2 ounces small red or green mustard leaves (about 4 cups, loosely packed)

2 ounces arugula leaves (about 4 cups, loosely packed)

¼ cup thinly sliced red pearl onions or shallots

4 ounces aged goat cheese, rind removed, shaved

¼ cup spiced pumpkin seeds (page 77)

ROAST THE SQUASH:

Preheat oven to 400°F. Line 2 rimmed baking sheets with parchment paper. Place acorn squash slices on one tray and sliced delicata on the other. Drizzle each tray with 1 tablespoon olive oil, ¼ teaspoon sea salt, and a pinch of black pepper; toss to combine. Place in oven and roast for 30 minutes; turn each slice of squash over, rotate the trays, and roast for another 10 to 15 minutes or until browning. Remove from oven and set aside to cool.

MAKE THE DRESSING:

Whisk dressing ingredients together in a bowl and sitr in cooked wheat berries.

ASSEMBLE THE SALAD:

Spread half the greens over a serving platter or bottom of a wide bowl, then add half of each of the following: acorn and delicata squash, pearl onions, goat cheese, and pumpkin seeds. Drizzle with half the dressing and repeat with remaining ingredients. Toss lightly, and serve immediately.

SHAVED FENNEL BEET SALAD
WITH BLOOD ORANGE AND CRUSHED HAZELNUTS

A vibrant, robust salad like this is perfect for brightening gray midwinter days. Once the beets are cooked, it comes together fast. The beet-and-fennel marinade creates the dressing, and everything else is tossed together right before serving. If you want to plan ahead, you can cook the beets and marinate them with the fennel a day in advance. Since all the ingredients in this salad are assertive, I suggest serving it as a starter followed by a warming soup or stew or even a simple pasta. Pecorino or another hard, nutty cheese can be used in place of the aged goat cheese.

SERVES 4

5 baby red beets (10 ounces)

1 medium fennel bulb, stems and tough outer layer removed, cored, and shaved (about 2 cups)

2 tablespoons unpasteurized apple cider vinegar

1 tablespoon white balsamic vinegar

½ teaspoon sea salt

2 medium blood oranges, segments removed

1 small to medium head radicchio (6 ounces), leaves torn into bite-size pieces

3 tablespoons extra virgin olive oil

4 ounces aged goat cheese, rind removed, shaved

¼ cup toasted hazelnuts (page 78), crushed

Place beets in a small pot, cover with filtered water, and bring to a boil. Cover pot, reduce heat to low, and simmer for 25 to 30 minutes or until tender. Test them by inserting a toothpick or tip of a sharp knife into the beets; it should glide in easily. Drain beets and slip off their skins under cold running water. Halve and thinly slice beets. Place in a salad bowl; add shaved fennel, apple cider vinegar, white balsamic vinegar, and salt. Set aside for 10 minutes, or refrigerate up to one day to marinate.

Add blood orange segments and radicchio to beets and fennel; toss to combine. Add olive oil, shaved cheese, and hazelnuts; toss gently again. Taste for seasoning, and serve immediately.

ROASTED WINTER VEGETABLES AND ARUGULA SALAD
WITH MUSTARD DRESSING

This salad, and the many variations of it, is one of my signature dishes. It seems to delight everybody who eats it and can easily be adapted to include whatever vegetables you happen to have in your kitchen. Roasting is a great way to cheer up the older root vegetables that you find at the market in January and February. Any combination of roasted winter squash or root vegetables—with the deep, caramelized flavors that come from spending time in the oven—will taste good when added to the bitter greens, chickpeas, toasted nuts, and an assertive grainy mustard dressing.

SERVES 4 TO 6

ROASTED VEGETABLES:

1 medium sweet potato, halved lengthwise and cut in ¼-inch slices

1 medium parsnip, halved lengthwise and cut in ¼-inch slices

2 medium carrots, cut in ¼-inch diagonal slices

1 medium golden beet, halved and thinly sliced

3 tablespoons extra virgin olive oil

1 teaspoon sea salt

Freshly ground black pepper

DRESSING:

1 tablespoon whole-grain Dijon mustard

1 tablespoon unpasteurized apple cider vinegar

1 teaspoon balsamic vinegar

2 tablespoons fresh orange juice

1 teaspoon fresh lemon juice

¼ teaspoon sea salt

¼ cup extra virgin olive oil

SALAD:

1 cup cooked chickpeas (see page 68)

⅓ cup chopped toasted walnuts (page 78)

6 cups baby arugula leaves (about 3½ ounces)

ROAST THE VEGETABLES:

Preheat oven to 400°F. Line 2 rimmed baking sheets with parchment paper and set aside.

In a large bowl, toss sliced sweet potato, parsnip, carrots, and beet with olive oil, salt, and a pinch of black pepper. Divide between trays, spreading vegetables out in a single layer, and roast for 20 minutes. Stir, rotate trays, and roast for another 20 to 25 minutes or until vegetables are browning. Remove from oven and set aside to cool.

MAKE THE DRESSING:

Combine all dressing ingredients in a jar and shake to combine; set aside.

MAKE THE SALAD:

Place chickpeas, toasted walnuts, roasted vegetables, and arugula in a large salad bowl, and toss to combine. Drizzle dressing over the salad and toss again. Serve immediately.

SIMPLE PRESSED SALAD

I often forget just how tasty and refreshing a simple pressed salad can be. Pressed salads are actually light, quick, Japanese-style pickles that require no dressing or oil and take hardly any time to put together. In winter, they add a welcome bright flavor served alongside simple brown rice and go with anything from Quinoa Congee (page 146) to the Bento Bowl (page 278). Many vegetables can be prepared this way: cucumbers, Japanese turnips, celery, and rehydrated seaweed all work, and you can change up the flavor by adding scallions, lemon zest, or grated ginger. Leave pressed salads under a weight for one hour or several; they're not fussy, they'll just get more pickle-like as time progresses.

NOTE: Using a mandoline for the daikon and radishes will give you nice thin slices and speed up prep time.

SERVES 4 TO 6

6 cups sliced Napa cabbage (about ½ medium cabbage), cut in ½-inch slices

2 medium carrots, cut in matchsticks

8-inch piece daikon, peeled, halved, and thinly sliced

8 radishes, thinly sliced

2 teaspoons sea salt, plus more to taste

¼ cup plus 2 tablespoons brown rice vinegar

Toasted black sesame seeds (page 77), to garnish

Thinly sliced scallions to garnish

Place all ingredients (except sesame seeds and scallions) in a medium bowl and toss to combine. Lightly squeeze vegetables with your hands to help soften and release their juices. Place a plate on top of salad and place a weight on top of plate; another bowl or large jar filled with water will work—anything heavy that will help press out the liquid. Set aside for 1 hour or longer.

Remove weight, drain off liquid, and season to taste. Gently squeeze salad to remove more liquid as you transfer it to a serving bowl. Sprinkle with black sesame seeds and scallions and serve. Any leftover salad can be stored in a jar in the fridge for up to a week. The salad softens over time as the pickling process continues. For a crisper, sharper-tasting salad, consume within two days.

NOTE: If you are making the salad in advance, I suggest sprinkling the sesame seeds over it just before serving, as the color in black sesame seeds bleeds.

snacks, nibbles, and drinks

When I was catering parties in London and New York, creating elaborate displays of seasonal ingredients for guests to congregate around and graze on was one of the things I enjoyed most, and I still find myself doing it when entertaining at home. As much as I love an intimate, sit-down dinner, there's something exciting about preparing and decorating a feast of smaller dishes—and people love the promise of tasting an array of flavors and nibbling convivially.

In this chapter, you'll find everything you need to create a beautiful party table of dips and spreads that can be paired with an abundance of local seasonal vegetables, both roasted and raw; fresh crusty bread; and a great selection of local cheeses, including your own homemade Cashew Cheese (page 217). And don't forget the drinks! I have included my favorites from all seasons. You will also find a few much-loved light meals like Summer Rolls with Macadamia Lime Sauce (page 206) and Greens and Grains Roll with Avocado and Carrot Dipping Sauce (page 210), which are ideal for warm-weather eating. If you and your friends are crowding in the kitchen, sharing the Curried Socca with Cilantro Coconut Chutney (page 209) straight out of the pan is the best way to eat it, and the Crispy Smashed Baby Potatoes with Caper Garlic Yogurt Dip (page 207) are a flavorful, cozy snack to serve with wine on a chilly night. No matter what the occasion or season, you'll find the recipes here.

SUMMER ROLLS WITH MACADAMIA LIME SAUCE

There is a macadamia farm down the mountain from where I grew up. There my family would pick up macadamia nut butter and the most fragrant, fresh-pressed macadamia nut oil when we'd drive by on our weekly shopping trips. We used macadamia nut butter everywhere you might use peanut butter, including in sauces like this one. After leaving home, it didn't take me long to realize what a luxury product macadamias are and how lucky we were back then.

These rolls are like a beautiful, bundled-up salad; each bite is a burst of freshness, with a velvety cloak of tasty macadamia sauce. They make a perfect light summer meal.

MAKES 6 ROLLS CUT IN 6 PIECES EACH

Sea salt

6 large collard leaves

2 ripe avocados, sliced lengthwise

1 tablespoon Black Sesame Gomasio, plus more to garnish (page 114)

2 medium cucumbers, halved lengthwise, each half sliced into 6 strips

2 medium carrots, cut in matchsticks

1 large red bell pepper, seeded and thinly sliced lengthwise

3 scallions, thinly sliced

½ cup mint leaves

½ cup basil leaves

½ cup cilantro leaves

1 cup loosely packed sunflower sprouts (1 ounce)

¾ cup purple radish sprouts (¾ ounce)

Bring a large pot of water to a boil and add a large pinch of sea salt. Holding collards by the stems, submerge 3 leaves at a time in the boiling water and cook for 20 seconds or until bright green and tender. Remove and lay them in a single layer on a clean towel to cool. Repeat with remaining leaves and pat them dry.

Cut off collard stems, plus an inch off the bottom of each leaf. Place a leaf facedown horizontally on cutting board. Carefully slice off back of stem to create a flat, pliable leaf.

Lay 3 slices of avocado across leaf about 1½ inches from bottom. Sprinkle avocado with ½ teaspoon gomasio. Top with 2 slices cucumber, a couple pinches of carrots, and 4 slices of red pepper. Top with some scallions, mint, basil, cilantro, and sprouts. Lift bottom of leaf up and over filling, tucking end in, then roll tightly. Place roll seam-side down, cut in half, and cut each half into 3 pieces. Repeat with remaining leaves and filling.

Serve with Macadamia Lime Sauce.

MACADAMIA LIME SAUCE

The sauce is scrumptious served over simple brown rice and sautéed veggies or used as a dressing for chilled noodle salads. Add a pinch of red chili flakes if you want a spicy kick; if you can't find macadamia nut butter, use cashew butter or peanut butter.

MAKES 2 CUPS

1 tablespoon extra virgin coconut oil

1 medium onion, diced

½ teaspoon sea salt, plus more to taste

4 garlic cloves, minced

1 tablespoon peeled and minced ginger

1 tablespoon mirin

¾ cup raw macadamia nut butter

½ cup filtered water

1 tablespoon tamari

3 tablespoons fresh lime juice

Warm coconut oil in a skillet over medium heat. Add onion and salt; sauté for 5 minutes or until golden. Add garlic and ginger, and continue sautéing for another 4 to 5 minutes, until the mixture is cooked and browning. Stir in mirin and remove from heat. Transfer to an upright blender and add macadamia nut butter, water, tamari, and lime juice. Blend until smooth, scraping sides as necessary. Season to taste with additional salt—keep in mind that you want the sauce well seasoned, as the roll only has a small amount of seasoning from the gomasio. Pour into a bowl and serve with rolls or place in a jar and store in the fridge for up to 3 days.

CRISPY SMASHED BABY POTATOES
WITH CAPER GARLIC YOGURT DIP

My partner, lover of potatoes in all shapes and forms, made these for me one night and they've since become our favorite way to enjoy all kinds of baby potatoes.

There are so many varieties available in markets these days—look for those with a buttery, creamy flesh for this recipe; fingerling potatoes also work well. The exact roasting time will depend on the size of the potatoes and how thinly you press them. After their time in the oven, they become irresistibly golden and crackly, with some crunchy bits among pockets of soft, creamy flesh.

SERVES 4

1½ pounds baby potatoes
4 teaspoons extra virgin olive oil
½ teaspoon sea salt
Freshly ground black pepper

Place potatoes in a medium-large pot and cover with filtered water. Bring to a boil over high heat; cover, reduce heat to low, and simmer for 10 to 12 minutes or until potatoes are soft but not falling apart. Test the center of a potato with a toothpick or tip of a sharp knife; if it is still slightly firm, continue cooking for a couple more minutes and test again.

While potatoes cook, preheat oven to 400°F. Line a rimmed baking sheet with parchment paper; set aside.

Drain potatoes in a colander and shake off any excess water. Place on parchment-lined tray, drizzle with olive oil, add salt and a generous pinch of black pepper; toss well. Spread potatoes out over the tray and use the palm of your hand (or a flat spatula) to press potatoes down until flattened—be careful, they're hot! Roast for 30 minutes, rotate tray, and continue baking for another 15 to 20 minutes or until golden brown and crispy around the edges. Serve warm with caper garlic yogurt dip.

CAPER GARLIC YOGURT DIP

This cool, garlicky caper dip tastes like an aioli but is made with yogurt, not eggs. It's a perfect accompaniment to the potatoes, but it could also be used as a dip for any roasted or raw vegetables.

MAKES ABOUT 1¼ CUPS

1 cup thick whole-milk yogurt
2 tablespoons capers,
    rinsed and finely chopped
1 garlic clove, pressed
¼ cup chopped parsley
2 tablespoons extra virgin olive oil
2 teaspoons minced scallions or chives
¼ teaspoon sea salt, plus more to taste
Freshly ground black pepper

Place yogurt, capers, garlic, parsley, olive oil, scallions, and salt in a medium bowl. Stir well, and season to taste with black pepper and additional salt. Serve with smashed potatoes, or place in a jar and store in the fridge for up to three days.

CURRIED SOCCA WITH CILANTRO COCONUT CHUTNEY

Socca is a crisp pancake-like flat bread made from chickpea flour, olive oil, and salt that is popular in the south of France and neighboring Liguria, where it is called farinata. It's gluten-free and scrumptious, and although I love it made plain, I find it carries Indian flavors really well; probably because chickpea flour is used so much in Indian cooking. Here, I make the socca with ghee for its buttery quality; to make a vegan version, replace it with extra virgin coconut oil. The cilantro and lime in the chutney adds a bright, fresh element to the socca, but it's also good eaten without it.

Socca is best straight out of the pan, so gather around the stove—although the batter needs to sit for an hour before cooking, once it's prepared, it cooks pretty fast and can easily be made while chatting.

NOTE: The exact time needed under the broiler will depend on how hot your broiler gets, so be sure to watch it. Also make sure the skillet you use for the socca is ovenproof.

MAKES ABOUT SIX 9-INCH SOCCA
SERVES 6 TO 8

3 cups chickpea flour

2¼ teaspoons sea salt

3 cups warm filtered water, divided

2 tablespoons melted extra virgin coconut oil

2 tablespoons ghee, plus more for cooking socca

2 teaspoons black mustard seeds

5 teaspoons homemade Curry Powder (page 112)

2 red onions, finely sliced

Place chickpea flour and salt in a bowl, and whisk to combine. Pour in 1½ cups warm water, and whisk until completely smooth. Add remaining warm water and coconut oil; whisk again and set aside.

Warm 2 tablespoons ghee in a skillet over medium heat. Add mustard seeds and cook until they begin to pop, about 30 seconds. Stir in curry powder, remove from heat, and add to chickpea flour mixture; stir well. Cover bowl with a towel and let batter sit for an hour at room temperature.

Preheat broiler.

Warm about 1 teaspoon ghee in an oven proof, 10-inch, cast-iron skillet over medium heat. Pour in ¾ cup chickpea batter and, moving quickly, distribute ⅙ of the onions over batter. Cook for 2 minutes, or until edges are set and small bubbles form. Place directly under broiler, and cook for 4 to 8 minutes or until top is beginning to brown. Remove from broiler (be careful as the handle will be extremely hot!) and loosen edges of socca with a pallet knife or flat spatula. Slide onto a cutting board, cut into wedges, and serve immediately with the chutney. Repeat with remaining batter.

CILANTRO COCONUT CHUTNEY

This bright, herbaceous chutney get lots of body and flavor from dried coconut that is soaked in boiling water to soften before blending. The recipe makes more than you'll need for the socca but since it lasts for up to four days in the fridge, consider using it to brighten up plain cooked rice, simple curries, and dals. London's newspaper The Guardian *spotted it on my blog and published the recipe in the "Cook" section of the paper in spring 2012.*

MAKES ABOUT 1½ CUPS

¾ cup dried, unsweetened, shredded coconut

1 cup boiling filtered water

3 cups roughly chopped cilantro (leaves and stems)

½ cup mint leaves

1 garlic clove, roughly chopped

1-inch piece fresh ginger, peeled and roughly chopped

1 serrano chili, seeded and roughly chopped

3 tablespoons fresh lime juice

1 teaspoon raw honey

¾ teaspoon sea salt

¼ cup mild extra virgin olive oil

Place coconut in a small bowl and cover with boiling water; set aside for 15 minutes or until rehydrated and softened. Pour into a strainer to drain, reserving soaking liquid. Set aside to cool completely.

Add cilantro, mint, garlic, ginger, chili, lime juice, honey, salt, and drained coconut to a food processor and blend until finely ground, scraping sides as necessary. While the motor is running, drizzle in olive oil and blend until combined. Add 5 tablespoons reserved coconut soaking liquid and blend until smooth, adding more liquid to get desired consistency. Serve immediately or store in a jar in the fridge for up to four days.

GREENS AND GRAINS ROLL
WITH AVOCADO AND CARROT DIPPING SAUCE

Tasty and refreshing—this is exactly what I feel like eating on a hot summer day or night. But don't let that stop you from making it any time of year. The peppery greens paired with the naturally sweet carrot sauce make a really delectable combination. These rolls would work well with plain cooked millet in place of the rice if you're in the mood to change it up.

**MAKES 4 ROLLS,
CUT IN 6 TO 8 PIECES EACH**

4 toasted nori sheets (see sidebar)

3 cups cooked brown and sweet rice (page 63)

1 ripe avocado, quartered

8 cups (about 5 ounces) mix of trimmed arugula, spinach, and watercress

Place 1 sheet nori, shiny side down, on a sushi mat. Wet your hands with cold water to prevent rice from sticking to them. Gently press ¾ cup cooked rice thinly over the surface of the nori, covering all but a 2-inch strip at the end farthest from you. Cut each quarter of avocado into 3 long slices, and place them along the edge closest to you. Place a quarter of the greens over the avocado.

To roll, moisten the exposed strip of nori with a little water. Carefully lift the end closest to you up and over the filling, squeezing firmly. Lift the mat up and continue rolling until you reach the moistened nori; seal the roll. Wrap the mat around the whole roll and squeeze gently to secure.

Remove mat and place roll seam-side down. Use a moistened knife to slice into 6 to 8 pieces. Repeat with remaining ingredients.

CARROT DIPPING SAUCE

Sweet, tangy, and full of flavor, the sauce is a cinch to make. Once you taste it, you'll want to drizzle it over everything. When used as a dressing, it lends a lovely Asian flavor to crisp lettuces or slaws.

MAKES 1¼ CUPS

1½ cups grated carrots

2 tablespoons unpasteurized apple cider vinegar

1 tablespoon unpasteurized sweet white miso

1 teaspoon umeboshi paste

½ garlic clove

¼ teaspoon fresh ginger juice (see sidebar on page 174)

½ cup filtered water

¼ teaspoon sea salt, plus more to taste

½ teaspoon toasted sesame oil

3 tablespoons extra virgin olive oil

Place carrots, vinegar, miso, umeboshi paste, garlic, ginger juice, water, and salt in an upright blender; blend until completely smooth, about 1 minute. Add sesame oil and olive oil, and blend for another 20 seconds or until creamy. Pour into a bowl and serve with rolls, or place in a jar and store in the fridge for up to three days.

HOW TO TOAST NORI

Many brands of seaweed sell their nori pretoasted, which is handy for eating right out of the package. It keeps fresh for a long time when stored in a sealed bag or container. If the nori you purchased is raw, you can easily toast it yourself. Turn on a gas flame to medium, and hold the nori about 4 inches away. It will immediately begin to turn a brighter shade of green; keep it moving over the flame until the whole sheet is bright green. This is also a good way to refresh old or stale pretoasted nori.

1. WHITE BEAN ARTICHOKE AIOLI 2. BEET
MARMALADE 3. RUSTIC PEA SPREAD 4. LABNEH
5. ROASTED RED PEPPER MACADAMIA PÂTÉ

RUSTIC PEA SPREAD

I love serving this spread on Garlic-Rubbed Whole-Wheat Bruschetta. Garnished with a fresh pea shoot, it makes a beautiful beginning to a spring dinner party, especially served with champagne. If you want to add richness, shave a little aged goat or sheep's cheese over it. You can also try this spread on oatcakes, in sandwiches, or as a side dish. And you needn't restrict yourself to making it only in spring; frozen peas make it super easy and are just as tasty as fresh.

MAKES 2 CUPS

3 cups shelled English peas, fresh or frozen

2 tablespoons extra virgin olive oil

3 garlic cloves, pressed

Sea salt

Freshly ground black pepper

Fresh pea shoots, to garnish (optional)

If using fresh peas, bring a medium pot of water to a boil, add peas, and cook until tender, about 2 to 3 minutes. Remove from heat, drain, and set aside.

Warm a medium skillet over medium heat. Add olive oil and garlic, and sauté for 3 to 4 minutes or until golden. Stir in peas and a pinch of salt and pepper. Cook for 3 minutes or until cooked through. If using frozen peas, continue cooking until completely defrosted. Remove from heat and place in a food processor; blend until well combined but not completely smooth. Season with salt and pepper to taste, and pulse to combine. Place in a bowl and garnish with pea shoots. Serve with crackers or bruchetta.

BRUSCHETTA

Whole-wheat sourdough bread, cut in ⅓-inch slices

Extra virgin olive oil

1 large garlic clove, cut in half

Heat a grill pan on stovetop over high heat for 4 to 5 minutes. Preheat oven to 300°F. Brush each side of sliced bread with olive oil. Place in heated pan in a single layer, and lower heat to medium. Top sliced bread with a weight (such as a heavy pot or kettle filled with water), and grill for 2 minutes on each side. Transfer to a sheet pan and place in oven to keep warm while you grill the remaining bread. When ready to serve, rub each slice of bread with cut garlic clove and serve immediately.

WHITE BEAN ARTICHOKE AIOLI

Luscious, creamy and garlicky, this versatile dip gets a slight tang from the artichokes and a splash of vinegar. In the warmer months, when the farmers' market is brimming with freshly picked vegetables, I whip up a batch of this aioli to accompany them. It's also great spread on crostini, or served with roasted vegetables, simple grains, or salads. You can also blend in more olive oil and use it as a "mayonnaise" for sandwiches or burgers.

Because of their soft texture, this is one of the only recipes where I think canned beans work better—unless you have a pressure cooker, of course. Using a can of beans adds to the simplicity of the recipe, and if you roast the garlic ahead of time, it comes together in an instant.

MAKES 2 CUPS

2 large garlic bulbs

¼ cup plus 3 tablespoons extra virgin olive oil, divided

Sea salt

1 15-ounce can cannellini beans, drained and rinsed (1¼ cups soft-cooked beans, see page 68)

2 teaspoons ume plum vinegar

1 teaspoon fresh lemon juice

1 teaspoon unpasteurized apple cider vinegar

6 artichoke hearts from a can or jar, drained

Freshly ground black pepper

Preheat oven to 400°F. Slice ¼-inch off top of each garlic bulb, drizzle with 1 tablespoon olive oil, and sprinkle with a pinch of salt. Wrap bulbs in a piece of parchment paper, then in foil, and seal tightly. Place in oven, and roast for 1 hour or until cloves are soft and golden brown. When cool enough to handle, remove garlic from foil and squeeze out cooked cloves; you should have about ¼ cup roasted garlic pulp.

Place beans, ume plum vinegar, lemon juice, apple cider vinegar, artichoke hearts, remaining (6 tablespoons) olive oil, ¼ teaspoon salt, and roasted garlic in a food processor. Blend for 2 minutes, scraping down sides as necessary; the mixture should be very smooth. Season with black pepper and salt to taste. Blend for another 2 minutes or until supersmooth and creamy. Blending the mixture for several minutes is key to achieving this texture and allowing air to whip into it.

Place in a bowl to serve, or store in a jar in the fridge for up to three days.

BEET MARMALADE

Rich and tasty, this deep crimson marmalade is surprisingly simple to make. Mirin, balsamic vinegar, and garlic complement the sweet earthy flavor of the beets and also give the dish a succulent sheen. Serve this marmalade with fresh bread or crackers, as a topping for simple grains, or as part of a cheese board—it goes really well with fresh goat cheese or Cashew Cheese (page 217).

MAKES ABOUT 3 CUPS

4 tablespoons extra virgin olive oil, divided

1 medium red onion, thinly sliced

½ teaspoon sea salt, plus more to taste

3 garlic cloves, pressed

2 medium red beets (12 ounces), peeled and grated (about 3 cups)

¼ cup filtered water

3 tablespoons balsamic vinegar

1 tablespoon mirin

Freshly ground black pepper

Warm 2 tablespoons olive oil in a wide skillet over medium heat. Add onions and sauté for 5 minutes. Reduce heat to medium-low, and cook for another 8 to 10 minutes or until caramelized. Stir in salt and garlic, and cook 2 minutes more. Stir in beets, increase heat to medium, and cook 2 minutes. Add water, stir, cover skillet, and simmer for 5 minutes or until beets have cooked.

Remove lid; add balsamic vinegar, mirin, and remaining olive oil. Continue cooking for 3 to 4 minutes or until liquid has evaporated and the mixture has thickened. Season to taste with salt and pepper, and remove from heat. Serve at room temperature, or store in a jar in the fridge for up to four days.

LABNEH

Labneh is a delightfully smooth cheese made by straining the whey out of yogurt; the longer you strain it, the thicker it gets. Labneh, or strained yogurt, is common in Middle Eastern and Mediteranean cuisine, where you'll find it eaten as a side dish or as part of mezze. It makes a great base for a variety of flavorings—stir in chopped fresh herbs, garlic, or any spices you like. Here, I add olive oil and season the labneh with sea salt and pepper. It can also be left plain and used as a dessert topping.

When making labneh from a quart of yogurt, you will be left with about 2 cups of whey. This cloudy liquid is full of amino acids, protein, minerals, and probiotic enzymes. It can be used when making pickles to help the fermentation process or added to soaking grains to further increase their digestibility. Stored in a jar in the fridge, it will keep for about two weeks.

MAKES ABOUT 1½ CUPS

1 quart whole-milk yogurt

1 tablespoon extra virgin olive oil, plus more for drizzling

¼ teaspoon sea salt, plus more to taste

Pinch freshly ground black pepper

Chopped chives, to garnish (optional)

Line a medium strainer with a clean, thin kitchen towel, several layers of cheesecloth, or a nut milk bag; place over a bowl, making sure strainer is suspended with plenty of room for whey to drain out. Pour yogurt into cloth-lined strainer and fold excess cloth over top to cover yogurt. Place in the fridge for 4 to 6 hours, or overnight for a thicker cheese.

Lift cloth and invert labneh into a bowl, reserving whey. Add olive oil and salt; stir to combine. Season to taste with pepper and additional salt. If labneh is too thick for your liking, stir in a tablespoon or more of reserved whey to get desired consistency. Drizzle with olive oil and garnish with chives. Serve, or store covered in the fridge for four to five days.

PISTACHIO PUMPKIN SEED DUKKAH

Dukkah is an Egyptian spice blend that can be made with a variety of nuts and seeds. I first sampled a dukkah blend with pistachios at an organic farmers' market in Melbourne, Australia. There, it's found in many cafés and restaurants sprinkled over everything from poached eggs and soft cheeses to roasted vegetables and watermelon slices. Traditionally, it is served by dipping bread into olive oil and then into the dukkah. I like serving it combined with a generous amount of olive oil and warm bread for dipping or sprinkled over Labneh (page 215). This recipe makes a decent amount of dukkah, but it stores well for weeks, and once you taste it, you'll find yourself sprinkling it over everything too.

MAKES ABOUT 1½ CUPS

4 teaspoons cumin seeds

4 teaspoons coriander seeds

1 tablespoon fennel seeds

2 teaspoons ground sumac (see sidebar)

1 teaspoon fleur de sel or other flaky sea salt

1 cup toasted pistachios (page 78)

½ cup toasted pumpkin seeds (page 77)

Extra virgin olive oil, to serve

Warm a small skillet over medium heat. Add cumin, coriander, and fennel seeds; reduce heat to low, and toast for 1 to 1½ minutes or until seeds are fragrant; be careful not to burn them. Remove from heat. Place in an electric spice grinder and grind until fine. Place in a bowl or wide-mouth jar, mix in sumac and salt, and set aside.

Place pistachios and pumpkin seeds in a food processor and pulse until coarsely ground. Add to spice mixture and stir to combine. Store mixture in an airtight jar in a cool place for up to two months.

To serve as a dip for bread, place a few tablespoons of dukkah in a shallow bowl and cover with olive oil.

Sumac is a lemony flavored berry that is dried and sold as a spice. It is used in many Mediterranean and Middle Eastern dishes. You can purchase it whole or ground.

ROASTED RED PEPPER MACADAMIA PÂTÉ

Roasted red peppers always take me back to the days of running my catering business in London with my dear friend Rosada Hayes. They add richness and sweetness to tarts, salads, foccacia bread, and sushi. We also made many versions of this pâté: with sage or rosemary, with different types of nuts or no nuts at all; the variations are endless. When I was last sitting in Rosada's kitchen in Sydney, she made a batch with Brazil nuts and ground it in a mortar and pestle. The mix was rustic and chunky and absolutely heavenly smeared on fresh Turkish bread. As long as you have well-roasted peppers, this recipe will not disappoint no matter how you interpret it.

MAKES ABOUT 2 CUPS

½ cup raw macadamia nuts

5 medium red bell peppers (2 pounds), seeded and chopped in 1½-inch pieces

4 tablespoons extra virgin olive oil, divided

1 teaspoon sea salt, divided

Freshly ground black pepper

1 medium onion, diced

1 medium red chili, seeded and chopped

5 garlic cloves, chopped

2 teaspoons white balsamic vinegar

Preheat oven to 300°F. Line a rimmed baking sheet with parchment paper and add macadamia nuts; roast for 10 minutes or until lightly golden and fragrant. Remove from oven and transfer to a plate to cool.

Raise oven temperature to 400°F. Place peppers on lined baking sheet. Drizzle with 3 tablespoons olive oil, and sprinkle with ½ teaspoon salt and a pinch of pepper. Toss well, spread out in a single layer, and roast for 20 minutes. Stir; roast for another 15 minutes or until peppers are soft and beginning to brown. Remove from oven and set aside.

While peppers roast, warm remaining 1 tablespoon olive oil in medium skillet over medium heat. Add onions and sauté for 5 minutes or until golden. Stir in chili, garlic, and remaining ½ teaspoon sea salt. Reduce heat a little, and cook for another 10 minutes or until caramelized. Set aside.

Place macadamia nuts, roasted peppers, onion mixture, and white balsamic vinegar in a food processor and pulse until combined. Don't blend for long, as you want the mixture to be a little chunky. Season with salt and pepper to taste. Serve with fresh bread or crackers, or store in a jar in the fridge for up to four days.

CASHEW CHEESE

Everybody in my life, including the passionate cheese connoisseurs, love this cheese. It's especially good for those avoiding dairy, as it provides the rich, creamy texture and delicate, tangy flavor of a good soft dairy cheese. Cashew cheese is surprisingly simple to make but requires a little advance planning—a day or so to culture and then a night in the fridge. The probiotics (acidophilus powder) gives the cheese a slightly tangy flavor and also provides you with some beneficial bacteria. One of my favorite ways to enjoy it is spread over rice cakes and topped with Marinated Beets (page 104) and chopped chives.

NOTE: A Vitamix is the best tool for achieving a silky smooth consistency when blending the cashews. I have also used a food processor with good results. Regular domestic blenders are usually not powerful enough.

MAKES ABOUT 2½ CUPS

2 cups raw cashews, soaked 2 to 6 hours
   in 3 cups filtered water
1 teaspoon sea salt, plus more to taste
10 capsules plain acidophilus powder (about 2 teaspoons)
1 cup filtered water, divided

Drain and rinse cashews. Place in a food processor or Vitamix; add salt, acidophilus powder, and half the water (or all the water if you're using a Vitamix). Blend for about 1 minute, scraping down sides as necessary. Add remaining water, and continue blending until completely smooth. Taste mixture, and add a little more salt if needed.

Transfer to a clean bowl (I find a 3- or 4-cup Pyrex storage container the best for this as I can use it to store the cheese as well), cover with a kitchen towel, and allow to sit at room temperature (about 70°F) for 24 hours. Check cheese; it should look aerated, have a slight cheesy-fermented smell, and taste mildly tangy. If it does not, replace towel and set aside for another 4 to 6 hours, checking again until cheese is ready. (Keep in mind that the flavor will improve after a night in the fridge.) Cover and place in the fridge for an additional 24 hours before serving. Serve or store in an airtight glass container in the fridge for two to three weeks.

NOTE: The weather will affect the exact amount of time needed to ferment this cheese. A moderate temperature is best. In spring and summer, I find 24 hours is enough time to achieve a perfectly tangy flavor; in winter, place the cheese in a warmer, draft-free spot.

BLACK SESAME RICE CRACKERS

One of the few snack foods I buy are Sanji's black sesame crackers. I find their combination of black sesame and tamari irresistible, and I love eating them unadorned, straight out of the package. Although the crackers in this recipe are much thinner and have a more subtle flavor, they were inspired by Sanji's. I use black rice to keep with the black theme.

These crackers are great plain or with any of the dips in this chapter, especially the Rustic Pea Spread (page 214)—pea and sesame is a great combination, and the colors are striking together.

NOTE: This is the only recipe in this book where I haven't soaked the grain before cooking it— I found the texture of soaked black rice too difficult to work with here. Even so, rolling these crackers takes a little practice, as the dough is very sticky. It's important to roll the dough out as thinly and evenly as possible. If you happen to have two Silpat baking mats, they come in handy here, making the rolling easier because they don't absorb moisture like parchment paper does.

MAKES 2 TRAYS OF CRACKERS

½ cup forbidden black rice

1¼ cup filtered water

Sea salt

1 cup toasted black sesame seeds (page 77), divided

2 tablespoons brown rice flour, plus more to roll out crackers

Tamari, to brush crackers

Place rice in a small pot, and fill it with water. Swish the grains around with your fingers, let them settle, then pour the water off through a strainer and repeat. Return the grains to the pot, add water and a pinch of salt, and bring to a boil over high heat. Cover pot, reduce heat to low, and cook for 1 hour or until all liquid is absorbed. Remove from heat and set aside for 10 minutes, then remove lid and cool completely.

Preheat oven to 350°F. Cut 4 sheets of parchment paper, about 13 × 18 inches each, and set aside.

Add ¾ cup sesame seeds, black rice, and ½ teaspoon salt to a food processor; blend until just combined. Pulse in rice flour until incorporated. Continue blending until mixture forms a ball and is very sticky. If dough is too sticky to handle, lightly dust parchment and your hands with brown rice flour. Divide dough in half; place one half on a piece of parchment paper and cover with a second sheet of parchment. Roll out into a large rectangle as evenly and thinly as possible. Carefully peel off top sheet of parchment and brush surface with tamari. Sprinkle with half the remaining sesame seeds and bake 10 minutes; rotate tray, and continue baking for another 10 minutes or until crisp. Remove from oven and set aside to cool. Repeat with second half of dough, using remaining unused sheets of parchment paper and remaining sesame seeds.

Once crackers are cool, you can tell if some parts aren't cooked, as they will not be crisp. Just break off what is crisp and return remaining dough to oven for 5 more minutes. Cool completely before breaking into shards and serving, or storing in an airtight container for up to two weeks.

NOTE: If you have leftover cooked brown rice, this recipe is a great way to use it up. You'll need 1¾ cups to replace the black rice in this recipe, and depending on how moist your grain is, you may or may not need to dust the parchment paper with brown rice flour.

RHUBARB ROSE INFUSION

This recipe is adapted from a drink called In the Pink Spring Tea, a rhubarb-infused herbal tea in Rebecca Wood's much-loved book *The New Whole Foods Encyclopedia*. When I worked at Angelica Kitchen, we made a version of this drink every spring; it was a great way to use the abundance of rhubarb we received from our local farmers. Here, I add rosebuds for a delicate floral note. A bud in each glass makes the drink even prettier, complementing the bright pink color that comes from the pink-stemmed rhubarb. When making this recipe, be sure to choose pink- or even red-stemmed rhubarb with as little green as possible; otherwise, your drink will come out a murky green color.

MAKES ABOUT 8 CUPS

2 pounds rhubarb, trimmed and sliced in ½-inch pieces (about 5 cups)

7 cups filtered water

¼ cup dried organic rosebuds, plus more to garnish

½ cup fresh mint leaves

Raw honey to taste

Place rhubarb and water in a large pot. Bring to a boil over high heat. Cover, reduce heat to low, and simmer for 20 minutes. Remove from heat, add rosebuds and mint. Re-cover pot and steep for 5 minutes. Strain into a bowl or large heat-proof jar, and add honey to taste. Allow to cool, then pour into glass bottles or jars and place in the fridge to chill before serving. Garnish each glass with a rosebud.

TURMERIC LEMONADE

As with many Australians, my family has had a connection to Bali for as long as I can remember. When I was last there, the guesthouse in Ubud where we stayed made fresh turmeric juice, which they mixed with lemon and honey—a potent, neon orange drink used in Ayurvedic medicine. Turmeric has been used in Ayurvedic treatments for thousands of years for its balancing and purifying qualities and also because it is tridoshic—meaning it is healing for all three body types identified in the healing system.

Fresh turmeric has a uniquely earthy, tropical flavor that enhances any dish where you would normally use dried turmeric. The fresh root can often be found in well-stocked health-food stores and Indian markets. If it isn't available, you can replace it with ½ to 1 teaspoon dried turmeric powder. Increase the amount as you become used to the flavor. This drink can be served warm in winter and at room temperature or chilled in summer.

MAKES ABOUT 3½ CUPS

2 tablespoons finely grated, unpeeled fresh turmeric root

1 teaspoon finely grated fresh ginger

3 cups boiling filtered water

Tiny pinch sea salt

2 tablespoons raw honey

¼ cup plus 2 tablespoons fresh lemon juice

¼ cup fresh orange juice

Place turmeric and ginger in a heatproof jar or pot, and add boiling water and salt. Steep uncovered for 10 minutes, stir in honey until dissolved, and strain into another jar or pitcher. Allow to cool to room temperature, then stir in lemon and orange juices. Drink as is, or place in the fridge to chill before serving. Stored in a jar in the fridge, the lemonade will last up to a week. To serve as a warming tea, place ½ cup in a mug and top with boiling water.

Turmeric is rich in anti-inflammatory, antibacterial, and antioxidant properties. It helps cleanse and tone the liver, boost immunity, and enhance digestion and circulation. If you find you like its flavor, try increasing the amount used in this recipe.

CONCORD GRAPE LIME INFUSION

To keep out the hot sun of the Southern Hemisphere, part of the verandah of my childhood home was shaded by a Concord grapevine. In late summer, my sister and I would sit under it after school, picking and eating grapes with our friends until our lips and fingers turned purple. We had more grapes than we knew what to do with, so my mother made grape juice by steaming large pots of them. This recipe is based on hers but with the addition of lime juice—which is the perfect complement to the rich, sweet flavor of the grapes.

NOTE: Without the lime juice added, this infusion will last up to a month in the fridge; just add a splash of lime to each glass before serving.

MAKES ABOUT 7 CUPS

2 pounds Concord grapes, on the vine

3 cups filtered water

2 cups apple cider or apple juice

4 to 6 tablespoons fresh lime juice, or more to taste

Combine grapes, water, and cider in a medium pot, and bring to a boil over high heat. Cover pot, reduce to low heat, and simmer for 30 minutes. Remove from heat and strain into a large bowl. Press out as much liquid as possible from grapes, and compost the skins and seeds. Allow liquid to cool to lukewarm before placing in the fridge to chill thoroughly. Stir in lime juice and serve cold.

HIBISCUS INFUSION WITH CITRUS AND GINGER

I first tried the refreshing combination of hibiscus and lime while working at Angelica Kitchen in a drink called the Hibiscus Cooler—it was the perfect summer thirst quencher for parched New Yorkers. Every year when it appeared on the menu, we could hardly keep up with the demand. This recipe is based on the one I learned there but with a strong kick of fresh ginger, orange juice, and a touch of honey. It looks pretty in a glass bottle, and it's a lovely drink to bring to a party, as it also makes a great mixer.

MAKES ABOUT 8 CUPS

8 cups filtered water

½ cup dried hibiscus flowers (1½ ounces)

⅓ cup mild raw honey, plus more to taste

½ cup strained fresh orange juice

4 teaspoons fresh ginger juice (see sidebar on page 174)

Bring water to a boil in a large pot over high heat. Add hibiscus flowers, cover pot, reduce heat to low, and simmer for 10 minutes. Remove from heat and strain into a large bowl. Compost the flowers. Allow to cool for 5 minutes, before stirring in the honey. Cool to room temperature; stir in orange, and ginger juices. Pour into jars or glass bottles, and chill before serving. Stored in the fridge, it will keep up to a week.

MULLED CONCORD GRAPE JUICE

One of my favorite things about bundling up to go to the farmers' market in the fall is the smell of mulled cider that floats in the air around the farm stands. This mulled drink is less sweet than apple cider and has a gorgeous, deep purple color from the Concord grapes. It's festive and comforting all at once and fills your kitchen with an inviting, spicy aroma.

MAKES 6 TO 7 CUPS

1½ pounds Concord grapes, on the vine

3 cups filtered water

3 cups apple cider or apple juice

1 cinnamon stick, broken in half

3 whole star anise

2 whole cloves

10 cardamom pods

2 large strips orange zest

Place grapes in a medium pot. Add water, cider, spices, and zest, and bring to a boil over high heat. Cover pot, reduce heat to low, and simmer for 40 minutes. Remove from heat and strain into a large bowl. Press out as much liquid as possible from grapes; compost grapes and spices. Pour into cups or mugs, and serve warm. Any leftover juice can be cooled and stored in a jar in the fridge for up to a month; just warm it up in a pot over medium heat before serving.

whole meals

soft polenta with nettles, peas, and goat cheese / 235

dill roasted plum tomato tart with pine nut crust / 236

squash blossom orecchiette with aged sheep's cheese and red chili / 238

beet tartlets with poppy seed crust and white bean fennel filling / 243

late summer stew with heirloom beans and parsley pistou / 247

fragrant eggplant curry with cardamom-infused basmati rice, tangy apricot chutney, and cucumber lime raita / 251

tempeh portobello burgers / 255

sweet corn tofu frittata with roasted cherry tomato compote / 259

beet chickpea cakes with tzatziki / 263

spicy black bean stew with crispy sweet corn polenta and tomatillo avocado salsa / 264

roasted fall vegetable cannellini bean stew with spelt berries and kale / 269

butternut squash lasagna with whole-wheat noodles and sage tofu ricotta / 270

spicy chickpea stew and quinoa pilaf with golden raisins and almonds / 273

coconut curry with tamarind tempeh and forbidden black rice / 274

bento bowl / 278

heirloom bean bourguignon with celery root mash / 283

It's through cooking in harmony with nature and bringing people together to share a meal that we can find the inspiration and connectedness we yearn for. These are the recipes I rely on as crowd-pleasers; they're the ones my clients request over and over; and they also happen to be the ones that I think best commemorate the fleeting moments of the ever-changing seasons.

The recipes in this chapter reflect my favorite flavor combinations and what I'm excited to cook when ingredients are at their peak. In spring, it's sautéed fresh peas and nettles, verdant like freshly rain-soaked earth, nestled over smooth polenta with the fresh goat cheese softly melting in. Summer brings a bounty of plump-to-bursting tomatoes; a pretty tart with a crisp pine nut crust is the perfect vessel to complement and highlight their flavor. In autumn, the bright orange, sweet flesh of winter squash draws us back inside to the warmth of the oven and inspires a comforting lasagna to ward off the chill in the air. Dried heirloom beans, with their multitude of shapes and flecks of color, are harvested and stored to carry us through the winter months— simmer them with fragrant herbs and wine and ladle over creamy mashed roots. Then gather friends, light candles, and enjoy the long, cozy nights.

Many of these recipes are a little more involved than the others in the book, some requiring several steps, but I promise your efforts will be greatly rewarded. So, before setting your heart on a particular meal from these pages, let the season be your guide. Your local produce will always be perfectly suited to the weather and mood and will delight everyone who joins you— whether it's on a picnic blanket under a sunny sky or a at a candlelit table on a cold winter's night.

SOFT POLENTA WITH NETTLES, PEAS, AND GOAT CHEESE

I crave the comfort of soft polenta most at the beginning of spring, when the weather is still cool and often wet. It makes a nice change to my whole-grain rotation and delivers a sweet, soothing meal in about 20 minutes. Using corn grits to make polenta gives a satisfying, coarser texture that won't lump as easily as the finer ground Italian polenta. It's fun to try different types of locally grown stone-ground corn grits; any type will work here, but the exact cooking time will depend on how coarse they are—just taste periodically until the raw flavor is gone and it is thick and creamy.

Stinging nettles are a wild herb with a lovely, grassy flavor that can be found from spring right through summer here in New York. They're not generally carried in grocery stores, so look for them at your local farmers' market. Nettles are a kidney tonic, high in iron, calcium, and magnesium. They help enrich the blood and build vitality. You can steep the leaves and stems in boiling water to make a tasty, fortifying tea. If nettles are not available spinach can be used in their place.

NOTE: Nettles are prickly and will sting you, so handle with care and use gloves when plucking the leaves from the stems, or hold the bunch with a cloth and cut leaves off with scissors. Cooking removes their sting.

SERVES 4

POLENTA:

6 cups filtered water

4 bay leaves

½ teaspoon sea salt

1½ cups corn grits

2 tablespoons extra virgin olive oil

PEAS AND NETTLES:

2 cups freshly shelled or frozen English peas

2 tablespoons extra virgin olive oil, plus more for drizzling

4 garlic cloves, thinly sliced

2 medium leeks, thinly sliced

Sea salt

6 cups nettle leaves, roughly chopped (see note)

6 ounces fresh goat cheese, divided

Zest of 1 lemon, divided

1 tablespoon fresh lemon juice

Freshly ground black pepper

MAKE THE POLENTA:

Add water and bay leaves to a medium pot and bring to a boil over high heat. Cover pot, reduce heat to low, and simmer for 5 minutes. Remove and compost bay leaves and add salt. Raise heat to high and slowly pour in corn grits, whisking constantly, until mixture is boiling again—be careful, it may splutter. Reduce heat to low and cook uncovered for 20 to 25 minutes, whisking every minute or so to prevent mixture from sticking. Taste to check that grits are soft and cooked; if not, continue cooking for 5 minutes more or until the raw flavor is gone. Remove from heat, stir in olive oil, and season to taste. Cover pot, and set aside while you prepare peas and nettles.

MAKE THE PEAS AND NETTLES:

If using fresh peas, bring a small pot of water to a boil. Add peas and cook 2 minutes or until tender. Remove from heat, drain, and set aside to cool. If using frozen peas, skip this blanching step.

Warm olive oil in a wide skillet over medium heat. Add garlic and sauté for 1 minute; add leeks and a pinch of salt, and continue cooking for 4 to 5 minutes or until softened. Stir in nettles, and cook for 2 to 3 minutes or until wilted and tender. Add peas and stir until heated through. Crumble in half of the goat cheese, half of the lemon zest, and add lemon juice. Remove from heat and stir to combine. Season with salt and pepper to taste.

TO SERVE:

Divide polenta into bowls and top with nettle and pea mixture. Crumble a little remaining goat cheese over each portion, sprinkle with remaining zest, and drizzle with olive oil.

DILL ROASTED PLUM TOMATO TART
WITH PINE NUT CRUST

Tasty roasted tomatoes, buttery pine nuts, fresh dill, and a tangy filling—it's no surprise that everyone is won over by this perfect summertime tart. Not only does it taste great, but it also looks stunning and needs nothing more than simply dressed greens to accompany it. I have made many variations of this tart over the years, and after you make it once, you can, too—try using basil or rosemary in place of the fresh dill in the filling, or use halved cherry tomatoes or roasted sliced zucchini instead of the plum tomatoes. The pastry here is inspired by a sesame seed crust from Peter Berley's excellent cookbook, *The Modern Vegetarian Kitchen*. The filling is a new take on a tofu ricotta that gets its deep flavor from sweet sautéed onions and vinegar.

I won't lie to you: there are a few steps involved here, but the flavor and beauty of the tart is well worth the effort. You can press the crust, make the filling, and roast the tomatoes a day ahead; just store them all separately in the fridge until you're ready to assemble and bake the tart.

NOTE: These roasted tomatoes are great to have on hand, they make a tasty addition to simple marinated beans, pasta, and sandwiches, and they are also excellent on avocado toast.

SERVES 6 TO 8

**EQUIPMENT: 9- TO 10-INCH
FLUTED TART PAN WITH REMOVABLE
BOTTOM AND 1¼-INCH SIDES**

ROASTED TOMATOES:

2 pounds (12 medium to large)
  plum tomatoes, quartered lengthwise

2 tablespoons extra virgin olive oil

½ teaspoon sea salt

Freshly ground black pepper

1 tablespoon dill seeds

1 tablespoon balsamic vinegar

CRUST:

½ cup pine nuts

½ cup regular rolled oats

¼ cup brown rice flour

½ teaspoon aluminum-free
  baking powder

½ teaspoon sea salt

1 cup whole spelt flour, divided

¼ cup extra virgin olive oil

3 tablespoons plain soy milk
  or plain almond milk

FILLING:

¼ cup plus 1 tablespoon
  extra virgin olive oil, divided

1 medium onion, diced

5 garlic cloves, chopped

1 15-ounce block plain, firm tofu,
  drained, rinsed, and patted dry

2 teaspoons fresh lemon juice

1 tablespoon ume plum vinegar

2 tablespoons brown rice vinegar

¾ teaspoon sea salt

Freshly ground black pepper

⅓ cup chopped fresh dill

Fresh dill flowers to garnish, optional

ROAST THE TOMATOES:

Preheat oven to 400°F. Line a rimmed baking sheet with parchment paper, and add tomatoes. Drizzle with olive oil, and sprinkle with salt and a pinch of pepper. Toss gently to coat with oil; arrange tomatoes in a single layer, cut-side up, and sprinkle with dill seeds. Roast for 20 minutes, rotate tray, and gently move any tomatoes that are browning to center of tray, keeping them facing up. Return to oven for another 15 minutes or until browning and reduced. Remove from oven, drizzle with balsamic vinegar, and set aside.

MAKE THE CRUST:

Reduce oven temperature to 350°F. Lightly oil tart pan and set aside.

Place pine nuts, oats, rice flour, baking powder, salt, and ¼ cup spelt flour in a food processor. Blend for about 30 seconds or until oats are ground. Transfer to a medium bowl and stir in remaining ¾ cup spelt flour. Drizzle in olive oil, and using a fork or your fingers, mix until all flour is moistened. Stir in soy or almond milk, and squeeze pastry together with clean hands. It should be moist and hold together but not stick to your fingers. If it seems crumbly or dry, add a splash more soy or almond milk.

Wash and dry your hands, then press pastry evenly into prepared tart pan. Use your thumbs to press into the fluted sides of the tart pan, making sure corners are not too thick. Trim any excess pastry from edges. Prick bottom of crust with a fork several times, and bake for 12 minutes or until pastry is just set but not cooked through. Remove from oven and set aside.

MAKE THE FILLING:

Warm 1 tablespoon olive oil in a skillet over medium heat. Add onion, and sauté for 5 minutes or until golden. Add garlic, and continue cooking for another 3 minutes. Remove from heat and set aside.

Crumble tofu into a food processor; add lemon juice, ume plum vinegar, rice vinegar, salt, a pinch of black pepper, remaining ¼ cup olive oil, and half of the onion-garlic mixture. Blend until combined, scraping the sides as necessary. Add dill and pulse until incorporated; transfer to a bowl and stir in the remaining onion-garlic mixture. Spread evenly in tart crust. Arrange roasted tomatoes in circles on top of filling, place tart on a baking sheet, and bake for 45 minutes or until filling is set in the center and crust is golden around edges. Remove from oven, and allow tart to cool for 15 minutes before carefully removing from pan. Garnish with dill flowers, and serve warm or at room temperature. It will last in the fridge for a day or two, but it is best the day it is made.

SQUASH BLOSSOM ORECCHIETTE
WITH AGED SHEEP'S CHEESE AND RED CHILI

If you are ever fortunate enough to have an abundance of squash blossoms at your fingertips, make this pasta. It's like a bowl of sunshine that melts in your mouth. The squash blossoms and golden zucchini dissolve into a butter-like sauce, and the basil and chili add a nice little kick. Since the heat of fresh chilies varies so much, taste yours as you cut it—if it's hot, you may want to leave the dried chili out.

Anne from Saxelby Cheesemongers on the Lower East Side introduced me to a Vermont-made Coomersdale, a semihard sheep's milk cheese, similar to a young pecorino, that I fell in love with. A small amount is perfect here, melting just enough and adding a delicious nuttiness to the delicate zucchini. This recipe makes four moderate bowls of pasta but could also be eaten by two hungry people.

NOTE: Grate the cheese and the zucchini on the largest hole of a box grater.

SERVES 4

Sea salt

8 ounces whole-wheat orecchiette

3 tablespoons extra virgin olive oil

6 garlic cloves, chopped

⅓ cup thinly sliced red chili
 (about 1 large)

3 medium golden zucchinis, grated
 (about 2½ cups)

¼ cup torn basil leaves

½ teaspoon chili flakes, optional

8 ounces squash blossoms, cut in ¾-inch
 slices (about 45 blossoms)

½ cup grated aged sheep cheese,
 plus more to garnish

Fill a large pot with filtered water, add a generous pinch of salt, and bring to a boil over high heat. Add pasta, and cook 10 to 12 minutes or until al dente. Meanwhile, make sauce.

Warm olive oil in a wide skillet over medium heat. Add garlic and chili; sauté for 2 minutes or until garlic is golden. Stir in zucchini and a pinch of salt; sauté for 3 to 4 minutes or until softened and slightly reduced. Add basil and chili flakes (if using), and cook for another minute. Stir in squash blossoms, and cook for 3 to 4 minutes or until soft and completely wilted.

Drain cooked pasta, reserving ¼ cup cooking liquid. Stir drained pasta and reserved cooking liquid into squash blossom mixture. Remove from heat, add cheese, briefly stir, and season to taste. Divide pasta among bowls and garnish with extra cheese.

BEET TARTLETS WITH POPPY SEED CRUST AND WHITE BEAN FENNEL FILLING

These tartlets are one of my favorite ways to show off the beauty of beets in all their vibrant colors; together, they look like a collection of jewels. If red beets are all that are available, I encourage you to make them, as they still look gorgeous, and the combination of flavors is excellent, no matter what color the beets are. The fennel-scented, white bean filling is so tasty that it can also be used as a dip or spread on its own. As with many tarts, the components here can be made ahead of time—press the crusts, marinate the beets, and blend the filling, then assemble when you're ready to bake them. For a light meal, all these tarts need is some simply dressed leaves to accompany.

SERVES 6

EQUIPMENT: SIX 4¾-INCH TARTLET PANS WITH REMOVABLE BOTTOMS

BEET TOPPING:

2 pounds beets (about 12 small),
    in different colors

2 tablespoons
    unpasteurized apple cider vinegar

2 tablespoons extra virgin olive oil

½ teaspoon sea salt

FILLING:

¼ cup plus 1 tablespoons
    extra virgin olive oil, divided

2 medium onions, quartered and sliced

2 teaspoons toasted and
    ground fennel seeds (see note)

½ teaspoon sea salt, divided

5 garlic cloves, cut in ¼-inch slices

1½ cups cooked navy beans (see page 68)
    or 1 15-ounce can navy beans,
    rinsed well and drained

1 teaspoon ume plum vinegar

1 tablespoon white balsamic vinegar

Freshly ground black pepper

CRUST:

½ cup toasted sunflower seeds
    (page 77)

½ cup regular rolled oats

¼ cup brown rice flour

½ teaspoon aluminum-free
    baking powder

½ teaspoon sea salt

1 cup whole spelt flour, divided

4 teaspoons poppy seeds

¼ cup plus 2 tablespoons
    extra virgin olive oil,
    plus more to oil the tart pans

¼ cup plus 1 tablespoon plain soy milk
    or plain almond milk

PREPARE THE BEETS:

Place red, pink, and golden beets in separate pots—beets bleed, so boiling them separately keeps each color true. Cover beets with water, and bring to a boil over high heat. Cover each pot, reduce heat to low, and simmer until a toothpick or tip of a small knife is easily inserted into centers of beets. Cooking time will vary, depending on the size of the beets; start checking them at 20 minutes, though larger ones may take up to 45 minutes.

Drain beets, slip off skins, and rinse under cool running water. Cut beets in ⅛-inch slices and place in separate bowls. In another small bowl, combine vinegar, oil, and salt. Divide the mixture over each bowl of beets; toss to coat. Set aside to marinate for about 30 minutes at room temperature or up to three days in the fridge.

MAKE THE FILLING:

Warm 1 tablespoon olive oil in a skillet over medium heat. Add onion, and sauté for 8 minutes or until golden brown; stir in ground fennel. Reduce heat to low and continue cooking for 10 more minutes, stirring every minute or so until caramelized. Stir in ¼ teaspoon salt and set aside.

Warm remaining ¼ cup olive oil in a small pot over medium heat. Add garlic, reduce heat a little, and simmer until golden, about 2 minutes. Remove from heat and set aside.

Place beans in a food processor and add ume plum vinegar, balsamic vinegar, remaining ¼ teaspoon salt, garlic-oil mixture, and half of caramelized onions. Blend for 2 minutes or until smooth, scraping sides as needed. Transfer to a bowl, stir in remaining caramelized onions, and season with salt and pepper to taste. Place in the fridge while you prepare pastry, or for up to two days if you're making components ahead.

MAKE THE CRUST:

Preheat oven to 350°F. Lightly oil 6 tartlet pans; place them on a baking sheet and set aside.

Place sunflower seeds, oats, rice flour, baking powder, salt, and ¼ cup spelt flour in a food processor. Blend for about 30 seconds or until oats are ground. Transfer to a medium bowl and stir in remaining spelt flour and poppy seeds. Drizzle in olive oil, and using a fork or your fingers, mix until all flour is moistened. Stir in soy or almond milk, and squeeze pastry together with clean hands. It should be moist and hold together but not stick to your fingers. If it seems crumbly or dry, add a splash more soy or almond milk.

Wash and dry your hands, then press pastry thinly and evenly into oiled tart pans. Use your thumbs to press pastry into fluted sides of pans, making sure corners are not too thick. Trim any excess pastry from edges.

Prick bottoms of crust with a fork several times and bake for 15 minutes or until lightly cooked. Remove from oven. Divide filling between tartlets, and use the back of a spoon or spatula to spread it out evenly. Lay beets over filling in a circular pattern, overlapping as you go. Return tarts to oven and bake for another 10 minutes. Remove from oven and set aside to cool for 10 minutes before removing from pans. Serve slightly warm or at room temperature.

NOTE: To toast fennel seeds, warm a small skillet over medium heat. Add seeds, and stir constantly for 2 minutes or until fragrant. Use a spice grinder or mortar and pestle to grind until fine.

LATE SUMMER STEW
WITH HEIRLOOM BEANS AND PARSLEY PISTOU

As the warm evenings wind down and cool seeps into the air, this flavorful, brothy stew is a lovely way to bid farewell to summer. The creamy heirloom beans add body and depth to an otherwise light stew. I like to use large, white beans called white runners or white bordals, which are similar to scarlet runners (see the Resources section). You can replace them with other large beans like lima beans or fresh shelling beans, which you can find at farmers' markets toward the end of summer.

In this recipe, I roast the zucchini before adding it to the stew, giving it more flavor and a less watery texture. Once the zucchini has vanished from the farmers' market, it can be replaced with butternut squash, which also combines beautifully with the tomatoes, herbs, and beans; just roast it for 5 to 10 minutes longer or until brown and soft inside. Either way, this stew is taken to another level with a drizzle of lively parsley pistou. And be sure to serve it with warm, crusty bread to sop up all the flavorful juices.

SERVES 4

BEANS:

1 cup white runner beans, sorted and soaked for 12 to 24 hours in 4 cups filtered water, or 3 pounds fresh shelling beans in pods

4 cups filtered water

2-inch piece kombu

4 bay leaves

ROASTED ZUCCHINI:

5 medium (1½ pounds) golden zucchini, sliced in ½-inch rounds

2 tablespoons extra virgin olive oil

Sea salt

Freshly ground black pepper

STEW:

2 tablespoons extra virgin olive oil

1 large onion, quartered and thinly sliced

½ teaspoon sea salt, plus more to taste

5 garlic cloves, thinly sliced

1 cup loosely packed basil leaves, divided

4 teaspoons chopped fresh thyme

2 tablespoons finely chopped fresh oregano

3 pounds tomatoes (about 8 large), peeled and chopped (see note)

Freshly ground black pepper

COOK THE BEANS:

Cook beans with kombu and bay leaves as directed on page 68. Drain beans, reserving 2 cups cooking liquid, and compost kombu and bay leaves. (You will have about 3 cups cooked beans.) If you're using fresh shelling beans, boil shelled beans with 4 cups water, kombu, and bay leaves for 30 minutes or until soft inside. Remove and compost kombu and bay leaves. Drain beans, reserving 2 cups cooking liquid, and set aside.

ROAST THE ZUCCHINI:

Preheat oven to 400°F. Line a rimmed baking sheet with parchment paper and add zucchini. Drizzle with olive oil, a pinch of salt, and black pepper; toss to combine. Spread out in a single layer over baking sheet and roast for 30 minutes. Turn zucchini slices over, and roast for another 5 to 10 minutes or until golden brown. Remove from oven and set aside.

MAKE THE STEW:

Warm olive oil in a large pot over medium heat. Add onions and sauté for 5 minutes or until golden. Stir in salt and garlic and cook for another 2 to 3 minutes. Chop ½ cup basil leaves; add to pot along with thyme and oregano; cook for another minute. Stir in tomatoes, raise heat, and bring up to a simmer. Cover pot, reduce heat to low, and simmer for 5 to 10 minutes or until tomatoes are cooked.

Add beans and 1½ cups reserved cooking liquid to tomato and herb mixture. If you prefer a thicker stew, reduce amount of cooking liquid or omit it entirely. Tear remaining basil leaves and add to pot. Raise heat, return to a simmer, and cook uncovered for 10 minutes or until flavors marry. Add more cooking liquid as needed to get desired consistency. Stir in roasted zucchini, and season to taste with salt and black pepper. Remove from heat, divide into bowls, and serve topped with pistou and with some warm, crusty bread on the side. Once cool, the stew can be stored in jars for up to four days.

NOTE: To peel tomatoes, bring a large pot of water to a boil. Score the tomatoes with an X at the stem end. Carefully place them in boiling water for 30 seconds or until the skin begins to peel back. Drain and peel once they're cool enough to handle.

PARSLEY PISTOU

Pistou is like a lemony pesto but without nuts or cheese. From soups and stews to grilled and steamed veggies, it adds a bright, herby flavor to everything it's drizzled over.

MAKES ABOUT ½ CUP

1 cup chopped flat-leaf parsley

¼ cup plus 2 tablespoons extra virgin olive oil

4 teaspoons lemon juice

1 clove garlic, pressed

Scant ¼ teaspoon sea salt

Freshly ground pepper

Place parsley, olive oil, lemon juice, garlic, salt, and a pinch of black pepper in a bowl; stir to combine. Season to taste. Store any leftover pistou in a jar in the fridge and use within a couple of days.

FRAGRANT EGGPLANT CURRY
WITH CARDAMOM-INFUSED BASMATI RICE, TANGY APRICOT CHUTNEY, AND CUCUMBER LIME RAITA

I think eggplants were made for curry; the way their buttery flesh melts and mingles with fresh ginger and aromatic spices is a delight in texture and taste. The addition of tomatoes in this recipe adds a juicy, tangy layer of flavor, and when served with the rice, chutney, and raita, the meal is a taste sensation. Although any eggplant tastes great in this recipe, I eagerly await the arrival of the slim, firm-fleshed Asian eggplants; their long, skinny shape makes them easy to prepare, and you get to see more of their beautiful deep purple skin.

SERVES 6

3 pounds Asian eggplant (about 10 medium), roll cut into 1½-inch pieces (see page 172)

6 tablespoons extra virgin coconut oil, melted and divided

Sea salt

1½ teaspoons black mustard seeds

2 medium onions, cut in 1-inch dice

2 tablespoons peeled and minced ginger

5 large garlic cloves, minced

2 tablespoons plus 1 teaspoon homemade Curry Powder (page 112)

2½ pounds (about 8 medium) tomatoes, peeled and chopped (see note on page 248)

1 cup cilantro leaves, roughly chopped (optional)

Preheat oven to 400°F. Line 2 baking sheets with parchment paper and set aside.

Place eggplant in a large bowl, add 4 tablespoons of the coconut oil and ½ teaspoon salt, and toss together. Divide over baking sheets in a single layer, placing larger cut-side down. Roast for 25 minutes, turn pieces over, rotate trays, and roast for another 15 minutes or until golden brown and soft inside. Remove from oven and set aside.

Warm remaining coconut oil in a large pot over medium heat. Add mustard seeds and stir until first seed pops, about 1 minute. Add onion and 1 teaspoon salt; cook for 2 minutes. Reduce heat to low and cover pot; cook for 10 minutes or until onions are soft and golden, stirring occasionally. Return heat to medium and add ginger and garlic; cook for another 3 minutes. Stir in curry powder, add tomatoes, and bring up to a simmer. Cover pot, reduce heat to low, and cook for 10 minutes or until tomatoes are soft and sauce-like. Gently stir in roasted eggplant and simmer uncovered for 10 minutes. Season to taste, add cilantro (if using), and transfer to a bowl to serve alongside rice, chutney, and raita.

CARDAMOM-INFUSED BROWN BASMATI RICE

Cooking basmati rice with cardamom is a great way to further enhance its delicate, fragrant flavor, and it's a nice change from my favorite short-grain rice. The lighter, fluffy texture is a perfect complement to the curry.

SERVES 6 TO 8

1½ cups brown basmati rice,
    washed and soaked 12 to 24 hours
    in 4 cups filtered water

2⅓ cups filtered water

10 cardamom pods

3 bay leaves

3 whole star anise

Large pinch sea salt

Drain and rinse rice. Place in 2-quart pot with a tight-fitting lid and add filtered water, cardamom pods, bay leaves, star anise, and salt. Bring to a boil, cover pot, reduce heat to low, and simmer for 50 minutes or until all liquid is absorbed. Remove from heat and allow to sit covered for 5 to 10 minutes. Remove and compost cardamom pods, bay leaves, and star anise before serving.

TANGY APRICOT CHUTNEY

Simple, pungent, and extremely tasty, this chutney is a breeze to make. Any leftover can be used to jazz up a simple bowl of rice or dal—add a dab of yogurt and a sprinkle of chopped cilantro, and you have a quick meal.

MAKES 1¾ CUPS

1 cup (packed) unsulfured dried apricots, thinly sliced

1 teaspoon peeled and minced fresh ginger

1 teaspoon minced garlic

¼ cup unpasteurized apple cider vinegar

1½ cups apple juice or apple cider

Pinch cayenne pepper, or more to taste

¼ teaspoon salt, plus more to taste

Chopped toasted pistachios (page 78), to garnish

Place all ingredients except pistachios in a small pot, and bring to a boil. Cover pot, reduce heat to low, and simmer for 20 to 25 minutes, stirring every 5 minutes. Chutney is cooked once apricots are soft and the liquid is has reduced. Allow to cool, then add more juice or water as needed to get desired consistency; season to taste and sprinkle with pistachios just before serving.

CUCUMBER LIME RAITA

This lime-kissed raita is great with any curry, but the flavors really shine when paired with the eggplant, basmati rice, and apricot chutney already described. I like making this raita with a thick, whole-milk yogurt; if the yogurt you use is on the thinner side, squeeze out some of the juice from the cucumber after grating it.

MAKES 2 CUPS

1 large (8-ounce) Middle Eastern cucumber
    (or a regular cucumber, peeled and seeded)

1½ cups whole-milk yogurt

¾ teaspoon sea salt

1 tablespoon finely sliced mint leaves, packed

Zest of 1 lime

Fresh mint leaves to garnish

Grate cucumber on the largest hole of a box grater and place it in a medium bowl. Add the yogurt, salt, sliced mint, and lime zest; mix well. Transfer to a serving dish and garnish with mint leaves.

  Stored in a jar in the fridge, this will keep for a couple of days.

TEMPEH PORTOBELLO BURGERS

Whenever I make these burgers, the response is nothing short of ecstatic, so although they require a few extra steps, the results are too rewarding to miss. Thanks to the great flavor and texture of the tempeh and its marinade, along with the sautéed portobello mushrooms and loads of fresh parsley, these burgers are hearty and beyond tasty. This recipe is my version of one I learned from my friends Leah Devde and Maria Jacecko, with whom I worked when I first moved to New York. Their recipe used premarinated, locally made tempeh that no longer exists, so with memory as my guide, I made my own, and love the result. I suggest marinating and even baking the tempeh a day or two in advance of making the burgers; otherwise, they require a few hours in the kitchen.

Although these burgers go well with any of your favorite condiments, my absolute favorite way to enjoy them is on a sprouted sesame bun with Miso Mayonnaise (page 114), avocado, browned onions (recipe follows), grainy mustard, fresh tomato, and some greens. You will not be disappointed!

MAKES 8 LARGE BURGERS

TEMPEH:

2 8-ounce packages
plain tempeh

1 cup apple juice or apple
cider

3 garlic cloves

2 tablespoons unpasteurized
apple cider vinegar

4 teaspoons tamari

¼ cup plus 2 tablespoons
extra virgin olive oil

1 teaspoon paprika

1 teaspoon ground cumin

BURGERS:

⅓ cup (about 10)
sun-dried tomatoes
(not oil-packed)

2 tablespoons extra virgin
olive oil, plus more for
brushing burgers and tray

1 medium onion, diced

5 garlic cloves, minced

½ teaspoon sea salt,
plus more to taste

½ teaspoon paprika

½ teaspoon ground cumin

7 medium portobello
mushrooms (1¾ pounds),
stems removed and caps
cut into ⅓-inch dice

½ cup regular rolled oats

¼ cup toasted sunflower
seeds (page 77)

1 teaspoon unpasteurized
barley or brown rice miso

1 cup chopped parsley

1 teaspoon tamari

Freshly ground black pepper

MARINATE AND BAKE THE TEMPEH:

Cut tempeh into 1 × 3-inch pieces (you should end up with
14 pieces). Lay each piece flat and cut in half horizontally to
make 28 thinner pieces. In a large baking dish (or two smaller
dishes), lay pieces flat in a snug, single layer.

Add apple juice, garlic, vinegar, tamari, olive oil, paprika,
and cumin to an upright blender; blend until smooth. Pour
marinade over tempeh, cover, and set aside to marinate for
an hour or up to two days in the fridge.

Preheat oven to 350°F. Bake tempeh for 45 minutes or until
marinade is mostly absorbed and tempeh begins to brown
around edges. Remove from oven and set aside to cool.

MAKE THE BURGERS:

Soak the sun-dried tomatoes in 1 cup boiling water for 30
minutes, then drain and mince them.

Warm olive oil in a wide skillet over medium heat. Add
onions, and sauté for 5 minutes or until golden. Add garlic
and salt and cook for another 2 minutes. Stir in paprika and
cumin. Add half the mushrooms, and cook for 2 minutes or
until they begin to reduce; add remaining mushrooms and
cook for 10 more minutes or until all liquid has evaporated
and mushrooms are cooked. Remove from heat and set aside.

Preheat oven to 350°F. Line a baking sheet with parchment
paper, lightly brush with olive oil, and set aside.

Place oats and sunflower seeds in a food processor, and
pulse several times until coarsely ground. Transfer to a large
mixing bowl and add cooked mushrooms, sun-dried tomatoes,
miso, parsley, tamari, and a large pinch of black pepper;
mix well. Crumble cooked tempeh into mushroom mixture
and mix until completely combined. Taste; add more salt
if needed.

Shape mixture into 8 burgers (I used a rounded ½-cup
measure as a guide) and flatten slightly to the size of your
bun. Place on prepared baking sheet and brush top and sides
with olive oil. Bake for 20 minutes. Carefully flip each burger
over with a flat spatula, return to oven, and bake another
10 minutes. Remove from oven, and serve with browned
onions and all the fixings. If your tempeh is freshly baked,
any leftover burgers can be stored in the fridge for three days.
But they won't last that long!

BROWNED ONIONS

2 tablespoons
extra virgin olive oil

2 medium onions,
cut in ⅓-inch rounds

Sea salt

Warm olive oil in a wide
cast-iron skillet over medium
heat. Add onion rounds in
a single layer; you will most
likely need to do this in two
batches. Cook for 4 to 5
minutes or until browning.
Using a flat spatula, carefully
turn them over, and cook
for another minute. Reduce
heat to low, and continue
cooking until soft and brown,
about 3 or 4 minutes.
Sprinkle with salt and
remove from pan. Repeat
with remaining onions.

SWEET CORN TOFU FRITTATA
WITH ROASTED CHERRY TOMATO COMPOTE

The delectable texture of this frittata comes from folding together a tasty whipped tofu cheese and a creamy polenta studded with sweet corn kernels, then baking it until golden. When topped with the juicy cherry tomato compote and served with a simple salad on the side, it's an absolute winner. Don't be tempted to make this meal with frozen corn and lackluster tomatoes; save it for summer—you'll be glad you waited.

SERVES 6

POLENTA:

3 cups sweet corn kernels, from 4 to 5 ears, divided

1 tablespoon plus 1 teaspoon extra virgin olive oil, divided

Sea salt

2½ cups filtered water

1 bay leaf

1 sprig rosemary

1 sprig oregano

1 sprig thyme

½ cup corn grits, plus more for dusting skillet

TOFU CHEESE:

4 tablespoons extra virgin olive oil, plus more for oiling the skillet

4 garlic cloves, cut in ¼-inch slices

1 15-ounce block plain, firm tofu, drained, rinsed, and patted dry

2 tablespoons plus 2 teaspoons brown rice vinegar

1 teaspoon ground flax seeds

¼ teaspoon turmeric

½ teaspoon sea salt

1 teaspoon minced fresh thyme

MAKE THE POLENTA:

Place 1 cup sweet corn, 1 teaspoon olive oil, and a pinch of salt in a bowl and toss to combine. Set aside to top frittata before baking.

Add water, bay leaf, rosemary, oregano, thyme, and ½ teaspoon salt to a medium pot; bring to a boil. Cover pot, reduce heat to low, and simmer for 5 minutes. Remove and compost bay leaf and herbs. Raise heat to high and slowly pour in corn grits, whisking constantly until mixture boils. Be careful, as it may splutter as it comes to a boil. Reduce heat to low, and cook uncovered for 15 minutes, whisking every minute or so to prevent it from sticking. Stir in 1 tablespoon olive oil and the remaining 2 cups corn kernels, and continue cooking on low for 8 to 10 minutes or until corn is tender and cooked. Remove from heat, cover pot, and set aside while you make tofu cheese.

MAKE THE TOFU CHEESE:

Preheat oven to 350°F. Oil a 9-inch cast-iron skillet, sprinkle bottom and sides with corn grits, and set aside.

Warm olive oil in a small skillet or pot over medium heat; add garlic and cook until golden, about 2 minutes. Remove from heat and set aside. Crumble tofu into a food processor. Add rice vinegar, flax, turmeric, salt, and garlic oil mixture. Blend until smooth, scraping sides as needed; add thyme and blend until incorporated. Remove lid from polenta and fold tofu cheese in, stirring until evenly combined. Spread in prepared skillet and distribute reserved sweet corn-olive oil mixture over surface. Bake for 45 to 50 minutes or until center is firm and set and the edges are golden. Remove from oven and allow frittata to sit for 10 minutes before serving. Serve topped with Cherry Tomato Compote (recipe at right). Any leftovers can be covered and reheated in the oven or steamed in a steamer basket.

ROASTED CHERRY TOMATO COMPOTE

You'll be hard-pressed to find a dish that this compote doesn't taste great on. I particularly love it for breakfast over avocado toast with poached eggs and lots of chopped parsley and chives. If you make extra while preparing it for the frittata, or make it to eat on its own, it will last about three days in the fridge; either way it's best served at room temperature or slightly warm.

SERVES 6 AS A SIDE DISH

4 cups (about 1 pound) cherry tomatoes, any color or a combination

2 tablespoons extra virgin olive oil

1 garlic clove, minced

10 fresh basil leaves, roughly torn

¼ teaspoon sea salt

Freshly ground black pepper

Preheat oven to 400°F. Place all ingredients in a rimmed baking dish that will hold tomatoes in a snug single layer. (An 8 × 12-inch pan works well.) Toss to combine and roast for 15 minutes; stir, and return to oven for another 15 minutes or until tomatoes are collapsed and juicy. Remove from oven and transfer to a serving bowl. Serve warm or at room temperature.

BEET CHICKPEA CAKES WITH TZATZIKI

Chickpeas and beets are two of my favorite ingredients. Whether eaten together or separately, I can't imagine a week without them appearing in at least a couple of my meals. The heartiness of chickpeas and the earthiness of beets lifted with a splash of vinegar make a most satisfying meal, but when shaped into cakes and topped with dill-packed, garlicky yogurt, they're taken to whole new level. These are great warm or at room temperature and also yummy tucked into warm pita bread with chopped tomatoes, crunchy lettuce, and a generous spoonful of the tsatziki.

NOTE: If you don't have a pressure cooker to cook your chickpeas, I suggest using canned chickpeas here, as they need to be completely soft to hold the cakes together.

MAKES 12 CAKES
SERVES 4

2 tablespoons extra virgin olive oil,
    plus more for brushing cakes and tray

3¼ cups cooked chickpeas (see page 68),
    or 2 15-ounce cans chickpeas, drained and rinsed well

2 medium red onions, finely diced

8 garlic cloves, finely chopped

2 teaspoon sea salt, plus more to taste

2 medium red beets (12 ounces),
    grated on largest hole of a box grater (4 cups grated)

2 tablespoons balsamic vinegar

¾ cup chopped fresh dill

Freshly ground black pepper

Tzatziki to serve (recipe follows)

Preheat oven to 375°F. Line a baking sheet with parchment paper, lightly brush with olive oil, and set aside.

Place chickpeas in a bowl and crush with a potato masher; set aside. (Don't mash the chickpeas completely. The mixture should be somewhat chunky.)

Warm olive oil in a wide skillet over medium heat. Add onions, and sauté for 5 minutes or until browning. Add garlic and salt, and cook for another 3 minutes. Stir in grated beets, and continue cooking for another 6 to 8 minutes or until beets are cooked. Add balsamic vinegar and remove from heat. Add to mashed chickpeas along with chopped dill, and mix well to combine. Season to taste with salt and pepper.

Use an oiled ⅓-cup measure to shape mixture into cakes. Place on prepared tray, and brush top and sides of each cake with olive oil. Bake for 15 minutes, rotate tray, and continue baking for another 15 minutes or until brown on the bottom. Remove from oven; allow to cool for 5 minutes before serving.

To serve, slide a thin spatula under each cake and flip onto plate so bottom side is up. Top with tzatziki, or serve it on the side.

TZATZIKI

Tzatziki is a fantastic Greek yogurt dip or side dish made with cucumbers, dill, garlic, and olive oil. The first time I ate it was on a trip to Greece with my best friend, Guinevere, many years ago. The tzatziki we had was served with cooked beets and beet greens, and the simple and extremely tasty combination has stuck with me ever since. Don't save it just for these cakes; tzatziki is delicious served with roasted vegetables, simple grains, and crunchy summer salads.

MAKES 2 CUPS

1 large (8-ounce) Middle Eastern cucumber
    (or a regular cucumber, peeled and seeded)

1½ cups whole-milk Greek yogurt or Labneh
    (page 215)

¼ cup chopped fresh dill

2 garlic cloves, pressed

¾ teaspoon sea salt, plus more to taste

2 tablespoons extra virgin olive oil,
    plus more for drizzling

Freshly ground black pepper

Grate cucumber on the largest holes of a box grater, place in a strainer, and squeeze out juice with your hands. Drink or discard juice, and add cucumber to a medium bowl along with yogurt, dill, garlic, salt, olive oil, and a pinch of black pepper. Stir to combine, season to taste, and serve drizzled with olive oil. Store any leftovers in an airtight container in the fridge for up to three days.

SPICY BLACK BEAN STEW
WITH CRISPY SWEET CORN POLENTA
AND TOMATILLO AVOCADO SALSA

I happily eat this scrumptious stew alone or with a simple garnish of toasted pumpkin seeds and avocado; however, when paired with the golden crispy polenta and flavorful salsa, it's fit for a festive feast with friends. Roasting the squash before simmering it with the stew adds a rich, sweet flavor that complements the cumin and cilantro beautifully. For a refreshing, colorful, and crunchy side dish, serve this meal with Quick Pickled Red Cabbage (page 102). You can cook the beans and roast the squash a day or two ahead of time. The stew also tastes great for a few days; it will thicken as it cools, so warm it up with a splash of water or reserved bean cooking liquid before serving.

NOTE: If you want to use canned beans, you will need about three 15-ounce cans. Make sure you drain and rinse them thoroughly before using. And use water in place of the bean cooking liquid.

SERVES 4 TO 6

BEANS:

2 cups dried black beans,
  sorted and soaked 12 to 24 hours
  in at least 6 cups filtered water

8 cups filtered water

8 bay leaves

2-inch piece kombu

3 large garlic cloves, peeled

Sea salt

STEW:

½ medium butternut squash, peeled,
  seeded, and cut in ¾-inch triangles
  (about 3½ cups)

3 tablespoons extra virgin olive oil,
  divided

1½ teaspoons sea salt, divided

1 medium onion, diced

5 garlic cloves, finely chopped

2 medium jalapeños,
  seeded and chopped (about ¼ cup)

3 tablespoons minced fresh oregano

¼ cup plus 2 tablespoons
  finely chopped cilantro stems

1 teaspoon toasted ground cumin

2 celery stalks, diced

3 medium carrots,
  roll cut in ¾-inch pieces
  (see page 172)

Tamari to taste, optional

¼ cup chopped cilantro leaves,
  plus more to garnish

COOK THE BEANS:

Drain and rinse beans. Place in a large pot and add water, bay leaves, kombu, and garlic. Bring to a boil over high heat. Remove any foam that rises to the surface with a small strainer or slotted spoon. Cover pot, reduce heat to low, and simmer for 1 hour or until soft and creamy inside. (If using a pressure cooker, reduce water to 6 cups and cook the beans for 25 minutes. See page 68.) Remove from heat; remove and compost bay leaves and kombu. Drain beans, reserving 2½ cups liquid, and add it back to the beans along with a large pinch of salt. Stir to break up the garlic cloves. Set aside.

ROAST THE SQUASH:

Preheat oven to 400°F. Line a rimmed baking sheet with parchment paper. Add squash, and toss with 1 tablespoon olive oil and ½ teaspoon salt. Roast for 30 minutes, stir, and continue roasting for another 10 to 15 minutes or until squash is browning and cooked through. Remove from oven and set aside.

Warm remaining 2 tablespoons olive oil in a large pot over medium heat. Add onion, and sauté for 5 minutes or until golden. Stir in garlic and jalapeños and remaining 1 teaspoon salt; cook for 3 more minutes. Add oregano and cilantro stems, and cook for another minute. Reduce heat to low and stir in the cumin. Add celery, carrots, and bean mixture. Raise heat and bring to a boil. Cover pot, reduce heat to low, and simmer for 20 minutes or until vegetables are tender. Add roasted squash, return to a simmer and cook uncovered for 15 to 20 minutes or until stew is thick and creamy. Stir in cilantro leaves and season to taste with tamari. Serve garnished with extra cilantro leaves.

Toasting and grinding whole cumin seeds yourself will give you the absolute best flavor, and it's easy to do. Warm a skillet over medium heat, add 2 tablespoons cumin seeds, and toast for 2 minutes, shaking pan until seeds are fragrant. Use a spice grinder or mortar and pestle to finely grind seeds, and store in a small jar for up to two months.

CRISPY SWEET CORN POLENTA

This polenta is made with corn grits, which gives it a bit more texture than the finer ground Italian polenta. After the grits have been cooked, the mixture is spread out in a thin layer to set before cutting, brushing with olive oil, and baking until crisp and golden. Stirring in fresh corn kernels adds a burst of sweet flavor—frozen corn will work when fresh isn't available.

NOTE: This recipe makes 8 rectangles (16 triangles) in a rimmed 13 × 9-inch baking sheet, sometimes called a quarter sheet pan. If you don't have that size, you can pour polenta into two or more smaller baking dishes, just as long as the mixture is ¼ to ⅓ inch thick. The polenta can be set and refrigerated for up to three days before cutting and baking. Pat off any moisture that may have formed on the surface with a clean towel before cutting, brushing with olive oil, and baking.

SERVES 4 TO 6

3 cups filtered water

3 bay leaves

1 teaspoon sea salt

1 tablespoon extra virgin olive oil, plus more for oiling the pan and brushing polenta

¾ cup corn grits

¾ cup fresh or frozen sweet corn kernels (defrost if using frozen)

Oil a rimmed 13 × 9-inch baking sheet or a baking dish; set aside.

Add water and bay leaves to a medium pot and bring to a boil over high heat. Cover pot, reduce heat to low, and simmer for 5 minutes. Remove and compost bay leaves; add salt. Raise heat to high and slowly pour in corn grits, whisking constantly until mixture returns to a boil—be careful as it may splutter. Reduce heat to low and cook uncovered for 20 minutes, whisking every minute or so to prevent sticking. Stir in sweet corn kernels, and if you're using fresh corn, continue cooking for another 10 minutes or until tender. If you're using frozen corn, cook for 3 minutes. Remove from heat and pour into prepared pan. Smooth out evenly (it should be quite thin—see note above), and set aside to cool until firm. Once mixture has stopped steaming, place it in the fridge to set for about 30 to 40 minutes or until completely firm.

Preheat oven to 400°F. Line a rimmed baking sheet (larger than the one you used for the polenta) with parchment paper, brush with oil, and set aside.

Cut polenta into 8 rectangles and cut each of those into 2 triangles. Place them on lined and oiled baking sheet, making sure they do not touch, and lightly brush with olive oil. Bake for 30 minutes or until crispy and golden. Remove from oven and serve warm.

TOMATILLO AVOCADO SALSA

Like tomatoes, tomatillos are in season in summer through midfall. When their papery husk is removed, they look like a small green tomato and often feel sticky. Tomatillos have a bright, lemony flavor that mellows nicely when either blanched or broiled, and they are a taste sensation when paired with avocado. Serve this zesty salsa as a snack with tortilla chips, or use it as a topping for tacos or just about anything.

MAKES ABOUT 2½ CUPS

1 pound tomatillos (about 10 medium), husks removed

¼ cup minced white onion

1 medium jalapeño, seeded

2 garlic cloves

½ teaspoon sea salt, plus more to taste

½ cup chopped cilantro

2 ripe avocados, diced

1 tablespoon fresh lime juice

Fill a medium pot with about 6 cups filtered water and bring to a boil. Carefully add tomatillos and boil for 5 minutes. Drain and rinse under cold water. Set aside to cool for at least 5 minutes.

Place minced onion in a strainer, rinse under cold running water, and set aside to drain.

In an upright blender, add tomatillos, jalapeño, garlic, and salt; blend until smooth. Stop and stir if necessary to get contents moving. Add cilantro and pulse a couple of times to combine. Pour into a bowl and stir in drained onion, avocado, and lime juice. For best flavor, serve right away. If you have anything left over, it can be stored for a day or two in the fridge.

ROASTED FALL VEGETABLE CANNELLINI BEAN STEW
WITH SPELT BERRIES AND KALE

Here is a flavorsome and complete meal in all one: beans, grains, greens, and vegetables. It's the kind of hearty, creamy, bean-based dish that I crave once autumn sets in. Roasting the vegetables before simmering them in the stew adds richness, texture, and a deeply sweet flavor. Soaking and cooking the beans and spelt berries together creates a full-bodied base for the stew, and adding the rosemary and thyme stems infuses them with even more flavor.

NOTE: As with all the recipes, I leave the skin on all the vegetables for this stew. Peel the squash if the skin is rough or particularly hard.

SERVES 4 TO 6

1¼ cup cannellini beans, sorted

¼ cup spelt berries

6 cups filtered water,
    plus more for soaking

5 bay leaves

2-inch piece kombu

10 whole sage leaves

3 cups kobocha or red kuri squash,
    cut in 1-inch triangles

5 medium Japanese (Hakurei) turnips,
    quartered, or halved if small
    (about 2 cups)

2 medium carrots,
    roll cut in ½-inch pieces (see page 172)

½ pound Jerusalem artichokes,
    cut in ½-inch slices (2 cups)

4 tablespoons extra virgin olive oil,
    divided

1 teaspoon sea salt, divided

Freshly ground black pepper

1 medium onion, diced

4 garlic cloves, finely chopped

2 teaspoons minced thyme,
    stems reserved for cooking beans

2 teaspoons minced rosemary,
    stems reserved for cooking beans

1 tablespoon chopped sage

2 stalks celery, diced

1 medium leek, cut in ¼-inch slices

1 teaspoon
    unpasteurized apple cider vinegar

2 teaspoons tamari

2 cups thinly sliced Lacinato kale leaves

Combine beans and spelt berries in a medium pot. To wash, fill pot with water, swish beans and grains around with your hands, let them settle, then pour off the water. Repeat and drain. Cover with at least 4 cups filtered water and soak 12 to 24 hours. Drain and rinse, return to pot and add 6 cups water, bay leaves, kombu, sage, and reserved herb stems. Bring to a boil over high heat; skim off any foam that rises to top with a small strainer or slotted spoon. Cover pot, reduce heat to low, and simmer for 1 to 1½ hours or until beans are soft and creamy and spelt berries are plump. Remove and compost kombu, bay leaves, and herbs. Drain, reserving cooking liquid, and set aside.

Preheat oven to 400°F. Line a rimmed baking sheet with parchment paper, and add squash, turnips, carrots, and Jerusalem artichokes. Drizzle with 2 tablespoons olive oil, and sprinkle with ½ teaspoon salt and a pinch of black pepper. Toss well, spread out in a single layer, and roast for 25 minutes. Remove from oven, stir gently, and return to oven for another 15 to 20 minutes or until browning and cooked through. Remove from oven and set aside.

Warm remaining 2 tablespoons olive oil in a medium to large pot over medium heat. Add onions, and sauté for 5 minutes or until golden. Stir in garlic and cook another 2 minutes. Add thyme, rosemary, sage, celery, leek, and remaining ½ teaspoon salt; cook for 2 more minutes. Cover pot, reduce heat to low, and cook 10 minutes or until celery is tender. Add cooked beans and spelt berries, 2½ cups reserved cooking liquid, and roasted vegetables. Bring up to a simmer, and cook uncovered for 5 to 10 minutes to allow flavors to meld. Add more bean cooking liquid to get the desired consistency. Stir in vinegar, tamari, and kale; cook for 2 more minutes or until kale is tender. Season to taste and serve warm.

NOTE: To cook beans and spelt berries in a pressure cooker, reduce water to 4½ cups and bring to a boil over high heat; skim off any foam that rises to the top. Lock lid in place and bring up to high pressure, then reduce heat to low and cook for 25 minutes. Remove from heat and allow pressure to release naturally. Remove lid and proceed with the recipe.

BUTTERNUT SQUASH LASAGNA
WITH WHOLE-WHEAT NOODLES AND SAGE TOFU RICOTTA

This lasagna was inspired by butternut squash ravioli with sage, one of my favorite Italian dishes. The texture of the squash and tofu ricotta is velvety smooth with a layer of succulent caramelized onions and folds of nutty, whole-wheat noodles to give it structure. This dish is always a crowd-pleaser and makes a wonderful vegetarian main course for Thanksgiving or any holiday celebration.

NOTE: If you can't find no-boil whole-wheat noodles, make the recipe with regular whole-wheat noodles. Just cook them according to the directions on the package, drain, and rinse well before layering.

SERVES 8

EQUIPMENT: 8 × 12-INCH OR 9 × 13-INCH LASAGNA PAN

SQUASH PURÉE:

2 medium-large butternut squash (6 pounds)

Extra virgin olive oil for brushing squash

1½ teaspoons sea salt

Freshly ground pepper

CARAMELIZED ONIONS:

2 tablespoons extra-virgin olive oil

4 medium yellow onions, quartered and thinly sliced

1 teaspoon sea salt

TOFU RICOTTA:

½ cup extra virgin olive oil, plus more for oiling pan

10 garlic cloves, cut in ¼-inch slices

2 15-ounce blocks plain, firm tofu, drained, rinsed, and patted dry

5 tablespoons brown rice vinegar

1 tablespoon ume plum vinegar

1 teaspoon sea salt

Freshly ground black pepper

⅓ cup chopped sage, plus 8 whole leaves to garnish

1 package no-boil whole-wheat lasagna noodles

MAKE THE SQUASH PURÉE:

Preheat oven to 400°F. Line a baking sheet with parchment paper. Cut neck off butternut squash, and cut neck and bottom in half lengthwise. Rub squash with olive oil and place cut-side down on parchment-lined tray. Roast for 50 minutes or until you can pierce the flesh easily with a knife. Remove from oven and set aside to cool while you cook the onions. Once squash is cool enough to handle, scoop out seeds with a spoon and peel off skin. Compost seeds and skin. Add squash to food processor with 1½ teaspoons sea salt and a pinch of black pepper. Blend until completely smooth; place in a bowl and set aside. Rinse out food processor.

CARAMELIZE THE ONIONS:

Warm oil in a large skillet over medium heat; add onions. Sauté for 10 minutes or until beginning to brown. Add salt, lower heat slightly, and continue cooking for 15 to 20 minutes or until onions are soft and caramelized. Remove from heat and set half the onions aside for layering in the lasagna. Place remaining onions in a food processor.

MAKE THE TOFU RICOTTA:

Warm olive oil in a small pot over medium heat. Add garlic, reduce heat a little, and simmer until soft and golden, about 10 minutes. Remove from heat and set aside. Crumble tofu into food processor with onions and add brown rice vinegar, ume plum vinegar, sea salt, a pinch of black pepper, and garlic-oil mixture. Blend until smooth, scraping down sides as necessary. Add chopped sage and process until incorporated. Place in a bowl and set aside a heaping ½ cup of ricotta mixture for garnishing top of lasagna.

ASSEMBLE THE LASAGNA:

Preheat oven to 375°F. Brush lasagna pan with olive oil. Spread ¾ cup squash purée over bottom of pan and top with a single layer of noodles. Spread 1½ cups squash purée over noodles, then top with half of tofu ricotta. Repeat with another layer of noodles and another 1½ cups squash purée. Spread caramelized onions over squash and top with a final layer of noodles. Cover with remaining tofu ricotta, and top with remaining squash purée. Spoon 8 dots of reserved tofu ricotta evenly over top, press a sage leaf into each one, and sprinkle with freshly ground black pepper. Cover with parchment paper and then with foil; bake for 50 minutes or until noodles are tender and lasagna is heated through. To test, insert a knife into center; you shouldn't feel any resistance. If noodles are still firm, continue cooking covered for another 5 to 10 minutes. Remove cover, and bake 10 minutes more or until top layer of squash looks set. Remove from oven and allow to sit at least 10 minutes before cutting. Serve warm.

Store any leftover lasagna in an airtight container in the fridge for up to three days. Warm covered in the oven until heated through.

SPICY CHICKPEA STEW
AND QUINOA PILAF WITH GOLDEN RAISINS AND ALMONDS

I often turn to this meal when I'm looking for a tasty, rich, and satisfying dinner to serve guests. When accompanied by Labneh (page 215), Quick Pickled Red Cabbage (page 102), and some steamed greens, you will have a scrumptious, colorful feast. This stew gets its heat from the Harissa paste stirred in at the end; you can stir in more or less, depending on how spicy you want the dish. Here I use my own Harissa (page 112); it's superfast to make and lasts months in the fridge.

NOTE: I highly recommend that you cook your own chickpeas for this stew. The flavor of home-cooked chickpeas is worth the effort, and the cooking liquid adds a nice body to the stew as well. You will need about 1 cup dried chickpeas to end up with 2½ cups cooked chickpeas. If you want to use canned beans, you will need about two 15-ounce cans. Make sure you drain and rinse them thoroughly before using. And use water in place of chickpea cooking liquid.

SERVES 6

1 medium butternut squash, peeled, seeded, and cut in ¾-inch triangular pieces (about 6 cups)

3 tablespoons extra virgin olive oil, divided

Sea salt

Freshly ground black pepper

2 medium onions, diced

8 large garlic cloves, finely chopped

¼ cup finely chopped parsley stems

1½ teaspoons toasted ground cumin (see page 266)

1 teaspoon paprika

3 medium carrots, roll cut in ½-inch pieces (see page 172)

1 cup chickpea cooking liquid, or filtered water

1 28-ounce can crushed tomatoes

2½ cups cooked chickpeas (see page 68)

3 to 4 teaspoons Harissa (page 112), or to taste

½ cup chopped parsley leaves, plus more to garnish

Preheat oven to 400°F. Line a rimmed baking sheet with parchment paper, and add butternut squash. Add 1½ tablespoons olive oil, sprinkle with ½ teaspoon salt and a pinch of pepper, and toss well. Spread out in a single layer and roast for 30 minutes. Stir, and continue roasting for another 10 to 15 minutes or until browning and cooked through. Remove from oven and set aside.

Warm remaining 1½ tablespoons olive oil in a large pot over medium heat. Add onions, and sauté for 5 minutes or until golden. Stir in garlic and cook 3 minutes more. Add parsley stems, cumin, paprika, and ½ teaspoon salt; cook for 1 to 2 minutes. Stir in carrots and 1 cup chickpea cooking liquid (or water), and bring to a boil over high heat. Cover pot, reduce heat to low, and simmer for 10 to 12 minutes or until carrots are cooked. Add tomatoes and chickpeas. Raise heat and bring up to a simmer; re-cover pot, reduce heat to low, and cook for 10 more minutes. Stir in Harissa paste, chopped parsley leaves, and roasted squash; simmer uncovered for another few minutes to allow flavors to meld. Season to taste and serve warm.

QUINOA PILAF WITH GOLDEN RAISINS AND ALMONDS

Cooking quinoa with raisins gives the grain a delicate, sweet taste, and an added burst of flavor. The almonds deliver crunch and great contrast to the dish—feel free to use toasted pistachios or walnuts in their place.

SERVES 6

1½ cups quinoa, washed and soaked 12 to 24 hours in 4 cups filtered water

1¾ cups filtered water

½ teaspoon sea salt

⅓ cup unsulfered golden raisins

⅓ cup toasted almonds, chopped (page 77)

Rinse and drain quinoa. Place in a 2-quart pot and add filtered water, salt, and raisins. Bring to a boil over high heat. Cover pot, reduce heat to low, and cook for 15 minutes or until all water is absorbed. Remove from heat, and let sit for 5 to 10 minutes before fluffing with a fork. Add almonds and mix gently to combine. Serve warm.

COCONUT CURRY WITH TAMARIND TEMPEH AND FORBIDDEN BLACK RICE

I'm always on the lookout for a Thai curry that rivals the ones I ate on the beach in Thailand. The little café where I dined daily made its curry with fresh coconut milk; nothing beats the way the clean, bright flavors of Kaffir lime, Thai basil, and lemongrass taste when simmered in fresh, sweet-tasting coconut milk. Over the years, I made many different variations before settling on this recipe, which is made with homemade coconut milk—I use dried, unsweetened coconut, as most fresh coconuts have to be irradiated when they're imported. The delicate texture of the milk allows the distinct Thai flavors to come through, and the dense-fleshed winter squash adds a rich, sweet flavor. When served with the forbidden black rice and tamarind tempeh, the meal is a vibrant, colorful taste sensation.

NOTE: If you're planning on serving this curry with the tamarind tempeh, marinate the tempeh before starting the curry. The tempeh can be marinated and coconut milk can be made up to two or three days in advance.

SERVES 4 TO 6

COCONUT MILK:

3 cups dried, shredded, unsweetened coconut

6 cups filtered water

CURRY:

1 cup Thai basil leaves, divided stems reserved

2 stalks lemongrass, tough outer layer removed, roughly chopped

8 large Kaffir lime leaves

3 tablespoons kuzu

1 cup plus 3 tablespoons filtered water, divided

2 tablespoons plus 2 teaspoons extra virgin coconut oil, divided

1 medium onion, quartered and thinly sliced

2 tablespoons peeled and minced fresh ginger

6 garlic cloves, minced

Sea salt

½ teaspoon turmeric

2 small red chilies, sliced (about 2 tablespoons)

1 medium leek, thinly sliced (white and light green parts)

½ large kabocha or red kuri squash, seeded, peeled, and cut into 1 ½-inch wedges, then cut in half into large triangles

1 medium red bell pepper, seeded and thinly sliced

¾ cup roughly chopped cilantro leaves

4 cups (3½ ounces) baby spinach leaves

MAKE THE COCONUT MILK:

Line a large strainer with a nut milk bag, clean, thin kitchen towel, or several layers of cheesecloth; place it over a large pot, and set aside. Add 1½ cups coconut and 3 cups filtered water to an upright blender. Blend on high speed until smooth, about 2 minutes. (Alternatively, if you have a large blender with an 8-cup capacity, you can do this all in one batch.) Pour into nut milk bag or cloth-lined strainer. Repeat with remaining coconut and water. Gather up edges of nut milk bag or excess cloth, and gently squeeze coconut milk through, getting as much liquid out as possible. Compost pulp, and set pot aside.

MAKE THE CURRY:

Set aside ½ cup Thai basil leaves. Roughly chop stems; place remaining leaves and all stems into pot with coconut milk. Add lemongrass and Kaffir lime leaves, and bring to a boil over high heat. Cover pot, reduce heat to low, and simmer for at least 30 minutes (up to 2 hours) to infuse milk with Thai flavors. Milk may separate and turn a slightly green color, but this is natural. In a small bowl dissolve kuzu in 3 tablespoons water, and slowly whisk into simmering coconut milk. Continue whisking until mixture returns to a simmer and thickens to a nice, silky consistency. Remove from heat, cover pot, and set aside.

Warm 2 tablespoons coconut oil in another large pot over medium heat. Add onions, and sauté for 5 minutes or until golden. Stir in ginger, garlic, and 1 teaspoon salt; cook for 3 minutes. Lower heat if the mixture begins to stick. Add turmeric, red chilies, and leeks; cook for 2 more minutes. Arrange squash inside facing up in pot over onion-leek mixture in a single layer. Add remaining cup of water and bring to a boil over high heat. Cover pot, reduce heat to low, and simmer for 15 to 20 minutes or until squash is tender. Remove from heat, keep covered, and set aside.

Warm remaining coconut oil in a wide skillet over medium heat. Add bell peppers and a pinch of salt, and sauté for 5 minutes or until tender and beginning to color. Remove from heat and set aside.

Strain coconut milk into pot with cooked squash and compost the Kaffir lime leaves and basil. Bring up to a simmer over medium-high heat. Stir in reserved Thai basil leaves, cilantro, and baby spinach. Simmer for 2 minutes or until spinach has wilted. Add sautéed red bell peppers and stir gently to combine. Season to taste, remove from heat, and serve warm.

TAMARIND TEMPEH

Tangy, nutty, and a bit sweet from orange and apple juice, this tempeh is a delicious addition to the Coconut Curry (page 274), although you could make it to go with plain rice too. This recipe serves a few slices each on the side of the curry. If you want more protein, then double this recipe and use 1 pound of tempeh.

NOTE: If you have a large, wide skillet, you can do this all in one batch; if not, be sure to divide the marinade and clean the skillet between batches, as the marinade sticks.

SERVES 4 TO 6

1 8-ounce package plain tempeh, cut in ¼-inch slices

6 whole star anise

4 teaspoons strained tamarind pulp (see sidebar)

2 garlic cloves

1 tablespoon mirin

¼ cup plus 2 tablespoons fresh orange juice

¼ cup apple juice

2 tablespoons tamari

Unrefined, untoasted sesame oil
    or extra virgin coconut oil, to cook tempeh

Lay tempeh in a single layer in a rimmed dish (a baking dish works well), scatter with star anise, and set aside. Add tamarind pulp, garlic, mirin, orange juice, apple juice, and tamari to an upright blender; blend until smooth. Pour over tempeh, cover, and marinate for at least an hour or up to two days covered in the fridge.

Warm 2 tablespoons sesame or coconut oil in a wide skillet over medium heat. Remove tempeh from marinade (reserving marinade) and place in skillet in a single layer. Cook for 3 to 4 minutes or until beginning to brown. Flip and cook for 2 to 3 more minutes. Add marinade and star anise, and raise heat to high. Once the mixture is simmering, reduce heat to low and cook until marinade has thickened, about 4 to 5 minutes. Remove star anise before serving.

Tamarind is a sticky pastelike tropical fruit with a tart flavor. You can find it sold as a concentrate or as a solid block with seeds in Indian, Asian, and Mexican markets.

To make tamarind pulp place about ¼ cup of tamarind (block with seeds) in a small bowl and pour ⅓ cup boiling water over it. Allow to sit a few minutes, then stir to combine. Press through a mesh strainer to extract the pulp and compost the seeds. Use the pulp within a week; the block can be kept in the fridge indefinitely.

FORBIDDEN BLACK RICE

Black rice cooks up quite light and fluffy; its delicate tropical flavor and deep purple color make a beautiful and dramatic background for this coconut curry. It also tastes great eaten with avocado, scallions, and toasted sesame seeds.

SERVES 4 TO 6

1 cup forbidden black rice,
    washed and soaked 12 to 24 hours in 4 cups filtered water

1¾ cups filtered water

Pinch sea salt

1 5-inch piece lemongrass stalk, tough outer layer removed,
    split lengthwise (optional)

Rinse and drain rice. Place in a 2-quart pot, add water, salt, and lemongrass. Bring to a boil over high heat. Cover pot, reduce heat to low, and simmer for 1 hour or until all water is absorbed. Remove from heat and allow to sit for 5 to 10 minutes. Remove and compost lemongrass before serving.

BENTO BOWL

This meal is inspired by the daily bento that was served at Shizen, a Japanese macrobiotic restaurant in Amsterdam where I worked in the mid-1990s. Shizen and the exceptional chefs I learned from there were influential in shaping my style of cooking. Besides all the interesting people I met at the restaurant, eating and preparing this terrifically healthy and exquisitely presented meal was one of the highlights of working there.

A bento is a meal served in a lacquered box with divided compartments that house the different components that make up a complete Japanese meal—rice, seaweed, pickles, dipping sauce, vegetable dishes, and traditionally fish or meat. At Shizen, the daily bento always looked like a piece of art, brimming with beautifully prepared (vegan) dishes and delicate garnishes.

Most of my simple grain- and bean-based meals are served in bowls—due to all the components, this one requires more effort, but the result is a truly beautiful meal that leaves you feeling particularly clear and grounded. When I'm short on time, I often make the adzuki sweet rice and choose just one or two of the components—they all store well for a few days too. Other dishes that go well with this bento bowl include Arame with Carrots and Sesame (page 107), Kimchi (page 123), or Simple Pressed Salad (page 200). And I always like to serve this meal with plenty of steamed dark leafy greens.

NOTE: The portions in the following recipes are for serving together as a meal; if you choose to cook only one or two of the recipes, they may not serve as many people.

ADZUKI SWEET RICE

The earthy flavor of adzuki beans cooked with sticky, sweet brown rice is an exceptionally nourishing combination and one that I'll never tire of. While perfect as a component in the bento bowl, this dish is a complete, one-pot meal in itself, needing only a sprinkle of tamari and scallions or Black Sesame Gomasio (page 77). Most recipes you'll find for adzuki and brown rice require a pressure cooker to get the soft, sticky texture. However, if you soak the rice and beans overnight together, you will get the same nutty and sticky result in a pot.

SERVES 4

½ cup adzuki beans, sorted

½ cup sweet brown rice

½ cup short-grain brown rice

2-inch piece kombu

1 teaspoon tamari, plus more to serve

½ sheet nori, cut in thin 2-inch-long strips

Place adzuki beans, brown rice, and sweet rice in a medium pot. To wash, fill pot with water, swish grains and beans around with your hands, let them settle, then pour off water. Repeat and drain. Cover with at least 4 cups filtered water and soak 12 to 24 hours.

Rinse and drain rice and beans. Return to pot, add 2½ cups water and kombu, and bring to a boil over high heat. Cover pot, reduce heat to low, and cook 1 hour, or until all water is absorbed and beans are soft. Remove from heat and let sit covered for 5 to 10 minutes; remove and compost kombu. Sprinkle with tamari and stir gently to combine. Serve warm, topped with nori strips and tamari to taste.

QUICK CUCUMBER PICKLE

This simple and refreshing side dish can be set aside to pickle while you prepare the rest of the bento. It's also particularly good tossed into chilled soba or udon noodle salads in summer.

NOTE: If you can't find thin-skinned Middle Eastern cucumbers, you can use a large English cucumber, or a regular cucumber, peeled and seeded.

SERVES 4

4 4-inch Middle Eastern cucumbers, thinly sliced

½ teaspoon sea salt

4 teaspoons brown rice vinegar

Place cucumbers in a medium bowl, add salt, and mix until they begin to soften and release liquid. Set aside for 20 to 30 minutes, or up to 2 hours. Drain off liquid and lightly squeeze out cucumbers. Place in a serving bowl and stir in rice vinegar.

BURDOCK AND CARROT KINPIRA

Burdock—called *gobo* in Japanese—is a long, woody-looking root with dark brown skin and firm white flesh. Known for its detoxifying uses (especially regarding the liver) and blood-purifying properties, burdock is also used in herbal formulas to fight cancer. Its fresh, earthy, artichoke-like flavor complements the sweet taste of carrots perfectly.

Kinpira is a Japanese cooking style that means to sauté and simmer; it's a great way to coax the most flavor out of root vegetables in a relatively short amount of time. Most root vegetables can be prepared using this method, so if you can't find burdock, try parsnips, turnips, or extra carrots. Keep in mind you won't need to cook them as long as burdock.

SERVES 4

1 tablespoon unrefined, untoasted sesame oil

14-inch piece burdock root, cut in thin matchsticks (about 2½ cups)

1 large carrot, cut in matchsticks (about 2 cups)

Pinch sea salt

¼ cup filtered water

2 teaspoons mirin

2 teaspoons tamari, plus more to taste

2 teaspoons toasted unhulled sesame seeds (page 77)

Warm oil in a wide skillet over medium heat. Add burdock, and sauté for 8 minutes or until beginning to soften. Stir in carrot and a pinch of salt, and continue cooking for 3 minutes or until evenly coated with oil. Add water, cover skillet, reduce heat to low, and cook for 8 minutes or until vegetables are tender. Remove lid and add mirin and tamari; continue cooking for another 2 minutes or until all liquid has evaporated. Remove from heat, and season to taste with tamari. For best flavor, texture, and looks, stir in sesame seeds just before serving. Serve warm or at room temperature.

NOTE: Scrub the burdock with a vegetable brush to remove only the rough outer layer of skin. Don't peel it, as most of the flavor and nutrients are in the skin. Look for burdock at health-food stores, Asian markets, and your local farmers' market.

KABOCHA NISHIME

Nishime is a Japanese cooking style that means "long-cooked with little water." In macrobiotic cooking, it is said to create strong, calm energy and restore vitality. This amazingly simple method is perfect for root vegetables and winter squash, as they become super-sweet and meltingly tender.

When I worked at Shizen, Bastian, one of the chefs, would trim the edges and carefully cut a decorative design in each wedge of squash before it was cooked, making his bento look like a box of jewels.

SERVES 4 TO 6

½ medium (4-pound) kabocha or red kuri squash

4-inch piece kombu

¾ cup filtered water

1 teaspoon mirin

1 teaspoon tamari

Pinch sea salt

Remove seeds from squash, leave skin on, and cut into 1¼-inch wedges. Cut each wedge in half to make triangles. Place kombu in bottom of a medium-large pot or one that will snugly fit all squash in one layer. Lay squash skin-side down over kombu and arrange in a circle, with pointy end of squash facing the center.

Pour in water, and add mirin, tamari, and a pinch of salt to center of pot. Place over high heat and bring to a boil. Cover pot, reduce heat to low, and simmer for 20 to 30 minutes or until squash is cooked through. You can test it with a toothpick or tip of a small knife; cooking time will depend on the thickness of the flesh. Remove from heat and carefully lift squash into serving bowl.

The cooking liquid you are left with is sweet and flavorful and can be poured over the squash when serving. Or you can simply drink it, as I love to do.

HEIRLOOM BEAN BOURGUIGNON
WITH CELERY ROOT MASH

This dish was inspired by a jar of gorgeous heirloom beans called Christmas limas that I found in an Italian market. The name conjured up images of a rich, festive winter meal, and they became the reason I made this bourguignon for Christmas Eve dinner. Traditionally, bourguignon is made with beef simmered in a rich stock with herbs, garlic, mushrooms, and red burgundy. Here, the large creamy beans replace the meat and absorb all the familiar flavors of bourguignon as they simmer in a deeply layered, roasted vegetable stock—which is so good it can stand alone as a soup. Like a classic bourguignon, this dish has a few steps and takes some time to prepare, but you will get soul-satisfying results.

COOKING NOTES:

• Be sure to scrub but not peel the vegetables for the roasted vegetable stock, as much of the flavor and nutrients are in the skin.

• Use a large ceramic or glass rimmed baking dish to roast the vegetables, so you can scrape off any vegetables that stick to the sides. If you don't have one, line a metal pan with parchment paper.

• The stock can be made up to three days in advance.

• Any large creamy bean can replace the Christmas lima beans here. Try scarlet or white runner beans, or even kidney beans, if heirloom varieties are not available. The beans can be cooked and also marinated in wine up to two days in advance. (See the Resources section for ordering beans online.)

SERVES 6

ROASTED VEGETABLE STOCK:

1 medium onion, cut in 1-inch dice

2 large heads garlic, separated
(about 20 unpeeled cloves)

2 large carrots, cut in 1-inch dice

2 medium parsnips, cut in 1-inch dice

2 medium turnips, cut in 1-inch dice

6-inch piece burdock root, cut in 1-inch dice

6 sprigs thyme

4 sprigs sage

2 large sprigs rosemary

3 tablespoons extra virgin olive oil

¾ teaspoon sea salt

8 cups filtered water, divided

4 stalks celery with leaves, chopped

4 bay leaves

6 large sprigs parsley

Stems from 2 pounds crimini mushrooms
(from the bourguignon)

BOURGUIGNON:

1 cup Christmas lima beans,
sorted and soaked 12 to 24 hours
in at least 3 cups filtered water

2-inch piece kombu

3 bay leaves

4 cups plus 2 tablespoons filtered water, divided

15 sun-dried tomatoes
(not oil-packed; about ½ cup)

1 cup boiling filtered water

1¼ cups full-bodied red wine

2 tablespoons mirin

1 tablespoon tamari, plus more to taste

2 pounds crimini mushroom caps
(stems removed and used above),
cut in ¼-inch slices (about 10 cups)

5 tablespoons extra virgin olive oil, divided

Sea salt

Freshly ground black pepper

8 medium shallots, cut in ¼-inch slices

3 garlic cloves, minced

1 tablespoon minced fresh thyme

2 medium carrots, roll cut in ½-inch pieces
(see page 172)

3 tablespoons kuzu or arrowroot (see note on
page 193)

Chopped fresh parsley, to serve

MAKE THE STOCK:

Preheat oven to 400°F. Place onion, garlic, carrots, parsnips, turnips, burdock, thyme, sage, rosemary, olive oil, and salt in a large bowl; toss to combine. Divide between two baking dishes and roast for 1 hour, stirring every 20 minutes. Remove from oven and drizzle each pan with ½ cup water to deglaze. Scrape vegetables and any juice into a large pot, and add celery, bay leaves, parsley, mushroom stems, and remaining water; bring to a boil over high heat. Cover pot, reduce heat to low, and simmer for 1½ hours. Remove from heat, strain stock, and compost vegetables. You should have about 5 cups stock. Set aside, or if you are making this ahead of time, allow it to cool, pour it into jars, and then refrigerate until you're ready to use it. Stock will keep in the fridge for up to three days.

MAKE THE BOURGUIGNON:

Rinse and drain beans. Place in a medium pot with kombu, bay leaves, and 4 cups water; bring to a boil over high heat. Cover pot, reduce heat to low, and simmer until beans are soft and creamy in center but not falling apart. Check beans at 45 minutes, then every 10 to 15 minutes until they're cooked. (If using a pressure cooker, cook the beans for 30 minutes at high pressure. See page 68.) Remove and compost kombu and bay leaves. Drain beans and place in a medium bowl; set aside.

While beans cook, soak sun-dried tomatoes in 1 cup boiling water for 30 minutes. Drain and cut into ¼-inch slices. Add to drained beans along with red wine, mirin, and tamari; stir well. Set aside to marinate while you roast the mushrooms, or if you are making this ahead of time, allow to cool, and refrigerate until you're ready to use.

Preheat oven to 400°F. Line 2 rimmed baking sheets with parchment paper. Place mushrooms in a large bowl with 3 tablespoons olive oil, ¼ teaspoon salt, and a pinch of black pepper; toss to combine. Divide mushrooms between lined baking sheets and spread out in a single layer. Roast for 20 minutes, stir, and continue roasting for another 10 to 15 minutes or until all liquid is released and mushrooms begin to brown. Remove from oven and set aside.

Warm remaining 2 tablespoons olive oil in a large pot over medium heat. Add shallots, and sauté for 5 minutes or until golden. Add ¼ teaspoon salt and reduce heat to low; cover the pot and cook for 5 minutes or until softened. Remove lid, stir in garlic and thyme, and cook for another 2 to 3 minutes. Add carrots, beans, sun-dried tomatoes with their marinade, and reserved stock; bring to a boil over high heat. Cover pot, reduce heat to low, and simmer for 30 minutes. Add roasted mushrooms; continue cooking uncovered for another 30 minutes or until flavors have married and bourguignon tastes rich and flavorful.

Dissolve kuzu in remaining 2 tablespoons filtered water and slowly drizzle into simmering stew. Stir constantly until mixture thickens slightly and begins to simmer again. Season to taste and remove from heat. Sprinkle with parsley, and serve warm with Celery Root Mash (recipe follows).

CELERY ROOT MASH

This smooth mash is the perfect component for the rich juices of Heirloom Bean Bourguignon. Adding celery root, also called celeriac, to mashed potatoes lightens them up a bit and gives them a slightly aromatic flavor.

SERVES 6

2 large celery root (2½ pounds), peeled and cut into ¾-inch dice

5 large waxy potatoes (3 pounds), peeled and cut into 1½-inch dice

1 teaspoon sea salt, plus more to taste

3 tablespoons extra virgin olive oil

Freshly ground black pepper

Place celery root, potatoes, and salt in a large pot. Add enough water to cover vegetables, and bring to a boil over high heat. Cover pot, reduce heat to low, and simmer for 15 minutes or until potatoes and celery root are soft but not falling apart. Drain off all cooking liquid, and return celery root and potatoes to pot. Add olive oil and mash with a potato masher until completely smooth. Season to taste with salt and pepper, and serve warm.

desserts

It's no surprise to my family that I've spent a good deal of my career specializing in desserts. I grew up eating (and loving) mouth-watering gourmet sweets that my mother and her friends made. Whether it was a much-anticipated, multilayer birthday cake topped with strawberries from our garden or a simple chocolate nut slice, desserts were celebrated and enjoyed in my family. My introduction to making wholesome desserts was helping my mother peel and slice apples for our (almost) nightly crumble. A self-described sweet tooth, she claims that she planned dinner around dessert instead of the other way around. My sister and I often spent entire weekends pouring over her cookbooks and then hours in the kitchen assembling complicated, cream-filled cookies. Besides having plenty of fancy cake and dessert books, my mother also owned one of the first raw food cookbooks by Leslie Kenton. I was struck by the author's fresh-faced glow and found endless inspiration in the pages of colorful fruit and nut desserts.

It wasn't until I left home and moved to Sydney that I actually tasted a variety of vegan desserts and started experimenting with them myself. The desire to make things more healthful, yet still beautiful and delicious, has always been the driving force behind my creations. In the community where I was raised, everybody we knew cooked and baked everything from scratch, and since there wasn't a store-bought food product in sight, I never got a taste for commercially made desserts. It was a natural progression and a creative challenge to make the desserts I grew up eating without dairy or refined sugar, and it was how I found a place in professional kitchens.

Truth be told, I have always found vegan baking easier than baking with animal products; there is no fussy blind baking, no beating of room temperature butter and sugar for cakes, and no risk of custards breaking. You can also taste everything as you go and test fillings for the perfect consistency ahead of time. I hope you will be inspired by the sweet possibilities that await you in your own kitchen. Happy baking!

NOTES ON AGAR, ARROWROOT, AND KUZU

The secret to success in creating delectable vegan desserts is learning how to use agar and arrowroot or kuzu. Agar sets a dessert, and arrowroot or kuzu make it creamy; the perfect balance of the two results in a dreamy consistency that melts in your mouth. Once you understand this principle, you can achieve almost any result without the use of animal products. Read through the tips that follow to get the most out of your ingredients, whether you're following a recipe or experimenting on your own.

AGAR

Agar is a clear seaweed that dissolves in simmering liquid and sets like gelatin when cool. It is perfect for setting creamy custard fillings for tarts, thick buttercream-like frostings, kanten (a Japanese gelled fruit dessert), mousses, and delicate fruit glazes. You will find recipes for all of these on the following pages.

Agar can be found in flake, bar, or powder form. I choose flakes because they are widely available, easy to measure, and unlike some agar powder, they haven't been bleached. Agar is virtually tasteless, but if you use a lot of it in a delicately flavored dessert, its mild briny flavor can be too dominant. (See page 29 for nutritional information.)

When using agar for mousse, custard fillings, or fruit glazes, it's important to use the right amount: too little will result in a dessert that doesn't hold together; too much will create a rubbery, unpleasant texture. I highly recommend testing a small amount of any dessert you make before setting the whole batch, this gives you total control, and you can add more agar or more liquid to achieve the desired consistency. Frostings are less fussy as long as you have plenty of agar, which will enable you to achieve a thick, creamy consistency after setting and blending it. Even after more than twenty years of making vegan desserts, I still test the agar every time I make even the smallest changes to a recipe or when multiplying recipes.

DISSOLVING AGAR

For the best results, always use a heavy-bottomed pot with a tight-fitting lid when simmering agar. This will help prevent it from sticking (a greater concern with thicker liquids), and the tight-fitting lid will prevent evaporation, which will also affect the final consistency of your dessert. Agar dissolves fastest in thin liquids like fruit juice; the thicker the liquid, the longer it will take to dissolve. Thicker milks, like coconut milk from a can, will take the longest. I recommend dissolving agar in apple juice, apple cider, or nut or coconut milk. If your recipe calls for a juice that's high in acid content—like a citrus juice—always add it after you have dissolved and tested the agar mixture. Dissolving agar in any highly acid juice will prevent it from setting. Even the amount of citrus or oxalic acid (like in rhubarb) in a recipe will affect the consistency of the final product.

It is best to whisk the agar and liquid frequently as you bring it up to a boil; this helps prevent the thicker milks from sticking to the pot and keeps the mixture from boiling over. Once the mixture is boiling, cover the pot, reduce the heat to low, and simmer for between 5 and 15 minutes. Again, the amount of time varies, depending on the liquid and the amount of agar being dissolved.

Always check to see if the agar is completely dissolved before proceeding with the next step. Take a spoonful of the hot liquid and slowly pour it back into the pot; you will be able to see any flakes that have not dissolved on the spoon. They can be small, so look carefully. Re-cover the pot, and continue simmering until no flakes appear.

TESTING

Spoon a couple of tablespoons into a small cup, and place it in the coldest part of the fridge for 5 to 10 minutes or until cold. Cover the pot and remove it from the heat while you're waiting.

Once your sample is completely cold, touch the center and see how firm it is: for a custard filling, you want it to just stand up and hold its form when sliced with a knife; a mousse should melt in your mouth; and a glaze is best somewhere in between. If it needs to be firmer, add ½ to 1 teaspoon more agar and simmer it again. If it's too firm, add a little more liquid and test again. Tasting the sample is a great chance to see how your final dessert will taste.

NOTE: When making frosting, it's largely unnecessary to test a sample, since you want the mixture to set hard when it cools so it will blend into a thick, creamy frosting. In this case, a little too much agar won't harm the final result, but too little will result in a runny consistency after blending. So unless you're experimenting with a new base or have used less agar than the recipe calls for, there's no need to test. The same goes for kanten (pages 326 and 351), as they can be blended briefly in a food processor if the consistency isn't perfectly smooth after whisking.

ARROWROOT AND KUZU

Arrowroot and kuzu are natural, tasteless thickeners that are excellent for creating a smooth, creamy texture in custard fillings, sauces, and glazes. They are both healthy alternatives to cornstarch and can be used interchangeably, although you may find that you need less kuzu, as it tends to create more body than arrowroot. I used arrowroot in all the dessert recipes, as it's more readily available and considerably less expensive than kuzu, which is also used medicinally (see page 41).

When using arrowroot or kuzu, always dissolve them in a small amount of cool liquid first—usually a little more than the amount of the arrowroot or kuzu. You don't want to add too much liquid, as that will dilute the final texture of the dessert. Once it's dissolved, slowly drizzle it into simmering liquid, whisking constantly. When the mixture has returned to a simmer and thickened slightly, remove it from the heat, and continue as directed in the recipe. If you're experimenting, keep in mind that the liquid will thicken more as it cools, so you may not want to add the full amount of dissolved kuzu or arrowroot. Too much will result in a gluey consistency.

TARTS

*When deciding on tart recipes for this book, I quickly realized that I needed a
whole section dedicated to tart making in order to showcase the endless possibilities. Here, I have chosen my
favorites recipes, the ones I rely on when I want to impress a crowd or experiment with ingredients
I have on hand. Because what I make is undeniably dictated by the season, the tarts are divided into
two parts—spring/summer and fall/winter. I have also included a couple of my
favorite dessert toppings to accompany them.*

*To me, tarts are the perfect dessert, as you can make a crust out of any nuts and flours
you have around and make a filling from the best of the current produce—fresh berries and succulent fruits
in spring and summer, creamy sweet squash or tart cranberries in fall, and rich dark chocolate
or dried fruit in winter. Tarts are what I turn to when I'm looking for a light, sweet end to a
meal or a treat to serve with afternoon tea.*

*My intention is for you to be able to mix and match crusts and fillings, to ignite ideas and grow them
using these tips and recipes as a starting place. The crust recipes are based on a combination of ground oats; whole-
grain flours like spelt, brown rice, and barley; nuts; and/or dried coconut.
You will find a couple of gluten-free crusts and a nut-free one, too.*

*When swapping out crusts and fillings, keep in mind that you may have extra crust
and/or filling; make cookies with any remaining crust, and pour leftover
filling into ramekins to enjoy later.*

MAKING AND PRESSING GREAT CRUSTS EVERY TIME

After years spent creating my crusts by "feel" and hardly measuring a thing, I was inspired to
develop a method to teach my students how to make them from whatever ingredients they
have in the kitchen. Whether you're following a recipe, adapting one, or experimenting,
follow these steps to ensure your crust will be a success.

When using gluten-free flours, it's important to keep in mind that they act differently,
either absorbing much more moisture than regular flours, or not holding together as well.
When I am experimenting with a new gluten-free crust, I often make a flat crust (like the Date
Pistachio Praline Tart on page 313), because there is no risk of the sides not holding up. At first
I recommend basing your experiments on a crust that's already gluten-free, trading out one
gluten-free ingredient for another of your choosing. Note that when using sprouted flour in
crusts, you'll need to bake them for about 5 minutes longer, and they often need a little more
flour than ones made with regular whole grain flours.

1. THE DRY INGREDIENTS Choose one of the tart crust recipes to base your ingredient amounts on. Combine the (ground and/or chopped) nuts, oats, and flour(s) in the rough measurements of your chosen recipe. Add salt, using more or less of the suggested amount, or none at all. Stir in ground spices here if you're using any.

2. THE OIL You can use either extra virgin coconut oil (melted) or extra virgin olive oil. Both provide a delicious, buttery texture. Remember that the oil content of the nuts and/or coconut you're using will impact the amount of oil you need. Always start by drizzling in a few tablespoons of oil. Mix well; I find the best tool for this is a regular dinner fork—or your fingertips. The mixture should be damp and almost stay together when squeezed in your hand; it shouldn't be too wet, as you need "room" to add the maple syrup, which is what will make it stick together and give you the perfect amount of sweetness. If you have more flour and less ground nuts, then you may need to add a little more oil. If you added too much oil and the mixture is too wet, add a pinch or two more of flour, mix thoroughly, and continue adding flour until you have the correct consistency.

3. THE SWEETNESS I find maple syrup gives the best and most consistent results in achieving crisp, tender tart crusts. You can experiment with switching out some of it for coconut nectar or yakon syrup if you prefer. Rice syrup can make your crust dense, so use very little. Like the oil, it's best to add the maple syrup a bit at a time. Use a fork again to mix it, add a good splash of vanilla extract, then gather the dough in your hands to squeeze it together. (If you're using other extracts, add those now.) Test to see if you have the right amount of maple syrup by washing and drying your hands to get rid of any stickiness left from mixing, then squeeze a handful of dough in your palm. You want the crust to be moist and stick together but not stick to your hands. If the mixture is not holding together, add a little more syrup. Sometimes I add the smallest splash of water here to bring it together. If the mixture is too wet, it will sink while baking; set the pastry aside for 10 minutes to allow the flours and oats to absorb the moisture, then test again. If it's still too wet, add a tablespoon more of the flour, stir to combine, and test again. The beauty of these types of vegan crusts is that they don't become tough from overmixing. That said, it's not a good idea to knead or mix dough for long periods of time, as the oats will start absorbing moisture.

4. THE TASTE The flavor of your crust should be scrumptious. If it needs a little more sweetness or vanilla, add them now. Once you like the flavor and consistency, press the dough into your tart pan immediately; if it sits around, it will continue to absorb moisture and become difficult to press.

The pressed crust can always be covered and refrigerated raw and baked the following day, or it can be covered and frozen for up to three months before or after baking.

5. PRESSING THE CRUST I use two types of pans for crusts: fluted tart pans and springform cake pans. For the best results and lovely edges, oil your pan thoroughly. I find it better to oil fluted tart pans with olive oil, as coconut oil is solid when cold, and it can be difficult to remove the sides of the pan if you have chilled the tart. If you're removing the crust from the pan before filling and refrigerating, then coconut oil works fine.

With clean, dry hands, take about ⅓ cup of dough, roll into a 3- to 4-inch log between your palms and lay it against the sides of your pan (where the bottom meets the side). Use your thumbs to press the dough into the edges of the pan at a 45-degree angle. Don't worry about covering the sides or the bottom yet. Continue rolling logs and pressing it into the edges of the pan until you have made it all the way around. Now press the crust evenly up the sides of the pan using your thumbs, making sure there isn't any excess dough where the bottom meets the sides. For a fluted tart pan, scrape off the excess dough with your thumbs; for a springform pan, leave the edges rustic. With your fingertips press excess dough from the edges into the center to cover the bottom of the pan. Add more dough as needed, and use the palm of your hand to even out the surface. Continue pressing until the crust looks and feels even. I aim for my crusts to be between ⅛ and ¼ inch thick (unless it is a flat-bottomed crust, in which case it can be thicker). If you have extra dough, use it to make little thumbprint cookies.

6. BAKING THE CRUST Always prick the bottom of the crust several times with a fork before baking; this prevents it from puffing up in the oven and potentially cracking when you push it back down.

Some of the recipes here have partially baked crusts when the filling needs baking too. Partially baking a crust helps to seal it and prevent it from becoming soggy when baked with a wet filling.

When baking, the crust should smell heavenly and look golden, maybe browning slightly around the edges and in parts of the center when it is ready. It may still be soft to the touch, but it will firm up when cool if it has baked long enough. Don't be tempted to pull it out early like with a cookie, as you want it crisp and light, not chewy.

SPRING + SUMMER

STRAWBERRY VANILLA CUSTARD TART

The winning combination of fresh, fragrant strawberries over a vanilla bean–infused custard is truly irresistible and a sure way to please everyone. The custard is made from macadamia nut milk, which is simultaneously light and rich and manages to melt completely in your mouth. The thin, crisp, oaty crust encases both the custard and the strawberries perfectly.

NOTE: This tart crust is pressed pretty thin and should go about 1¼ inches up the sides of a springform pan. It doesn't contain nuts and can be used in many of these tart recipes if you need to avoid them. I have made it with extra virgin olive oil in place of coconut oil with excellent results.

**MAKES ONE 9-INCH TART
EQUIPMENT: 9-INCH SPRINGFORM PAN**

CRUST:

Olive oil for oiling the pan

¾ cup regular rolled oats

3 tablespoons barley flour

½ teaspoon aluminum-free baking powder

¼ teaspoon sea salt

¾ cup whole spelt flour

3 tablespoons plus 1 teaspoon melted extra virgin coconut oil

3 tablespoons maple syrup

1 teaspoon vanilla extract

CUSTARD FILLING:

¾ cup raw macadamia nuts, soaked 2 to 6 hours in 2 cups filtered water

2 cups plus 2 teaspoons filtered water, divided

1 vanilla bean

¼ cup brown rice syrup

3 tablespoons maple syrup

2 teaspoons agar flakes

Pinch sea salt

2 teaspoons arrowroot powder

STRAWBERRY TOPPING:

½ cup plus 1 teaspoon apple juice, divided

½ teaspoon agar flakes

½ teaspoon arrowroot

¾ pound strawberries (about 3 cups of medium strawberries), hulled, halved, and sliced

1 teaspoon maple sugar

1 teaspoon vanilla extract

MAKE THE CRUST:

Preheat oven to 350°F. Line bottom of springform pan with parchment paper (see sidebar on page 304) and lightly oil sides.

Add oats, barley flour, baking powder, and salt to a food processor; blend until oats are ground, about 30 seconds. Transfer to a medium bowl and stir in spelt flour, and salt. Drizzle in coconut oil, and mix with a fork or your fingertips until all flour is moistened. Add maple syrup and vanilla, and mix until evenly incorporated. Dough should be moist but not sticky. Wash and dry your hands, then press crust evenly into prepared pan to about a ⅛-inch thickness. Press crust 1¼ inches up sides of the pan, leaving the top edge uneven.

Prick the bottom of the crust with a fork several times, and bake for 16 to 18 minutes or until lightly brown and fragrant. Remove from oven and set aside while you make the filling.

MAKE THE CUSTARD FILLING:

Drain and rinse macadamia nuts; place in an upright blender with 2 cups water. Blend on highest speed until completely smooth, about 1 minute. Pour macadamia milk into a small heavy-bottomed pot. Split vanilla bean in half lengthwise and scrape out seeds with the tip of a small knife, then add seeds to pot along with whole bean. Add rice syrup, maple syrup, agar, and salt; place pot over high heat. Whisk to combine, and continue whisking frequently until mixture comes to a boil. Cover pot, reduce heat to low, and simmer for 15 minutes, whisking every 5 minutes. Check to see if agar has completely dissolved (see page 293). In a small bowl, dissolve arrowroot and remaining 2 teaspoons water; slowly drizzle it into simmering custard mixture. Continue whisking until custard has thickened slightly and returned to a simmer. Mixture should be the consistency of heavy cream. Remove from heat. Let cool, uncovered, for 10 minutes. Remove and compost vanilla bean. Whisk mixture again, then pour into baked crust. Once it has stopped steaming, place tart in the fridge and chill until completely set, about 1 hour.

MAKE THE STRAWBERRY TOPPING:

Place ½ cup apple juice and agar in a small heavy-bottomed pot. Bring to a boil over high heat, whisking constantly. Cover pot, reduce heat to low, and simmer for 5 minutes or until agar flakes are completely dissolved. In a small bowl, dissolve arrowroot in remaining apple juice and slowly whisk into simmering apple juice and agar mixture. Continue whisking until mixture has thickened slightly and returned to a simmer (you can increase heat to make this happen faster). Remove from heat and cover pot while you prepare strawberries.

Place strawberries in a bowl, add maple sugar and vanilla, and toss gently to combine. Pour warm agar juice mixture over berries and, working quickly, mix with a rubber spatula until all strawberries are coated. Spread over set custard filling, and return to the fridge for 30 minutes or until glaze has set. Keep tart refrigerated until ready to serve. Carefully release sides of pan before serving.

FRESH PEACH TART WITH WALNUT CRUST

This tart is straightforward and effortlessly scrumptious; a buttery, toasted walnut crust encasing a succulent peach filling held together by a simple glaze. It's just the right thing to end a summer meal. If you decide to top it with a dab of whipped cream, Cashew Cinnamon Cream (page 322), or Vanilla Bean Cream (page 321), then you're in for a real treat. Make this tart in summer only when the peaches are perfectly juicy, ripe, and at their best. If you don't have peaches, consider substituting ripe nectarines or sliced ripe pears. Either way, as long as the fruit is good eaten fresh, then you can't go wrong.

NOTE: This tart should only be served the day it's made, as the moisture from the peaches makes the crust soggy after a day in the fridge.

MAKES ONE 9-INCH TART
EQUIPMENT:
FLUTED 9-INCH TART PAN
WITH REMOVABLE BOTTOM

CRUST:

Olive oil for oiling the pan

1¼ cup toasted walnut halves (page 78)

¾ cup regular rolled oats

2 tablespoons brown rice flour

¼ teaspoon sea salt

¾ cup whole spelt flour

3 tablespoons extra virgin coconut oil

¼ cup maple syrup

1 teaspoon vanilla extract

FILLING:

1 cup plus 2 teaspoons apple juice, divided

1 teaspoon agar flakes

1 teaspoon arrowroot

4 ripe medium peaches (1½ pounds)

1 tablespoon maple sugar

½ teaspoon vanilla extract

MAKE THE CRUST:

Preheat oven to 350°F. Thoroughly oil tart pan and set aside.

Grind walnuts, oats, rice flour, and salt in a food processor until coarsely ground, about 20 seconds. Transfer to a bowl and stir in spelt flour. Drizzle in coconut oil; mix with a fork or your fingertips until all flour is moistened. Add maple syrup and vanilla, and mix until evenly incorporated. Dough should be moist but not sticky. Wash and dry your hands, then evenly press crust into prepared tart pan to about ¼-inch thickness. Trim any excess pastry from edge (you will be left with a small handful, enough to make a couple of cookies). Prick the bottom of the crust with a fork several times, and bake for 18 minutes or until deeply golden and fragrant. Remove from oven and set aside to cool.

MAKE THE FILLING:

Combine 1 cup apple juice and agar flakes in a small heavy-bottomed pot; bring to a boil over high heat, whisking frequently. Cover pot, reduce heat to low, and simmer for 5 minutes or until agar has completely dissolved (see page 293). In a small bowl, dissolve arrowroot in remaining 2 teaspoons apple juice, and slowly whisk into simmering apple juice and agar mixture. Continue whisking until mixture has thickened and returned to a simmer (you can increase heat to help this happen faster). Remove from heat; set aside uncovered while you prepare peaches or until mixture thickens slightly, but don't let it set. (If it does set, briefly return it to medium heat and stir until liquid again.)

Slice peaches into ¼- to ½-inch slices (you should have about 4 cups). Place in a bowl with maple sugar and vanilla, and toss gently to combine. Pour warm agar mixture over peaches; working quickly, use a rubber spatula to coat peaches completely. Immediately spoon into baked tart shell and use your hands to spread them out evenly, gently pressing into tart shell. Pour remaining juice-agar mixture over peaches (you may not need it all); tilt shell to distribute evenly. Place in the fridge for 30 minutes or until completely set. Serve cold topped with cream of your choice.

BLACKBERRY LEMON CREAM TARTLETS WITH TOASTED COCONUT CRUST

The lemon filling in these tartlets is delightfully creamy and light, with just the right amount of richness from the coconut and cashew milk base. The crisp and fragrant crust is also used for the Coconut Custard Tart (page 303) and is one of my favorite all-purpose crusts. If you have a little left over, use it to make thumbprint cookies. If blackberries are not in season, top these tartlets with raspberries or halved strawberries instead, or just eat them plain.

NOTE: The tiny pinch of turmeric in the filling gives it a lovely, lemony yellow hue. The color will deepen as the custard simmers, so don't be tempted to add too much.

MAKES 8 TARTLETS
EQUIPMENT: EIGHT 3¾-INCH TART PANS, PREFERABLY WITH REMOVABLE BOTTOMS

CRUST:

1½ cups dried, unsweetened, shredded coconut

¼ cup plus 2 tablespoons regular rolled oats

3 tablespoons brown rice flour

¼ teaspoon sea salt

1 cup whole spelt flour

¼ cup melted extra virgin coconut oil, plus more for oiling pans

¼ cup plus 2 tablespoons maple syrup

1 tablespoon vanilla extract

FILLING:

¾ cup raw cashews, soaked 2 to 6 hours in 2 cups filtered water

2¼ cups plain rice milk (see note)

¼ cup plus 2 tablespoons dried, unsweetened, shredded coconut

3½ teaspoons agar flakes

Pinch sea salt

¼ cup maple syrup (grade A or lightest color)

Tiny pinch turmeric

¼ cup fresh lemon juice

4 teaspoons lemon zest (from about 2 lemons), divided

TOPPING:

3 cups fresh blackberries

1 teaspoon maple sugar

½ teaspoon vanilla extract

MAKE THE CRUST:

Preheat oven to 300°F. Line a rimmed baking sheet with parchment paper, add coconut, and spread out evenly in a single layer. Place in oven and toast for 4 minutes; stir, and toast for another 2 to 3 minutes or until golden and fragrant. Remove from oven and set aside.

Raise oven temperature to 350°F. Thoroughly oil tartlet pans and set aside.

Grind oats, rice flour, salt, and ½ cup of the toasted coconut in a food processor until finely ground, about 30 seconds. Transfer to a bowl, and stir in spelt flour and remaining toasted coconut. Drizzle in coconut oil; mix with a fork or your fingertips until all flour is moistened. Add maple syrup and vanilla, and mix until evenly incorporated. Dough should be moist but not sticky. Wash and dry your hands, then press crust evenly into tartlet pans. Trim any excess dough from the edges. Prick each crust with a fork several times and place on a baking sheet. Bake for 16 to 18 minutes or until deeply golden and fragrant. Remove from oven and set aside to cool.

MAKE THE FILLING:

Line a medium strainer with a nut milk bag; clean, thin kitchen towel; or several layers of cheesecloth. Place over a medium heavy-bottomed pot, and set aside. Drain and rinse cashews, and add them to an upright blender, along with rice milk and shredded coconut. Blend on highest speed until smooth, about 1 minute. Pour through lined strainer into pot, gather up edges of nut milk bag or cloth, and gently squeeze out all liquid. Compost dry pulp that remains. Rinse blender and set aside.

Add agar, salt, maple syrup, and turmeric to the coconut-cashew milk mixture and whisk to combine. Bring to a boil over high heat, whisking every minute or so. Cover pot, reduce heat to low, and simmer for 15 minutes, whisking every 5 minutes. Check that agar has completely dissolved (see page 293); if not, re-cover and continue simmering until no flakes appear. Remove from heat and set aside, uncovered, for 10 minutes to cool slightly. Pour into rinsed blender; add lemon juice and blend for 20 seconds or until frothy. Add 3 teaspoons lemon zest and pulse to combine. Let mixture sit in blender for another 10 minutes to cool a little more. This step allows cream filling to thicken a bit more, which ensures tartlet crusts will remain crisp (thin, hot liquids seep into crusts and affect the texture).

Carefully remove tartlet crusts from pans and place on a baking sheet or flat tray that will fit in your fridge. Divide lemon filling between crusts, filling them all the way to the top. Sprinkle with remaining lemon zest. Once filling has stopped steaming, place in the fridge to set completely, about 30 minutes.

While tartlets set, gently combine blackberries, maple sugar, and vanilla in a medium bowl; set aside to macerate for 20 to 30 minutes or until ready to serve. Stir blackberries, then evenly distribute over tartlets, and serve.

NOTE: When using rice milk, be sure to purchase plain, not unsweetened—it has a bad aftertaste and lots of unnecessary additional ingredients. Plain rice milk isn't sweetened; it's made with rice, which tastes naturally sweet.

ROASTED FIG RASPBERRY TART WITH TOASTED ALMOND CRUST

This is a quick, fuss-free, easily adaptable dessert, perfect to serve at a summer dinner party. The toasted almond and salt-kissed crust, maple roasted figs, and fresh raspberries topped with organic whipped cream is an all-round hit. Most of the ingredients here can be found in a well-stocked pantry, so all you need to do is pick up some fruit or roast what you have on hand, and this tart comes together in a flash. When figs are not available, try making it with roasted pears (page 318), or roast summer fruits like nectarines, peaches, or apricots—they all go well with raspberries and taste great with the almond crust.

MAKES ONE 9-INCH TART
EQUIPMENT: 9-INCH SPRINGFORM PAN

CRUST:

3 tablespoons extra virgin olive oil, plus more for oiling the pan

⅔ cup toasted almonds (page 77), divided

¼ cup regular rolled oats

¼ teaspoon sea salt

⅔ cup whole spelt flour

3 tablespoons maple syrup

1 teaspoon vanilla extract

¼ teaspoon almond extract

FILLING:

1 pound fresh ripe figs, stemmed and cut in half

2 teaspoons extra virgin olive oil

2 tablespoons maple syrup, divided

¾ cup plus 1 tablespoon apple juice, divided

¾ teaspoon agar flakes

1 teaspoon arrowroot

½ teaspoon vanilla extract

2 cups fresh raspberries

MAKE THE CRUST:

Preheat oven to 350°F. Line the bottom of springform pan with parchment paper (see sidebar below), and lightly oil the sides.

Grind ⅓ cup almonds, oats, and salt in a food processor until coarsely ground, about 20 seconds. Transfer to a bowl and stir in spelt flour. Roughly hand-chop remaining almonds, add to bowl, and mix well. Drizzle in olive oil, and mix with a fork or your fingertips until all flour is moistened. Add maple syrup, vanilla, and almond extract; mix until evenly incorporated. Dough should be moist but not sticky. Wash and dry your hands, then press crust evenly into prepared pan. Press crust only ½ inch up sides, leaving top edge uneven; you may end up having a little dough left over, which you can make into a cookie. Prick bottom of crust several times with a fork, and bake for 18 minutes or until golden brown and fragrant. Remove from oven and set aside to cool.

MAKE THE FILLING:

Raise oven temperature to 400°F. Line a rimmed baking sheet with parchment paper. Add figs, and drizzle with olive oil and 1 tablespoon maple syrup; and toss gently to coat. Spread figs out evenly over tray and arrange cut-side up; roast for 25 minutes or until they begin to caramelize and soften. Remove from oven and set aside to cool.

Combine ¾ cup apple juice and agar flakes in a small heavy-bottomed pot, and bring to a boil over high heat. Whisk, cover pot, reduce heat to low, and simmer for 5 minutes or until agar has completely dissolved (see page 293). In a small bowl, dissolve arrowroot in remaining tablespoon apple juice and slowly drizzle into hot agar mixture, whisking constantly until mixture returns to a simmer and has thickened slightly. Remove from heat and whisk in remaining tablespoon maple syrup and vanilla. Set aside, uncovered, for about 5 minutes or until mixture has thickened a little but not begun to set.

Place roasted figs in a bowl and pour in warm agar mixture. Stir gently with a rubber spatula or with your hands to combine. Add raspberries, and toss gently until evenly distributed. Working quickly, transfer mixture to baked tart shell and carefully spread out filling in an even layer. Refrigerate for 20 to 30 minutes or until filling is completely set. Serve topped with cream of your choice.

LINING A SPRINGFORM PAN WITH PARCHMENT PAPER

Open the springform pan and place the base of the pan upside down on the counter. Lay a square piece of parchment paper over the base—the parchment should be at least an inch or two larger than the base on all sides. Now place the sides of the pan on the base and, keeping the paper flat against the base, slightly lift the base to fit in the groove of the pan. Secure sides, flip pan over and fold paper into the center. It's now ready to use. Fitting the base of the pan this way ensures an even edge with crusts and cakes, eliminates the need to oil the base before adding a parchment circle, and also prevents the paper from lifting when serving a slice of tart. If your pan has a "leak proof" seal you won't be able to fit parchment this way; just lightly oil the base and cut a circle to fit inside the pan.

COCONUT CUSTARD TART WITH TOASTED COCONUT CRUST

This tart is one of my signature desserts—I have made hundreds of variations and topped them with everything from berries and juicy nectarines in summer to roasted plums (page 329) and even caramel and chocolate sauces in the cooler months. With a toasted coconut crust and a light, silky custard filling, this tart is nothing short of sublime. The homemade coconut milk (from dried coconut) is the secret to creating the delicate texture and refreshing flavor of the custard—enriched with almonds and flecked with vanilla beans, you'll be amazed how good it tastes unadorned.

NOTE: Since organic blanched almonds are hard to come by, I soak whole raw almonds and then slip off their skins. If you have blanched almonds, feel free to use them instead; just soak them for a couple of hours to soften them up.

Don't be tempted to use canned coconut milk, as it will result in a heavy filling. If you have an upright blender that has an 8-cup capacity, then you can make coconut milk in one batch. It can be made up to two days in advance.

This tart depends on the right amount of agar for it to stand up when sliced. Since natural products like agar vary, I always test the filling (see page 293) to ensure a perfect consistency.

MAKES ONE TALL 9-INCH TART
EQUIPMENT: 9-INCH SPRINGFORM PAN

CRUST:

Toasted coconut crust (page 303)

Olive oil for oiling the pan

CUSTARD FILLING:

1 cup whole raw almonds, soaked
    8 to 24 hours in 2 cups filtered water

5½ cups plus 1 tablespoon filtered water,
    divided

3 cups dried, unsweetened,
    shredded coconut, divided

1 vanilla bean

4½ teaspoons agar flakes

¼ cup plus 1 tablespoon maple syrup
    (grade A or lightest color)

pinch of sea salt

2 teaspoons arrowroot

1 tablespoon vanilla extract

Fresh berries or seasonal fruit, to serve

MAKE THE CRUST:

Preheat oven to 350°F. Line the bottom of a springform pan with parchment paper (see page 304) and lightly oil the sides. Press crust evenly into bottom and all the way up sides of oiled pan, making sure there is no excess dough around the edges. Leave top edges uneven. (This looks nice and rustic, and it also makes it easier to remove the sides when the crust stays below the curve of the pan edge.) Prick bottom of crust with a fork several times, and bake for 18 to 20 minutes or until deeply golden and fragrant. Remove from oven and set aside to cool while you make filling.

MAKE THE FILLING:

Line a large strainer with a nut milk bag; clean, thin kitchen towel; or several layers of cheesecloth. Place over a large, heavy-bottomed pot and set aside.

Slip the skins off the almonds, rinse, and drain. Add half the almonds to an upright blender. Add 3 cups water and 1½ cups coconut and blend on high speed for 1 to 2 minutes or until smooth. Pour into lined strainer and repeat with 1½ cups water and remaining almonds and coconut.

Gather edges of bag or excess cloth and gently squeeze out liquid; you should be left with just under 6 cups milk. Compost dry pulp that remains. Split vanilla bean and scrape out seeds with the tip of a small knife, then add them and the pod to coconut milk, along with agar, maple syrup, and salt. Bring to a boil over high heat, whisking frequently. Cover pot, reduce heat to low, and simmer for 15 minutes or until agar has dissolved completely (see page 293). In a small bowl, dissolve arrowroot in remaining water, and slowly whisk into simmering coconut milk. Continue whisking until mixture has thickened slightly and returned to a simmer. Remove from heat, compost vanilla bean pod, and whisk in vanilla extract. Set aside uncovered to cool slightly for 10 minutes, then whisk again. Pour into prebaked crust.

Once filling has stopped steaming, place in the fridge and chill for about 3 hours or until completely cold and set. Serve cold, topped with fresh berries or seasonal fruit.

FALL + WINTER

PUMPKIN TARTLETS WITH CASHEW GINGER CRUST

These tartlets are perfect for sharing and make a lovely addition to a holiday dessert selection. They taste great plain but are really special and look lovely and festive topped with a dab of organic whipped cream—or for a vegan version, Vanilla Bean Cream (page 321) Using homemade pumpkin purée from sweet and dense-fleshed winter squash is key here for flavor and texture, so skip the canned version and fill your kitchen with the warm aroma of steaming squash.

NOTE: If you don't have mini tartlet pans you can use a 9-inch tart pan with a removable bottom. You will have leftover crust that can be made into little cookies or flattened and cut into shapes that can decorate the top of the baked tart.

MAKES 6 TARTLETS
EQUIPMENT: SIX 4¾-INCH TARTLET PANS WITH REMOVABLE BOTTOMS

FILLING:

½ large kabocha squash, peeled, seeded, and cut in ½-inch dice (about 4½ cups)

1 cup plus 2 tablespoons unsweetened full-fat coconut milk

½ cup plus 1 tablespoon maple syrup

2 teaspoons vanilla extract

1 teaspoon ground cinnamon

1 tablespoon arrowroot

Pinch sea salt

CRUST:

Olive oil to oil pans

1¼ cups raw cashews

½ cup plus 2 tablespoons regular rolled oats

½ teaspoon sea salt

¾ cup plus 1 tablespoon whole spelt flour

¼ cup brown rice flour

1 tablespoon ground ginger

¼ cup plus 1 tablespoon extra virgin olive oil or melted extra virgin coconut oil

¼ cup plus 2 tablespoons maple syrup

1 teaspoon vanilla extract

MAKE THE FILLING:

Place squash in a steamer, and cook for 10 to 12 minutes or until soft. Place in a bowl and mash well. Measure out 2¼ cups mash (it should be pretty close); set aside. Add coconut milk, maple syrup, vanilla, cinnamon, arrowroot, and salt to an upright blender and blend until evenly combined. Add mashed squash and blend until completely smooth. If squash was on the drier side, you may need to help it blend by scraping down sides of blender with a rubber spatula. Set mixture aside while you make the crust.

MAKE THE CRUST:

Preheat oven to 350°F. Thoroughly oil your tartlet pans and set aside. Place cashews, oats, and salt in a food processor; blend until coarsely ground, about 30 seconds. Transfer to a bowl and add spelt flour, brown rice flour, and ground ginger; mix to combine. Drizzle in oil, and mix with a fork or your fingers until all the flour is moistened. Add maple syrup and vanilla, and mix again. Let sit for 5 minutes; dough should be moist but not sticky. If it's still too sticky to work with, let it sit another 5 minutes. Wash and dry your hands, then press pastry thinly and evenly into oiled tartlet pans. Prick bottoms of crust with a fork several times, place on a baking sheet and bake for 15 minutes or until crust is set but not done. Remove from oven and divide filling between tartlets. Fill them all the way to the top, as filling will sink when cool.

Place tartlets in oven, and bake for 25 minutes or until center is set. Remove from oven and set aside to cool. Once cool, place in the fridge to chill completely, about 1 hour. Remove tartlets from their pans and serve cool with whipped cream on the side.

DATE PISTACHIO PRALINE TART

This is one of my favorite tarts—not only does it look stunning covered with the maple-coated pistachios, but I'm also crazy about the tropical caramely flavor that the combination of coconut sugar, vanilla beans, and dates provides. It can be made with or without butter. Both versions are great; however, if you're not vegan and you're looking for something a wee bit more decadent, then I say go with the butter. It's also particularly good topped with Greek yogurt, but you won't be disappointed if you eat it plain.

MAKES ONE 9-INCH TART
EQUIPMENT: ONE 9-INCH SPRINGFORM PAN

CRUST:

½ cup toasted almonds (page 77)

1 cup dried, unsweetened, shredded coconut

¼ cup coconut flour

¼ cup plus 2 tablespoons coconut palm sugar, packed

½ cup regular rolled oats

¼ teaspoon sea salt

¼ cup brown rice flour

5 tablespoons melted extra virgin coconut oil, plus more for oiling pan

3 tablespoons maple syrup

1 tablespoon vanilla extract

FILLING:

1½ cups pitted deglet noor dates

1 cup filtered water

5 cardamom pods

Pinch sea salt

2 3-inch strips orange zest

1 vanilla bean

2 tablespoons mirin or white dessert wine

2 tablespoons unsweetened raspberry jam (see the Resources section)

1 teaspoon vanilla extract

2 tablespoons unsalted or salted butter, optional

PRALINE TOPPING:

4 teaspoons maple sugar

4 teaspoons pure maple syrup

Pinch sea salt

½ teaspoon vanilla extract

1 cup raw pistachios, roughly chopped

MAKE THE CRUST:
Preheat oven to 350°F. Line bottom of springform pan with parchment paper (see page 304) and lightly oil the sides.

Add almonds, coconut, coconut flour, palm sugar, oats, and salt to a food processor and grind until fine, about 45 seconds. Transfer to a medium mixing bowl, and mix in rice flour. Drizzle in coconut oil, and use a fork or your fingertips to mix until all flour is moistened. Add maple syrup and vanilla; mix again. Dough should be moist but not sticky. Wash and dry your hands, and press crust evenly into bottom of prepared pan—do not press it up sides. Bake for 18 minutes or until set but not cooked through. Remove from oven and set aside. Leave oven on.

MAKE THE FILLING:
Place dates, water, cardamom pods, salt, and orange zest in a small pot. Split vanilla bean in half lengthwise, scrape out seeds with the tip of a small knife, and add to pot along with pod. Bring to a boil over medium-high heat, stirring frequently until mixture simmers. Cover pot, reduce heat to low, and simmer for 20 minutes or until dates are completely soft. Remove lid, stir in mirin or dessert wine, and continue cooking uncovered for 10 minutes or until all liquid has evaporated and dates are pasty. Remove from heat; stir in raspberry jam, vanilla extract, and butter (if using). Remove and compost cardamom pods, orange zest, and vanilla bean pod. Spread mixture over prebaked crust and set aside.

MAKE THE TOPPING:
Place maple sugar, maple syrup, salt, and vanilla in a medium bowl, and stir until smooth. Add pistachios and toss to coat. Sprinkle evenly over date layer, and bake for 20 minutes or until nuts are slightly golden and shiny. Remove from oven and allow to cool at least 15 minutes before running a knife around edge of pan, removing sides and cooling completely.

CRANBERRY ALMOND TART

This recipe is based on a tart my dear friend and former business partner, Rosada Hayes, used to make whenever we were due for a get-together. She was inspired by the English Bakewell tart and usually made hers with an apple or apricot filling. I have many treasured memories of sitting in her kitchen in London, enjoying her delicious cakes and tarts with bottomless pots of Earl Grey tea.

Here, the deep red color and tart, tangy flavor of cranberries cooked in orange juice pairs beautifully with the almond topping.

NOTE: If cranberries aren't available, try using blueberries, blackberries, raspberries, or a combination. Since these berries create enough juice on their own, leave out the orange juice and start with just 2 tablespoons maple syrup, increasing to taste, then thicken with arrowroot as in the recipe.

Zest the orange for the topping before juicing it for the filling.

MAKES ONE 9-INCH TART
EQUIPMENT:
9-INCH FLUTED TART PAN WITH REMOVABLE BOTTOM

CRUST:

¼ cup regular rolled oats

¼ cup dried, unsweetened, shredded coconut

¼ cup whole raw almonds

2 tablespoons brown rice flour

¼ teaspoon sea salt

¾ cup plus 2 tablespoons whole spelt flour

3 tablespoons extra virgin olive oil, plus more for oiling the pan

3 tablespoons maple syrup

1 teaspoon vanilla extract

FILLING:

2 teaspoons arrowroot

4 tablespoons fresh orange juice, divided

3 cups fresh or frozen cranberries, divided

¼ cup plus 2 tablespoons maple syrup

⅛ teaspoon cinnamon

TOPPING:

2½ cups almond meal

1 teaspoon aluminum-free baking powder

3 tablespoons extra virgin olive oil

¼ cup maple syrup

Zest of 1 orange

Zest of 1 lemon

⅛ teaspoon sea salt

1 teaspoon vanilla extract

½ teaspoon almond extract

3 tablespoons sliced almonds

MAKE THE CRUST:

Preheat oven to 350°F. Thoroughly oil tart pan and set aside.

Combine oats, coconut, almonds, rice flour, and salt in a food processor, and blend until finely ground, about 45 seconds. Transfer to a bowl and stir in spelt flour. Drizzle in olive oil; mix with a fork or your fingertips until all flour is moistened. Add maple syrup and vanilla, and mix again. Dough should be moist but not sticky. Wash and dry your hands, and press crust evenly into tart pan. Trim any excess dough from edges. Prick bottom of crust with a fork several times, and bake for 15 minutes; crust should be set but not done. Remove from oven and set aside. Leave oven on.

MAKE THE FILLING:

Place arrowroot in a small bowl and add 1 tablespoon orange juice; stir to combine and set aside. In a small pot, combine 2½ cups cranberries, remaining orange juice, maple syrup, and cinnamon. Bring to a boil over high heat, stirring frequently. Cover pot, reduce heat to low, and simmer for 5 minutes or until the cranberries are soft. Remove lid, stir arrowroot mixture again, and slowly drizzle into simmering cranberries, stirring constantly until mixture has thickened and returned to a simmer. Remove from heat and spread into prebaked tart shell.

MAKE THE TOPPING:

Combine almond meal and baking powder in a medium mixing bowl, breaking up any lumps of almond meal with your fingertips or a whisk. In another bowl, combine olive oil, maple syrup, orange zest, lemon zest, salt, and vanilla and almond extracts; whisk until emulsified. Pour into almond meal mixture and stir with a rubber spatula until completely combined—mixture will be quite wet. Scoop spoonfuls of mixture over cranberry filling, and use damp fingers to spread topping out a little, leaving it rustic with some filling showing in parts to allow cranberries to bubble up. Lightly press remaining ½ cup cranberries into topping and sprinkle with sliced almonds. Bake for 25 minutes or until puffed and golden. Allow tart to cool completely before removing from pan and serving.

ROASTED PEAR TARTLETS WITH PEAR CREAM FILLING

With their unmistakable taste, texture, and beauty, these tartlets are a celebration of pears prepared in my two favorite ways: roasted with maple syrup and blended to make a luscious cream filling. The pear cream is so mouth-wateringly good that you may be inspired to serve it in a parfait glass topped with berries and sprinkled with chopped toasted nuts. One of my favorite appetizers to serve in the fall is a sourdough raisin-walnut crostini spread with soft goat cheese topped with these maple-roasted pears.

Made with almonds, coconut, and brown rice flour, these gluten-free tartlet shells might just be the lightest pastry I have ever made. They can be baked ahead of time and stored refrigerated in airtight containers for up to three days. The pear cream can also be made up to three days ahead of time. Once filled, the tartlets can be stored in the fridge for up to 3 hours; after that the moisture from the cream will make the crust soggy.

NOTE: These crisp and delicate tartlet crusts can be a little difficult to remove from their pans, even if they have removable bottoms. For best results line the whole tartlet pan with an oiled parchment circle.

MAKES 8 TARTLETS

EQUIPMENT: EIGHT 3¾-INCH TARTLET PANS WITH REMOVABLE BOTTOMS

FILLING:

¾ cup cashews, soaked 2 to 6 hours in 2 cups filtered water

1 cup plus 1 tablespoon pear nectar, divided

¼ cup agar flakes

3 ripe Anjou or Bartlet pears (1½ pounds)

1 tablespoon arrowroot powder

1 tablespoon maple syrup

1 teaspoon vanilla extract

CRUST:

1 cup regular rolled oats

1 cup almond meal

¼ cup brown rice flour

¼ cup coconut flour

½ teaspoon sea salt

2 tablespoons extra virgin olive oil, plus more for oiling pans

2 tablespoons plus 2 teaspoons melted extra virgin coconut oil

¼ cup plus 2 tablespoons maple syrup

2 teaspoons vanilla extract

ROASTED PEARS:

3 firm ripe Anjou or Bartlet pears (1½ pounds)

1 tablespoon extra virgin olive oil

2 tablespoons maple syrup

MAKE THE FILLING:

Rinse and drain cashews, and set aside.

Whisk 1 cup pear nectar with agar flakes in a medium heavy-bottomed pot, and bring to a boil over high heat. Cover pot, reduce heat to low, and simmer for 10 minutes or until all agar is dissolved (page 293). While agar dissolves, peel, core, and cut pears into a ½-inch dice. You should have 3¼ cups diced pears. Add pears to pot, and raise heat to medium-high to bring mixture up to a simmer, stirring frequently. Cover pot, reduce heat to low, and cook for 5 minutes or until pears are soft. In a small bowl, dissolve arrowroot in remaining tablespoon pear nectar; drizzle slowly into simmering agar mixture, stirring constantly until mixture has thickened slightly and returned to a simmer. Remove from heat, and place in an upright blender along with drained cashews, maple syrup, and vanilla. Because mixture is hot, it will splutter when blending, so place a towel over blender lid and hold it down firmly. Start with blender on lowest setting (if you have a variable speed) and carefully increase speed, blending until completely smooth. Pour into a wide, shallow bowl or rimmed baking dish. Once mixture has stopped steaming, place in the fridge to cool and set, about 1 hour. Whisk thoroughly; mixture should be thick and smooth. Place in a container and refrigerate up to three days until ready to use.

MAKE THE CRUST:

Combine oats, almond meal, brown rice flour, coconut flour, and sea salt in a food processor and blend until finely ground, about 45 seconds. Transfer to a bowl, drizzle in olive and coconut oils, and mix to combine. Add maple syrup and vanilla, and mix again. The mixture will be wet; set aside for 20 minutes. Dough should now be moist but not sticky. If it's still sticky, set aside for another 5 to 10 minutes.

Preheat oven to 350°F. Thoroughly oil tartlet pans (or for best results line them with oiled parchment circles) and set aside. Evenly press about 3 tablespoons dough into each pan. Prick bottom of crusts with a fork several times, place on a baking sheet, and bake for 8 minutes, rotate trays, and bake another 8 minutes or until golden and lightly brown in parts. Remove from oven and set aside to cool completely. Leave oven on.

ROAST THE PEARS:

Increase oven temperature to 400°F. Line a rimmed baking sheet with parchment paper and set aside.

Peel pears, cut into quarters, core, and cut each quarter into 3 long slices. Place pears on baking sheet, drizzle with olive oil and maple syrup, toss gently to coat, and spread them out in a single layer. Roast for 25 to 30 minutes or until browning. Remove from oven and set aside.

Once cool enough to handle, remove from parchment paper and place in a bowl until ready to serve. If they're left on parchment, the maple syrup hardens and they stick.

ASSEMBLE THE TARTLETS:

Carefully remove cooled tartlet shells from pans. Divide pear cream filling between tartlets, and top each tart with a few slices of roasted pear. Serve immediately or keep in the fridge for up to three hours.

DARK CHOCOLATE TRUFFLE TART WITH BRAZIL NUT CRUST

There are so many things I love about this tart: the enchanting flavor combination of dark chocolate, tangy red berries, toasted nuts, and a touch of salt; the speed and ease with which it comes together; and the enthusiastic response it gets each and every time I serve it.

For a truly deluxe treat, try sprinkling the top with edible gold dust. When raspberries are in season, scatter a generous handful over each portion. This tart tastes best when served chilled and keeps well in the fridge for a couple of days.

NOTE: I find this tart tastes great (and comes together incredibly fast) made with plain Edensoy soy milk, but it also works well with strained almond milk (page 74).

MAKES ONE 9-INCH TART
EQUIPMENT: ONE 9-INCH
FLUTED TART PAN WITH
REMOVABLE BOTTOM

CRUST:

¾ cup raw Brazil nuts

Olive oil for oiling tart pan

¼ cup regular rolled oats

¼ cup dried, unsweetened, shredded coconut

¼ teaspoon sea salt

½ cup plus 2 tablespoons whole spelt flour

2 tablespoons plus 1 teaspoon melted extra virgin coconut oil

3 tablespoons maple syrup

1 teaspoon vanilla extract

FILLING:

½ cup unsweetened raspberry jam

1 cup plain soy milk

Pinch sea salt

9 ounces (70 percent) dark chocolate, roughly chopped

2 teaspoons vanilla extract

Cocoa powder or edible gold dust, to garnish

MAKE THE CRUST:

Preheat oven to 300°F. Line a rimmed baking sheet with parchment paper and spread out Brazil nuts in a single layer. Toast for 8 minutes or until fragrant. Remove from oven and set aside to cool.

Increase oven temperature to 350°F. Thoroughly oil tart pan with olive oil and set aside.

Combine Brazil nuts, oats, coconut, and salt in a food processor, and blend until coarsely ground, about 20 seconds. Transfer to a medium mixing bowl, and stir in spelt flour. Drizzle in coconut oil, and mix with a fork or your fingertips until all flour is moistened. Add maple syrup and vanilla, and mix again. Dough should be moist but not sticky. Wash and dry your hands, and press crust thinly and evenly into tart pan. Prick bottom of crust with a fork several times, and bake for 20 minutes or until fragrant and lightly brown. Remove from oven and set aside.

MAKE THE FILLING:

Warm jam in a small pot over medium heat. Stir until melted and beginning to bubble, about 1 minute. Pour into baked tart shell and spread evenly over bottom. Set aside to cool.

Place soy milk and a pinch of salt in a small pot, and bring to a boil over medium-high heat, stirring with a whisk to prevent sticking. As soon as milk begins to boil, remove from heat. Immediately add chocolate, cover pot, and let sit for 2 minutes. Remove lid and whisk vigorously until chocolate is melted and looks smooth and shiny. Stir in vanilla, and pour into tart shell. Place tart in the refrigerator for at least 1 hour to set and chill thoroughly. Remove from pan and dust tart with cocoa powder or edible gold dust.

To slice, warm a sharp knife in very hot water and dry thoroughly before cutting into tart. Serve cold.

VANILLA BEAN CREAM

This cream is a great vegan alternative to whipped cream. The flecks of vanilla bean and the creamy color make it a pretty addition to desserts. It's especially tasty served with the fruit-filled tarts in this section or layered with Strawberry Rose Kanten (page 326). It also pairs well with the roasted plums on page 329 and can serve as the base for a parfait when layered with fresh, juicy summer fruits and berries in glasses and topped with a sprinkle of toasted nuts.

NOTE: When using rice milk, be sure to purchase plain, not unsweetened—it has a bad aftertaste and lots of unnecessary additional ingredients. Plain rice milk isn't sweetened; it's made with rice, which tastes naturally sweet.

MAKES 3 CUPS; SERVES 8 TO 10 AS A TOPPING

1 cup whole raw almonds, soaked 8 to 12 hours in 2 cups filtered water

3 cups plain rice milk

1 cup dried, unsweetened, shredded coconut

1 vanilla bean

3 tablespoons agar flakes

3 tablespoons maple syrup (grade A or lightest color)

Pinch sea salt

1 teaspoon arrowroot

1 tablespoon filtered water

1 tablespoon vanilla extract

Line a medium strainer with a nut milk bag; a clean, thin kitchen towel; or several layers of cheesecloth. Place over a medium heavy-bottomed pot and set aside.

Slip the skins off the almonds, rinse and drain, and place them in an upright blender. Add rice milk and coconut, and blend until completely smooth, about 1 minute. Pour through lined strainer into pot; gather edges of bag or excess cloth, and gently squeeze out all liquid. Compost dry pulp that remains.

Split vanilla bean lengthwise and scrape out seeds using tip of a small knife. Add seeds and pod to pot with rice milk mixture. Whisk in agar, maple syrup, and salt; bring to a boil over high heat, whisking frequently. Cover pot, reduce heat to low, and simmer for 15 minutes or until agar is dissolved (see page 293).

In a small bowl, dissolve arrowroot in water. Slowly whisk into simmering rice milk mixture; continue whisking until mixture thickens slightly and returns to a simmer. Remove from heat, remove and compost vanilla pod, and pour cream into a wide shallow bowl or a rimmed baking dish. Once mixture has stopped steaming, place in the refrigerator to set, about 1½ hours. It's important that mixture is completely cold and set firm; otherwise, cream will not end up with a perfectly thick texture after blending.

Spoon set cream into a food processor, add vanilla extract, and blend until silky smooth (this will take a few minutes), scraping down sides as needed. Transfer to a bowl or storage container, and refrigerate for at least 20 minutes or until ready to serve. Stored in an airtight container, the cream will last up to four days.

CASHEW CINNAMON CREAM

This is a luscious vegan dessert cream that's an absolute breeze to make. Its subtly sweet flavor and rich creamy texture is the perfect way to dress up the simplest desserts. Try spooning it over berry crisps, poached pears, or chilled and layered in a glass with a fruit compote. I love it as a topping for the Fresh Peach Tart (page 300) or the Strawberry Rose or Pomegranate Kanten (pages 326 and 351). In a pinch, you can skip the cashew-soaking step, and provided you have a good blender, you'll still get a supersmooth result. This cream can be served as soon as it's made, but the flavor and texture get even better after a day in the fridge.

MAKES ABOUT 1½ CUPS

1 cup raw cashews, soaked for 2 to 6 hours in
    2 cups filtered water

¼ cup brown rice syrup

2 teaspoons vanilla extract

¼ teaspoon cinnamon

Pinch sea salt

2 tablespoons filtered water

¼ cup fresh orange juice

Drain and rinse cashews. Place all ingredients in an upright blender, and blend until completely smooth, scraping sides as necessary. Pour into a jar and refrigerate until ready to use. Cream will thicken slightly after it is chilled, so you may need to thin it out with extra water or orange juice to get desired consistency. The cream will keep for up to five days in the fridge.

SWEET TREATS FOR EVERY OCCASION

*This is my little box of treasured collectables—recipes that I pull out
when I'm looking for the perfect sweet treat to use as a starting point for the many adaptations and
experiments that happen in my kitchen. In this section, you'll find everything from my
reliable layer cake with chocolate ganache, which is perfect for birthday celebrations, to dinner-party desserts
like Coconut Vanilla Bean Ice Cream with Roasted Plums and Maple Coconut Crunch, plus
bars, cakes, and cookies to serve with tea. For the times when you're cleaning up your diet and restricting
sweeteners, or coming off of a formal cleanse but still want to make a dessert everyone
(including children) can enjoy, there are kantens—delicious and refreshing, sweetened with juice alone.
The golden amaranth bar with yakon syrup—a natural sweetener that's classified as a superfood—
makes the perfect high-protein snack. Many of these treats can be prepared ahead of time and savored
by everyone who passes through your kitchen. Whatever the occasion, I hope you
find inspiration and delight in these pages.*

STRAWBERRY ROSE KANTEN

Kanten is a delightfully light, simple, and refreshing dessert that also makes a wonderful afternoon pick-me-up in hot weather. While I worked at Angelica Kitchen in New York City, I experimented with lots of different flavored kantens, many of which I infused with herbs and flowers from our local farmers. Here, the dried roses infuse the kanten with a delicate floral flavor. When made in peak strawberry season, you won't need to add any sweetener—kanten is the perfect dessert if you're cutting out sugar, as the fruit alone is usually sweet enough. For something a little richer, try layering it in a glass with the Cashew Cinnamon Cream (page 322).

NOTE: Be sure to seek out unsprayed roses. You'll also find them used in the Rhubarb Rose Infusion (page 221).

SERVES 4

1¾ cups apple juice, divided

1¼ pounds strawberries (about 5 cups medium strawberries), hulled and halved, plus more to garnish

2 teaspoons mild raw honey, optional

¼ cup agar flakes

¼ cup dried organic rosebuds (about 30)

Place a fine mesh strainer over a medium bowl and set aside. Add ¾ cup apple juice and strawberries to an upright blender, and blend until completely smooth. Taste mixture for sweetness; if needed, add honey and blend again. Strain strawberry juice through strainer into a bowl and set aside; you should have 2¾ cups.

Combine remaining 1 cup apple juice and agar flakes in a small, heavy-bottomed pot and bring to a boil over high heat, whisking frequently. Cover pot, reduce heat to low, and simmer for 10 minutes or until all agar has dissolved (page 293). Add rosebuds, re-cover pot, and remove from heat. Set aside to steep for 10 minutes, then strain into bowl with strawberry juice, pressing the rosebuds to extract as much liquid as possible; and compost the rosebuds. Immediately whisk until combined. Place in the fridge for about an hour or until completely chilled and set. Remove from fridge, and whisk thoroughly until smooth. If kanten isn't as smooth as you would like, place it in a food processor and pulse briefly until smooth. Do not overblend, as it will become too runny.

Store in a jar in the fridge until ready to serve. Spoon into glasses or bowls and garnish with strawberries. Keep any leftover kanten in the fridge for up to a week.

Kanten is a Japanese dessert made from agar—a virtually tasteless seaweed that's dissolved in simmering juice and sets when cool. There are two ways you can serve kanten: one is set like Jello, and the other is smooth like a fruit mousse. Here, I serve it like a fruit mousse, but either way, it is light and refreshing and a great way to enjoy any seasonal fruit.

COCONUT VANILLA BEAN ICE CREAM
WITH ROASTED PLUMS
AND MAPLE COCONUT CRUNCH

Warm, tangy plums bursting with juice and rich, vanilla bean–flecked ice cream come together here to create a truly sensational dessert. It's the ideal thing to serve on a sultry, summer evening when plums are at their best, and only ice cream will hit the spot. Top with the golden maple coconut crunch and you'll have everybody at your table swooning.

NOTE: If you have a Vitamix or powerful upright blender, you won't need to strain the coconut-cashew mixture.

COCONUT VANILLA BEAN ICE CREAM
EQUIPMENT: ICE CREAM MAKER
SERVES 4 TO 6

¾ cup cashews, soaked 2 to 6 hours in 2 cups filtered water

2 13.5–fluid ounce cans unsweetened, full-fat coconut milk, divided

1 vanilla bean

Pinch sea salt

4 tablespoons mild raw honey

1 tablespoon vanilla extract

Line a medium strainer with a nut milk bag; clean, thin kitchen towel; or several layers of cheesecloth. Place over a medium-size pot and set aside. Drain and rinse cashews, and place in an upright blender. Add 1½ cans coconut milk, and blend on highest speed until completely smooth. Pour through strainer into pot. Gather edges of bag or excess cloth, and gently squeeze out liquid. Compost any solids. (There won't be much, if any, but this step ensures a completely silky consistency when using less powerful blenders.) Add remaining ½ can coconut milk to pot.

Split vanilla bean in half lengthwise and scrape out seeds with tip of a small knife. Add seeds and pod to coconut mixture; whisk to combine. Bring to a boil over medium-high heat, whisking frequently; cover pot, reduce heat to low, and simmer for 10 minutes, whisking every few minutes to prevent sticking. Remove from heat; allow to cool uncovered for 5 minutes, then whisk in honey and vanilla extract. Remove and compost vanilla bean pod. Pour into a bowl and set aside to cool. Once mixture has stopped steaming, place in the refrigerator until completely chilled.

Churn chilled coconut milk mixture in an ice cream maker according to manufacturer's directions; it should take about 15 to 20 minutes. Serve immediately—as with most nondairy ice creams, this one is perfectly thick and creamy when served immediately after churning. Any leftover ice cream can be stored in an airtight container and frozen. Remove from freezer 30 minutes before serving.

MAPLE COCONUT CRUNCH

Golden, crispy, and irresistible, this coconut crunch has a deep caramel-maple flavor and is nearly impossible to stop eating once it's cool enough to nibble. Fortunately, this recipe makes more than you'll need for this dessert, and because it stores well for a couple weeks, you can have it on hand for last-minute desserts—try crumbling it over Greek yogurt with stewed or roasted fruit or serving large shards of it along with fresh berries and tea.

MAKES 1 TRAY

2 tablespoons maple sugar

2 tablespoons maple syrup

1 tablespoon brown rice syrup

1 teaspoon vanilla extract

Pinch sea salt

2 cups dried, unsweetened, flaked coconut

Preheat oven to 300°F. Line a rimmed baking sheet with parchment paper and set aside.

Add maple sugar, maple syrup, brown rice syrup, vanilla, and salt to a medium mixing bowl; stir to combine. Add coconut, and toss gently to coat evenly with maple mixture, being careful not to break up flakes too much. Spread over parchment-covered baking sheet in a single layer, and bake for 12 to 14 minutes or until deeply golden and fragrant. Remove from oven and cool completely. Break coconut into shards and serve on top of roasted plums and ice cream, or store in an airtight container for up to two weeks.

NOTE: If the coconut doesn't have a snappy texture once it's cool, return it to the oven for a few minutes longer and cool again.

ROASTED PLUMS

With their meltingly tender flesh and rich maple-infused juices, these roasted plums taste decadent eaten just as they are. Paired with the coconut ice cream, they're over-the-top amazing. They also taste great served with thick yogurt or Vanilla Bean Cream (page 321).

NOTE: I like to use red plums in this recipe, as their skins soften perfectly and the flesh is succulent when roasted. If you use firmer varieties like Italian prune plums, you may need to increase the roasting time by 5 to 10 minutes for their skins and flesh to cook and soften completely. When plums aren't available, try roasting peaches, apricots, or nectarines the same way.

SERVES 4 TO 6

8 large plums (about 2½ pounds)

2 teaspoons extra virgin olive oil or melted extra virgin coconut oil

2 tablespoons maple syrup

1 teaspoon vanilla extract

Pinch cinnamon

Preheat oven to 400°F.

Cut plums in half and remove pits. Place in a rimmed baking dish that can hold the plums in a single layer. Add oil, maple syrup, vanilla, and cinnamon; toss to combine. Arrange plums so they're cut-side up, and roast for 20 minutes or until flesh is soft and pan is full of juices. Remove from oven and allow to cool slightly before serving. Store any leftover plums in an airtight container for up to three days in the fridge. Allow them to come up to room temperature before serving, or warm them in a pan over medium heat.

CHOCOLATE POTS DE CRÈME

Through many years of making vegan pastries professionally, I discovered the benefit of combining nut milks to create rich bases for various creams and fillings. Here, cashews, almonds, and dried coconut are combined to make a milk that doesn't taste strongly of any of them and carries the chocolate flavor without overpowering it.

The trick to creating a light-textured vegan mousse is to blend the final mixture before pouring it into cups or bowls to set. This method was born when a dessert my sister and I were making for a client's special dinner flopped at the last minute. After a few failed attempts to fix it, panic set in, and I threw the whole thing in the blender, hoping for the best. While the guests were enjoying their final course before dessert, we sat in the kitchen and nervously sampled the mousse. Our faces lit up with relief and delight as we cautiously dipped in; thankfully, it turned out to be the lightest vegan mousse ever!

NOTE: Since organic blanched almonds are hard to come by, I soak whole raw almonds and then slip off their skins. If you have blanched almonds, feel free to use them instead; just soak them the same amount of time as the cashews.

SERVES 6

½ cup whole raw almonds, soaked 8 to 24 hours in 1 cup filtered water

½ cup raw cashews, soaked 2 to 6 hours in 1 cup filtered water

1 cup dried, unsweetened, shredded coconut

3 cups filtered water

1 cup plain rice milk

¼ cup maple syrup

1 tablespoon agar flakes

Small pinch sea salt

¼ cup unsweetened cocoa powder, plus more to dust mousse

1¾ ounces dark (70 percent) chocolate, broken into pieces

1 tablespoon vanilla extract

Fresh raspberries to serve, optional

Line a medium strainer with a nut milk bag; a clean, thin kitchen towel; or several layers of cheesecloth. Place over a medium heavy-bottomed pot and set aside.

Slip the skins off the almonds, rinse and drain, and place them in an upright blender. Rinse and drain cashews; add to blender along with coconut and water. Blend on highest speed until completely smooth, about 2 minutes. Pour through strainer into pot; gather edges of bag or excess cloth, and gently squeeze milk out. Compost dry pulp that remains. You should have 2½ cups nut milk. Rinse blender and set aside.

Add rice milk, maple syrup, agar, and sea salt the pot with the nut milk. Whisk and bring to a boil over high heat. Cover pot, reduce heat to low, and simmer for 15 minutes, whisking every 5 minutes. Check that agar is completely dissolved (see page 293). Add cocoa powder and whisk until combined. Remove from heat, add chocolate, cover pot again, and let mixture sit for 2 minutes so chocolate can melt. Remove lid and whisk thoroughly until completely smooth. Stir in vanilla, and set aside uncovered for 10 minutes to cool slightly. Pour into blender and blend on highest speed for 1 minute.

Divide mixture among small bowls, cups, or glasses, and place in the fridge to set for at least an hour or until ready to serve. These can be made up to a day in advance. Dust surface with cocoa powder and top with raspberries; serve chilled.

CHOCOLATE HAZELNUT LAYER CAKE
WITH CHERRY FILLING AND CHOCOLATE GANACHE

For my sister's thirtieth birthday, my father and I came up with a clandestine plan for him to fly to New York from Australia to surprise her at her party. I was beside myself with the excitement of keeping his visit a secret and thrilled to see my plan unfold undetected. In between my father's arrival and the big day, I baked a large version of this cake. After the initial shock and delight of his surprise visit, we enjoyed this rich, moist, and decadent cake—it was a perfect ending to a wonderful night. The cherry filling pairs well with the chocolate and nuts, adding a burst of tangy sweet flavor. Use fresh cherries when available, and save some to garnish the top.

The cake batter here is based on a chocolate cake from Myra Kornfeld's brilliant book, *The Voluptuous Vegan*.

NOTE: For best results with the frosting, make it a day ahead, so it has plenty of time to cool and set. Be sure to assemble the cake when all components are completely cool. I recommend assembling it on either a round cardboard cake base or the bottom of a springform cake pan. This makes it easier to decorate the sides with hazelnuts, holding the base of the cake with one hand and pressing nuts into the sides with the other.

MAKES 1 TALL 8-INCH CAKE
EQUIPMENT: TWO 8-INCH CAKE PANS

CHOCOLATE GANACHE:

2 13.5–fluid ounce cans
  unsweetened full-fat coconut milk

¼ cup maple syrup

5 tablespoons agar flakes

Pinch sea salt

3½ ounces dark (70 percent) chocolate,
  broken into pieces

½ cup fresh orange juice, strained

4 teaspoons vanilla extract

CAKE:

2 cup toasted hazelnuts (page 78),
  skins removed, divided

2 cups whole spelt flour, divided

2 teaspoons aluminum-free
  baking powder

1 teaspoon baking soda

½ cup unsweetened cocoa powder

1 cup boiling filtered water

¼ cup ground flax seeds

½ cup melted extra virgin coconut oil,
  plus more for oiling the pan

1½ cups maple syrup

1 teaspoon unpasteurized
  apple cider vinegar

1 tablespoon vanilla extract

½ teaspoon salt

FILLING:

2½ cups pitted cherries (12 ounces),
  fresh or frozen

1 tablespoon maple syrup

¼ teaspoon cinnamon

Pinch sea salt

¾ teaspoon arrowroot powder

2 teaspoons filtered water

1 teaspoon vanilla extract

¼ teaspoon almond extract

½ cup unsweetened black cherry jam

MAKE THE GANACHE:

Add coconut milk, maple syrup, agar flakes, and salt to a medium, heavy-bottomed pot and whisk well. Place over high heat and bring to a boil, whisking frequently. Cover pot, reduce heat to low. Simmer for 20 minutes, whisking every 5 minutes. Check that the agar is completely dissolved (page 293). Remove from heat, add chocolate, and re-cover pot. Wait 2 minutes, then thoroughly whisk until completely smooth. Pour into a shallow bowl or rimmed baking dish, and allow to cool. Once mixture has stopped steaming, put it in the fridge until cold and completely hard and set, about 1½ to 2 hours.

Cut ganache into rough 1-inch pieces and place in a food processor with orange juice and vanilla; blend until completely smooth. Scrape down sides as necessary, and check for unblended lumps. If frosting separates, just keep blending until it comes together again—it can take up to 5 minutes to get it completely uniform and smooth. Transfer to a container and refrigerate until you're ready to frost cake.

MAKE THE CAKE:

Preheat oven to 350°F. Oil cake pans and line bottom of each with a parchment circle; set aside.

Place ⅔ cup toasted hazelnuts in a food processor, and add ¼ cup spelt flour; blend until finely ground, about 30 seconds. Place in a medium bowl. Sift in remaining 1¾ cups spelt flour, baking powder, and baking soda. Stir with a whisk to combine, and set aside.

In another medium bowl, whisk cocoa powder and boiling water until smooth. Add ground flax seeds, coconut oil, maple syrup, vinegar, vanilla, and salt, and whisk to emulsify. Add flour mixture, and use a whisk to mix batter. Divide batter between prepared cake pans, and bake for 35 to 40 minutes or until cake pulls away from sides of pan and a toothpick inserted in center comes out clean. Remove from oven and place on a wire rack to cool.

MAKE THE FILLING:

Combine cherries, maple syrup, cinnamon, and salt in a small pot, and bring to a boil over high heat. Cover pot, and reduce heat to low. Cook fresh cherries for 10 to 15 minutes or until softened and juicy; cook frozen cherries for 5 minutes. Dissolve arrowroot in water and drizzle into simmering cherries; stir constantly until mixture thickens slightly and returns to a simmer. Remove from heat, and stir in vanilla and almond extracts and jam. Pour into a shallow bowl, and place in the fridge to cool completely before filling cake.

ASSEMBLE THE CAKE:

Spread remaining 1⅓ cups toasted hazelnuts out on a rimmed baking sheet lined with parchment paper, and crush them with flat end of a rolling pin or a heavy jar; set aside.

Run a butter knife around edge of one cake pan and invert onto an 8-inch cardboard cake base or bottom of a springform pan. Remove parchment circle and spread surface with about 1 cup frosting. Top with cherry filling and spread out, leaving about a ½-inch border around edges. (This prevents it from spilling out when you top it with second cake layer.) Invert second cake onto a flat surface. (I like to use the bottom of a tart pan for this, as it is completely flat and will allow you to slide the top layer easily onto the bottom layer.) Remove parchment circle and slide cake onto bottom layer. Frost top and sides with remaining frosting, and press crushed hazelnuts into sides of the cake. Garnish with fresh cherries, if available, and place in the fridge until ready to serve. It will improve after a few hours as the flavors settle, and it can even spend the night in the fridge.

APPLE ALMOND SLICE

As I was deciding on recipes for this book, I combed through old notebooks, folders, and loose scraps of restaurant ordering pads containing hundreds of splattered dessert recipes. I found a vague scribble of ingredients with amounts listed in "handfuls" that was hardly readable on the oil-stained page. The cooking method read, "bake until done." This scribble was an attempt to re-create a stateside version of a much-adored apple cake that my friend Rosada baked in London. After a few tweaks, it evolved into this slice, which is wheat-free, supereasy, and fast to make, with all the flavors I miss about drinking tea on cozy afternoons in Rosada's Portobello flat.

NOTE: If you want to dress this slice up, you can brush it with the optional apricot glaze.

I like the look of the red skins left on the apples, but you can peel them if you like. If you do, keep in mind that they may take less time to cook.

MAKES ONE 9-INCH SQUARE SLICE
EQUIPMENT: 9-INCH SQUARE CAKE PAN

1 tablespoon melted extra virgin coconut oil

4 small Gala, Pink Lady, or other red-skinned apples (1¼ pounds),
    cored and cut in ½-inch slices

⅔ cup plus 1 tablespoon maple syrup, divided

4 teaspoons vanilla extract, divided

1½ cups regular rolled oats

2½ cups almond meal

½ cup barley flour

1½ teaspoons aluminum-free baking powder

½ cup extra virgin olive oil, plus more for oiling the pan

½ teaspoon almond extract

2 tablespoons unsweetened apricot jam, optional

Preheat oven to 350°F. Lightly oil a 9 × 9-inch square cake pan and line with parchment paper, covering bottom and about an inch up sides; set aside.

Warm coconut oil in a wide skillet over medium heat. Add apples and sauté for 5 minutes or until golden in parts. Stir in 1 tablespoon maple syrup and 2 teaspoons vanilla. Continue cooking for another 6 to 8 minutes, lowering heat if apples begin to brown. Cook until apples are soft but not falling apart. If they're still firm, reduce heat to low, cover skillet, and continue cooking for a few more minutes. Remove from heat and set aside.

Add oats to a food processor and blend until finely ground, about 30 seconds. Transfer to a medium bowl and mix in almond meal, barley flour, and baking powder. In another bowl, whisk remaining ⅔ cup maple syrup, remaining 2 teaspoons vanilla, olive oil, and almond extract. Pour into oat-almond flour mixture and stir to combine. Lightly press batter into prepared cake pan and bake for 15 minutes. Remove from oven (leave oven on), and arrange apples in 4 rows over surface of slice, leaving a ½-inch border around edge. Lightly press apples into cake and return to oven for another 20 to 25 minutes or until edges are golden brown. Remove from oven and allow cake to cool completely in pan. Invert cake onto a flat plate or cutting board, peel off parchment, and reinvert onto a serving plate.

To make the optional glaze, place jam in a small pot over medium heat and stir until melted, about 1 minute. Remove from heat and use a pastry brush to lightly brush glaze over surface of apples. Cut into 8 or 16 squares, and serve at room temperature. Store any leftovers in an airtight container in the fridge for up to three days.

CITRUS COCONUT CUPCAKES

I adore really moist—verging on dense—cakes with lots of body and flavor. Often vegan cakes are too crumbly and delicate to hold up as cupcakes, but not these! The whole cooked and blended orange, combined with lots of ground coconut, gives these cupcakes great texture and a less sweet, more adult flavor. The lemon-colored frosting is tangy and rich, just like a good buttercream, only better! There are a few steps to making these cupcakes, but they're worth it, and unlike many vegan desserts, they keep well for a few days in the fridge.

MAKES 12 CUPCAKES
EQUIPMENT: 1 STANDARD MUFFIN PAN

FROSTING:

2 13.5–fluid ounce cans
  unsweetened full-fat coconut milk

¼ cup plus 2 tablespoons agar flakes

¼ cup plus 2 tablespoons maple syrup
  (grade A or lightest color)

¼ cup brown rice syrup

⅛ teaspoon turmeric

Pinch sea salt

¼ cup fresh lemon juice

¼ cup fresh lime juice

⅓ cup fresh orange juice

1 tablespoon vanilla extract

CUPCAKES:

1¾ cups whole spelt flour

1½ teaspoon aluminum-free
  baking powder

¾ teaspoons baking soda

1¼ cups dried, unsweetened,
  shredded coconut, divided

1 medium navel or Valencia orange,
  boiled (see sidebar)

1 cup maple syrup

¼ cup plus 2 tablespoons
  extra virgin olive oil

2 teaspoons unpasteurized
  apple cider vinegar

½ teaspoon sea salt

1 tablespoon vanilla extract

Strips of lemon and orange zest to
  garnish, optional

MAKE THE FROSTING:

Add coconut milk, agar flakes, maple syrup, rice syrup, turmeric, and salt to a medium, heavy-bottomed pot; whisk to combine. Place over high heat and bring to a boil, whisking every minute or so. Cover pot and reduce heat to low. Simmer for 20 to 30 minutes, whisking every 10 minutes or until agar is completely dissolved (see page 293).

Remove from heat and whisk in lemon, lime, and orange juices. Pour into a rimmed baking dish or wide shallow bowl; once mixture stops steaming, place it in the fridge and chill until completely set and hard, about 1 hour.

Remove from fridge, and cut frosting into rough 1-inch pieces. Place in a food processor and add vanilla. Blend until completely smooth, scraping down sides as necessary. If frosting separates, just keep blending until it comes together again and texture is light and smooth—this can take up to 5 minutes. Place in a covered container and refrigerate until ready to use; it will continue to thicken as it cools.

MAKE THE CUPCAKES:

Preheat oven to 350°F. Line muffin pan with 12 paper liners and set aside.

Sift flour, baking powder, and baking soda into a medium bowl; set aside. Grind ¾ cup coconut in a food processor for 1 minute or until fine. Add to flour mixture along with remaining ½ cup coconut. Stir with a whisk to combine and set aside.

Cut boiled orange into quarters, remove any seeds, and cut each piece in half. Place in a food processor, and add maple syrup, olive oil, vinegar, salt, and vanilla. Blend until smooth, scraping down sides as necessary. Pour into flour mixture, and use a rubber spatula to stir until just combined; do not overmix.

Distribute batter among lined muffin pans, filling them almost to the top. Place in oven, and bake 25 to 30 minutes or until a toothpick comes out clean and centers are firm to the touch. Remove from oven and set aside to cool for a few minutes in pan; remove and place on a wire rack to cool completely. Once cool, frost each cupcake generously and garnish with strips of citrus zest.

Depending on how generously you frost your cupcakes, you may be left with a little or a lot of extra frosting. It can be frozen for up to six months and used as a frosting for cakes, or blended with a splash of almond milk or rice milk for a lovely lemon cream to serve with fruit crisps or tarts.

To boil oranges, place a whole orange in a medium pot, cover with filtered water, and bring to a boil over high heat. Cover pot, reduce heat to low, and simmer for 45 to 50 minutes or until soft. Remove from heat, drain, and set aside to cool.

Boil the orange up to three days in advance of making this recipe; you can also boil a few and freeze them for up to three months. The smell of boiling oranges makes your kitchen smell divine.

ALMOND BUTTER BROWNIES WITH SEA SALT

Toasted almonds, dark chocolate, and flaky sea salt are a divine combination. When you're in the mood for a rich, chocolaty treat, these brownies really hit the spot. Of course, they're made with 100 percent whole-grain spelt, which gives them great body and a delicious nutty flavor.

NOTE: I use regular dried deglet noor dates here, but you can use Medjool if you prefer, and if they're supermoist and soft, you can skip the soaking step.

MAKES FIFTEEN 3 × 2½-INCH BROWNIES
EQUIPMENT: 13 × 9-INCH PAN (ALSO KNOWN AS A QUARTER SHEET PAN)

½ cup packed pitted deglet noor dates

1½ cups whole spelt flour

¾ cup unsweetened cocoa powder

1½ teaspoons aluminum-free baking powder

¼ cup plus 2 tablespoons toasted almond butter,
    store-bought or homemade (page 117)

¾ cup extra virgin olive oil, plus more to oil pan

¾ cup maple syrup

¾ cup maple sugar

¼ cup plus 2 tablespoons homemade almond milk (page 74)
    or plain soy milk

½ teaspoon sea salt

1 tablespoon vanilla extract

3½ ounces dark (85 percent) chocolate, coarsely chopped and divided,
    or about ¾ cup chocolate chips

½ cup toasted almonds (page 77), chopped

Maldon or fleur de sel, or other flaky sea salt

Place dates in a medium bowl and cover with boiling water. Let soak for 20 minutes or until softened, then drain well.

Preheat oven to 350°F. Line pan with parchment paper; brush paper and sides of pan lightly with oil, and set aside.

Sift flour, cocoa powder, and baking powder into a medium bowl; whisk to combine and set aside.

Place almond butter, olive oil, maple syrup, maple sugar, almond milk, salt, vanilla, and drained dates in a food processor; blend until smooth. (It's okay if a few small date pieces are not blended.) Pour into sifted flour mixture, and stir with a rubber spatula until almost combined. Reserve 2 tablespoons chopped chocolate and stir remaining chocolate into batter, being careful not to overmix. Transfer batter to prepared pan and spread out evenly. Sprinkle with toasted almonds, remaining chocolate, and a large pinch of sea salt.

Bake for 30 minutes or until edges pull away from sides of pan and a toothpick inserted into center comes out clean. Remove from oven and allow to cool completely. For best results, refrigerate until completely cold before cutting. These brownies keep well for three or four days when stored in an airtight container in the fridge.

APRICOT COCONUT BARS

Serve this irresistible treat with tea, when you're in the mood for something buttery and sweet yet not too filling. The crust gets its rich body and snappy texture from a combination of ground coconut and coconut oil, perfectly offsetting the flavorful apricot filling and lemon-scented topping.

MAKES SIXTEEN 2 × 4-INCH BARS
EQUIPMENT: 13 × 9-INCH PAN
(ALSO KNOWN AS A QUARTER SHEET PAN)

CRUST:

1 cup dried, unsweetened, shredded coconut

½ cup regular rolled oats

¼ teaspoon aluminum-free baking powder

¼ teaspoon sea salt

¼ cup whole spelt flour

¾ cup barley flour

¼ cup melted extra virgin coconut oil, plus more for oiling pan

¼ cup maple syrup

1 teaspoon vanilla extract

FILLING:

⅓ cup thinly sliced unsulfured dried apricots (about 9)

½ cup unsweetened apricot jam

TOPPING:

1 cup dried, unsweetened, shredded coconut

⅓ cup raw cashews

¼ teaspoon aluminum-free baking powder

1 tablespoon maple syrup

1 tablespoon extra virgin olive oil

2 teaspoons vanilla extract

Zest of 1 lemon

1 cup dried, unsweetened, coconut flakes

MAKE THE CRUST:

Preheat oven to 350°F. Oil pan, and line bottom and sides with parchment paper; set aside.

Place coconut, oats, baking powder, and salt in a food processor; blend until fine, about 45 seconds. Transfer to a medium bowl, and mix in spelt and barley flours. Add oil, and mix with a fork or your fingertips until combined. Stir in maple syrup and vanilla, and mix again. Dough should be moist but not sticky. Wash and dry your hands, and press dough thinly and evenly over bottom of prepared pan. (Don't press it up the sides.) Prick crust with a fork, and bake for 20 minutes or until edges are just beginning to brown. Remove from oven and set aside; keep oven on.

MAKE THE FILLING:

Place apricots in a bowl and cover with boiling water. Set them aside to soften for 5 minutes; then drain well. Spread baked crust with apricot jam, and arrange drained apricot slices on top.

MAKE THE TOPPING:

Place shredded coconut, cashews, and baking powder in a food processor, and blend until ground and moist, about 45 seconds; transfer to a medium bowl. Combine maple syrup, olive oil, vanilla, and lemon zest in another bowl, and whisk to combine. Pour into ground coconut and cashew mixture; stir to combine. Mix in flaked coconut, being careful not to break up flakes too much. Crumble topping over apricots and preserves, leaving some filling showing. Bake 18 minutes or until golden on top. Remove from oven, and set aside to cool completely before cutting into bars. Store any leftover bars in an airtight container in the fridge for up to three days.

CINNAMON CARAMEL POPCORN

Something magical happens to popcorn when it's coated in this caramely mixture of cashew butter, vanilla, and brown rice syrup. Baked until crisp and golden, it seems to shatter when bitten but manages to remain a little chewy too. Subtly sweet, kissed with cinnamon and a touch of salt, this is a truly irresistible treat. Luckily, it's also superfast to make.

MAKES 1 TRAY THAT SERVES 4 TO 6

6 cups freshly popped popcorn (see sidebar)

½ cup brown rice syrup

3 tablespoons raw cashew butter

¼ teaspoon sea salt

1½ teaspoons vanilla extract

¼ teaspoon cinnamon, plus more to sprinkle

Preheat oven to 350°F. Line a rimmed baking sheet with parchment paper and set aside.

Place popcorn in a large mixing bowl; set aside. Add rice syrup to a small pot over medium heat, and bring to a simmer. Reduce heat to low and cook for 2 minutes, stirring frequently. Remove from heat, and add cashew butter, salt, vanilla, and cinnamon; mix until smooth. Pour mixture over popcorn, and mix well with a rubber spatula to combine. Spread over lined baking sheet and bake for 6 minutes; rotate tray, and continue baking for 2 to 3 more minutes. Remove from oven, and sprinkle with additional cinnamon. Allow to cool completely (if you can resist it!) before breaking into pieces.

If you have any left over, it can be stored in an airtight container for up to three days.

For 6 cups popcorn, you need to cook about ¼ cup popcorn kernels. Warm 2 teaspoons coconut oil in a large pot over high heat. Add popcorn and cover immediately; shake pot to coat corn with oil. Continue shaking pot until corn is popping rapidly, then lower heat slightly. Once popping slows to about 2 seconds between pops, remove from heat, shake again, and keep covered until all popping has stopped. Remove lid, measure out 6 cups, and use within an hour, as popcorn becomes stale quickly.

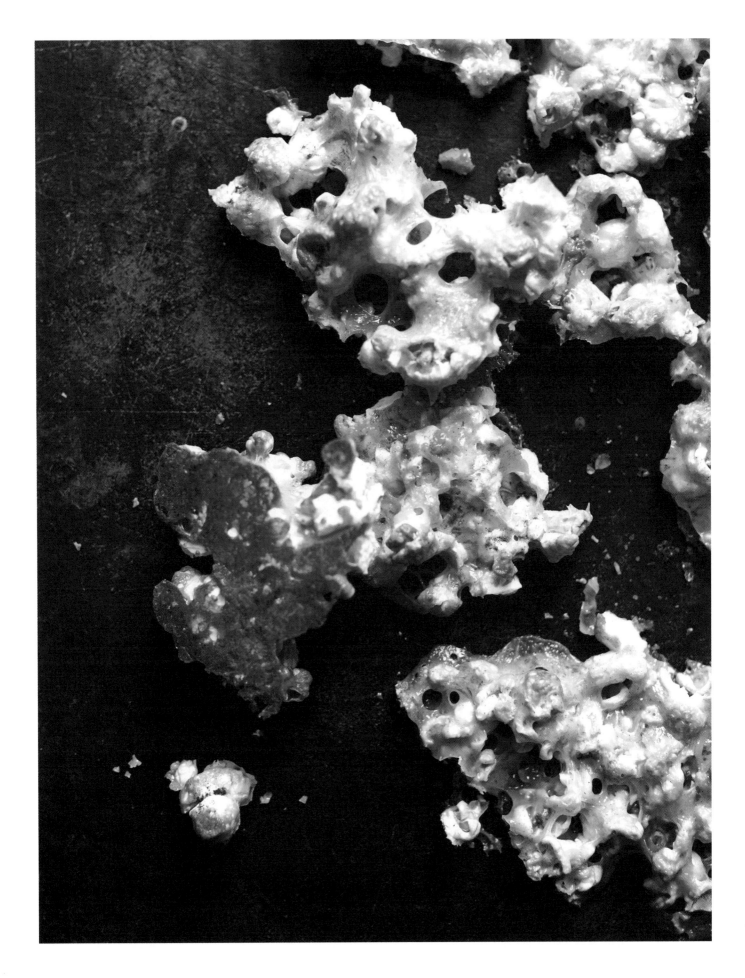

GOLDEN AMARANTH SUPERFOOD BARS

This bar is inspired by a recipe my friend and fellow chef Georgia Melnyk shared with me many years ago, when we met in the kitchen of a small natural-food restaurant called Terra 47 in New York. Georgia is a talented chef who possesses special capabilities when it comes to cooking truly delicious and healing food.

Not only do I love the tasty flavor and satisfying chewiness of this bar, but I also like its golden caramel color. Goji berries are an excellent (and obvious) addition to this recipe, so feel free to add some in.

EQUIPMENT: ONE 8-INCH SQUARE BAKING DISH
MAKES EIGHTEEN 2 × 1-INCH BARS

Olive oil for pan

1¼ cup puffed amaranth (see page 130)

1 cup dried, unsweetened, shredded coconut

¼ cup toasted unhulled sesame seeds (page 77)

¼ cup toasted sunflower seeds (page 77)

¼ cup hemp seeds

½ cup yakon syrup (see sidebar)

½ cup toasted almond butter, store-bought or homemade (page 117)

1 teaspoon vanilla extract

2 teaspoons lemon zest

1 cup toasted walnut halves (page 78), chopped

½ cup dried mulberries

Lightly brush pan with olive oil, or if using a metal cake pan, line with oiled parchment paper.

Place amaranth, coconut, sesame seeds, sunflower seeds, and hemp seeds in a medium-size bowl; toss to combine. Add yakon syrup and almond butter to a small pot over medium heat; stir well to work out any lumps. Continue stirring until mixture begins to bubble. Remove from heat, and stir in vanilla and lemon zest. Working quickly, pour into amaranth mixture and stir until evenly combined. Add walnuts and mulberries, and mix again. Using moist hands, press dough into baking dish until completely even and flat. Place in the fridge to cool for at least 1½ hours or in the freezer for 45 minutes.

Cut into 18 bars. Stored in an airtight container in the fridge, bars will keep for up to two weeks, although they are best eaten within a few days.

Yakon syrup is a low glycemic sweetener with half the calories of sugar. It is made from yakon, a highly nutritious root grown in Peru. One of the healthiest sweeteners available, yakon syrup has a pleasant, malty, tropical flavor. (See page 44 for more information.) If you don't have yakon syrup on hand, you can replace it with brown rice syrup, and the bar will still be delicious.

PISTACHIO GOLDEN RAISIN COOKIES
WITH CARDAMOM

These cookies will fill your home with the enticing and exotic scents of cardamom, vanilla, coconut, and pistachios. Packed with oats and studded with golden raisins, they're an exciting new take on the classic oatmeal raisin cookie.

MAKES SIXTEEN 2½-INCH COOKIES

2 cups regular rolled oats

1 cup whole spelt flour

1 cup almond meal

½ teaspoon aluminum-free baking powder

1 teaspoon ground cardamom (see note)

½ cup melted extra virgin coconut oil

¼ cup extra virgin olive oil

¾ cup maple syrup

1 tablespoon vanilla extract

½ teaspoon sea salt

Zest of 1 orange

½ cup unsulfured golden raisins

1 cup boiling filtered water

¾ cup toasted pistachios (page 78), roughly chopped

Combine oats, spelt flour, almond meal, baking powder, and cardamom in a medium bowl. In another bowl, combine coconut and olive oils, maple syrup, vanilla, salt, and orange zest; whisk until emulsified. Pour into dry ingredients and stir well; mixture will be very wet. Set aside for 10 to 15 minutes to allow dough to thicken.

Place golden raisins in a bowl, add boiling water, and soak for 10 minutes. Pour through a strainer, and set aside to drain well.

Preheat oven to 350°F. Line a baking sheet with parchment paper and set aside.

Add drained raisins and pistachios to cookie dough, and mix until combined. Using a damp ¼-cup measure, scoop cookie dough onto baking sheet, flatten slightly, and bake 15 minutes or until golden around the edges. Using a spatula, carefully transfer cookies to a wire rack. They will firm up when completely cool. Store any leftover cookies in an airtight container; in warm weather, store them in the fridge.

NOTE: If you don't have ground cardamom on hand, grind 18 cardamom pods as finely as possible in an electric spice grinder. Use a small strainer to sift the ground pods, and toss anything left in the strainer. You should have 1 teaspoon ground cardamom when you're done.

CHERRY PECAN COOKIES

Perfectly sweet, crisp around the edges, with pockets of chewiness and lots of nuts, these cookies are a yummy, gluten-free afternoon treat. I love the simple combination of oats, pecans, and cherries baked with cinnamon, but you can dress the cookies up with the zest of an orange or, if you are in the mood, a handful of chopped dark chocolate.

NOTE: If your dried cherries are not soft and chewy, pour boiling water over them, let them soak for a few minutes, then drain well before using. Be sure to purchase gluten-free rolled oats if you are allergic to gluten.

MAKES ABOUT FIFTEEN 2½-INCH COOKIES

1½ cups toasted pecan halves (page 78), divided

1½ cups regular rolled oats, divided

¼ cup brown rice flour

½ teaspoon aluminum-free baking powder

1 teaspoon cinnamon

¼ cup extra virgin olive oil or melted extra virgin coconut oil

3 tablespoons brown rice syrup

2 tablespoons maple syrup

1 tablespoon vanilla extract

¼ teaspoon sea salt

½ cup unsweetened dried cherries, large ones halved

Preheat oven to 325°F. Line a baking sheet with parchment paper and set aside.

Roughly chop or break up 1 cup pecans into large pieces; set aside. Place remaining ½ cup pecans and ½ cup oats in a food processor, and blend until finely ground, about 30 seconds. Transfer to a medium bowl, and add remaining 1 cup oats, brown rice flour, baking powder, and cinnamon; stir to combine.

In another bowl, whisk together oil, rice syrup, maple syrup, vanilla, and salt. Pour into oat nut mixture, and stir to combine. Mix in chopped pecans and cherries. Shape cookies into approximately 3-tablespoon mounds and place a couple of inches apart on lined baking sheet; press lightly to flatten dough a little. Bake for 15 minutes or until edges are golden and lightly browning. These cookies may not look done when they come out of the oven, but they firm up as they cool. Remove from oven, and set aside to cool for 10 minutes before transferring to a wire rack. Once cool, any leftover cookies can be stored in an airtight container for two to three days.

POMEGRANATE KANTEN

When I first arrived in Istanbul en route to southern Turkey for a sailing trip, I was excited to see people selling freshly squeezed pomegranate juice on almost every street corner. The vibrant, deep pink color and tart flavor was one of the highlights of walking around the city, and I happily drank it every day. This light and refreshing kanten (see page 326 for details on kanten) is the perfect way to bring the delicious freshness, brilliant color, and unparalleled health benefits of pomegranates into a dessert. If you want to add some richness to it, Cashew Cinnamon Cream (page 322) is a delightful addition.

NOTE: Apple juice tames the sourness of the pomegranate juice in this recipe, but you can add the optional honey if you want a sweeter dessert—it's excellent either way.

This kanten is exceptional made with fresh pomegranate juice; if you use the bottled variety, the color and flavor won't be as bright.

SERVES 4

2 cups plus 1 tablespoon apple juice

3 tablespoons agar flakes

1 teaspoon arrowroot

2 cups fresh pomegranate juice (see note)

1 teaspoon raw honey, optional

Pomegranate seeds to garnish

Combine 2 cups apple juice and agar flakes in a small, heavy-bottomed pot and bring to a boil over high heat, whisking frequently. Cover pot, reduce heat to low, and simmer for 10 minutes or until all agar is dissolved (page 293).

In a small bowl, dissolve arrowroot in remaining 1 tablespoon apple juice. Raise heat to medium, and slowly drizzle in dissolved arrowroot, whisking constantly until mixture thickens slightly and returns to a simmer. Remove from heat, and whisk in pomegranate juice and honey (if using). Pour mixture into a shallow bowl or rimmed ceramic baking dish, and refrigerate for about an hour or until completely chilled and set. Remove from fridge and whisk thoroughly until smooth. If kanten isn't as smooth as you would like, place it in a food processor and pulse briefly until smooth. Do not overblend, as it will become too runny. Store in a jar in the fridge until ready to serve. Spoon into glasses or small bowls and garnish with pomegranate seeds. Keep any leftover kanten in the fridge for up to a week.

You can juice a pomegranate the same way you would juice an orange. Just cut it in half and use a hand juicer or citrus press to extract the juice. Strain it if your juicer doesn't have a strainer, and squeeze out as much juice as possible from the pulp and seeds. You will need about 6 pomegranates to get 2 cups of juice.

EARL GREY FRUITCAKE

When I lived in Sydney many years ago, my favorite place to eat was a restaurant called Iku on Glebe Point Road. Back then, Iku was co-owned by Holly Davis, an excellent whole-food chef and cookbook author, who along with the other great chefs who worked there, created fantastic healthy meals and desserts daily. In the afternoons, they served a moist, nutty fruitcake called Bancha tea cake. Bancha tea is a Japanese tea similar in flavor to kukicha. Being the tea lover that I am, I wanted to re-create it using Earl Grey tea. You can use any tea you choose here—or even orange juice if you like. This gluten-free cake is simple to make, has no added sweetener or oil, and actually improves after it sits for a couple of days.

NOTE: Since bergamot is what gives Earl Grey tea its distinctive flavor, if you're lucky enough to find a fresh bergamot, substitute its zest for the orange zest.

MAKES ONE 8-INCH CAKE
EQUIPMENT: ONE 8-INCH CAKE PAN

Olive oil for brushing parchment paper

1½ cups toasted hazelnuts (page 78), skins removed and divided

½ cup unsulfured dried apricots, cut in ½-inch pieces

8 dried Black Mission figs, cut in ½-inch pieces

6 Medjool dates, pitted and cut in ½-inch pieces

1½ cups hot, strong, brewed Earl Grey tea, divided

2½ cups seedless raisins

¾ teaspoon cinnamon

¼ teaspoon freshly grated nutmeg

¼ teaspoon ground allspice

2 teaspoons vanilla extract

Zest of 1 orange

1½ cups toasted walnuts (page 78), chopped

Preheat oven to 300°F. Lightly oil a piece of parchment paper about 12 × 12 inches and line cake pan, oil-side up; set aside.

Grind 1¼ cups toasted hazelnuts in a food processor until fine, about 30 seconds; don't overblend, as they will turn into nut butter. Place in a medium bowl and set aside. Halve remaining ¼ cup hazelnuts, and set aside.

Place apricots, figs, and dates in a bowl, and cover with 1 cup hot tea; set aside for 10 minutes, then drain well.

Place raisins and remaining ½ cup tea in a medium pot, and bring to a boil over high heat; stir, cover pot, reduce heat to low, and simmer for 10 minutes. Remove lid, and continue cooking for a couple more minutes or until all tea has cooked off and raisins are plump. Transfer raisins to a food processor; add cinnamon, nutmeg, allspice, and vanilla. Blend until smooth. Add to bowl with ground hazelnuts, along with drained dried fruit and orange zest. Mix to combine, then stir in walnuts. Evenly press cake batter into prepared pan and garnish edge with reserved chopped hazelnuts. Bake for 1 hour or until firm and set. Remove from oven, and set aside to cool completely before removing from pan. Slice thinly and serve with tea. This cake keeps well stored in an airtight container for at least a week in a cool kitchen and for a couple of weeks in the fridge.

my life with tea

Tea—my enchanting and endlessly intriguing companion through life. I'm not sure I can remember a day that has gone by that I haven't woken up and prepared a pot of tea, then paused for at least another cup at some point during the day. When I was working long hours in restaurants and catering, a few stolen sips of tea here and there both rewarded me and kept me going. Then and now, brewing tea punctuates my life and work.

Long car trips always involve a full thermos and a good tea selection; I love nothing more than sipping a grassy cup of green tea on early morning drives out to the country. And whether I'm in a foreign city, on a deck gazing at the mountains, or at the beach, drinking a good cup of tea makes me feel at home wherever I find myself.

Green tea is always at the top of my list, and I will happily admit that I'm addicted to sencha: its smell; its bright, fresh taste, and the clear-headed buzz it provides. Although I go for long periods of time without black tea, it will always be a nostalgic favorite, especially a pot of Earl Grey with grated fresh ginger and a splash of soy milk. Most of my oldest and dearest friends drink it this way too, and when I brew a pot, it seems to reduce the sometimes vast distances between us. In the afternoons, I drink teas made from herbs and roots rather than drinking plain water. I use tea at this time of day as an opportunity to boost immunity, cleanse, or strengthen, depending on the time of year and how I'm feeling.

In spring and summer, I make tea from fresh nettles by steeping the leaves and stems in a jar with hot water. It's delicious warm and becomes a potent black tonic if left overnight. I drink this at room temperature throughout the day or add a shot to my cup and top it off with boiling water. Other lovely fresh herbs to steep are lemon verbena, lemon balm, and (of course) mint.

In fall and winter, I drink a warming ginger tea blend with black pepper and lemongrass from Yogi (see the Resources section). If I'm under the weather, I add a dropper of olive leaf extract, which is full of antioxidants and makes a great immunity-boosting tonic; I also love its invigorating, almost eucalyptus-like flavor.

I sometimes drink a medicinal Chinese blend of eight different herbs called Cold Prevention by Beyond Tea (see the Resources section). It's perfect for anyone prone to feeling cold and for protection against seasonal sniffles.

Kukicha, a roasted and aged twig-and-leaf tea is always in my tea drawer (and handbag); it's perfect for times when you're in need of something more grounding than herbal tea. It has an alkalizing effect on the blood and is high in calcium and vitamin C as well. Its tasty, woody flavor is perfect for sipping after dinner, as it has very low levels of caffeine. In summer, it's nice served at room temperature or chilled with a squeeze of fresh lemon or a splash of apple juice.

Here are some other teas I like to stock in my tea drawer:
- Dandelion root—for its strong liver-cleansing properties
- Dried burdock root—a great blood-cleansing and strengthening tea that can be added to broths when fresh burdock is unavailable
- Dried nettle—for times when I can't get it fresh; a kidney tonic that helps enrich the blood and build vitality
- Fennel—warming, sweet, and great for digestion
- Red clover—cleansing for the blood and delightfully light
- Rose—fragrant and beautiful, rose is said to nourish the heart
- Matcha—for a frothy, rich, caffeinated boost

Except for a couple of favorite tea blends that I've already mentioned, I generally prefer tea unmixed and straight up so that I can appreciate its unique flavor and properties. That said, it can be fun to experiment with making your own herbal blends with spices.

Whether your chosen tea is from a twig, root, bud, or leaf, may you find time to enjoy the ritual of drinking tea and take a moment of pause to enjoy its benefits.

cleansing

The concept of cleansing and detoxifying has different connotations: for some people, it's a fast of only water, juice, or brown rice; for others, it's simply eliminating animal products, refined foods, and sugar. Either way, it can be an uplifting experience to set aside time to improve mental focus, increase energy, and rebalance and rejuvenate your body, especially at the beginning of a new season. The idea that we can start anew with a clean slate is appealing, and although a period of cleansing can be helpful in marking the beginning of a healthy dietary transition, the best and most lasting changes are usually gradual. A daily diet consisting of truly whole and nutritionally dense foods is the most effective way to support the body in its natural cleansing and detoxification cycles. When the body is overloaded with too much stress, poor-quality food, animal products, and too little rest, it becomes overly acidic, and long-term acidic conditions can result in disease and illness. The simple act of increasing alkalizing foods such as vegetables, fruits, naturally fermented foods, and soaked grains can help maintain and promote a healthy acid-alkaline balance in the body.

Although extreme quick-fix detox programs are appealing, they are often too severe (unless you've taken adequate time to prepare) and can result in a post-fast binge that can increase stress on the body. Since there are many different approaches to cleansing, the best way to get the most out of any extreme or long-term cleanse and find the right one for your body type and lifestyle is with the guidance of an experienced practitioner.

Over the years, I have tried many different cleanses and found that unless the extreme ones are very short, they're too harsh and leave me cold and weak rather than refreshed and bounding with energy. Through recommendations from my friend Paul Pitchford, the author of *Healing with Whole Foods*, guidance from Dr. Drew DiVittorio, and what I continue to learn about Traditional Chinese Medicine, I find that gentle cleanses involving cooked food—soups, nutritional broths, and lots of greens—suit me better. My clients have also seen great results with this kind of program. This approach is based on a balanced vegan whole-food diet, where all the ingredients are nutritionally enhanced through soaking and sprouting, and meals are based around vegetables with a focus on greens, fermented foods, superfoods, sea vegetables, and a variety of protein sources. Portions are kept small, and the goal is to feel genuinely hungry three times a day and to only eat until 75 percent (or less) full.

If you are experienced with more extreme cleansing programs, this kind of plan can work well leading up to and following a fast or juice cleanse.

SOME GUIDELINES

Most of the meals suggested here can be made ahead, before beginning a cleanse, and can be eaten over a few days, which will give you time away from the kitchen. The more you can prepare ahead—shopping for ingredients and teas, making soups and broths, washing greens to steam, and so on—the more time you can spend doing things that assist you in the cleansing process, like getting eight hours of sleep, practicing yoga or Qigong, and taking baths!

Make sure all your meals are warm in fall, winter, and spring, and either warm or room temperature in summer. Serve salads only in the hotter months.

For the best results, avoid coffee, black tea, alcohol, and concentrated sweeteners before you begin and throughout the cleanse.

Many of the recipes in this book are used in my cleansing diet plan that I cook for my clients—cleanses can be a great time to celebrate beautiful, simple food rather than feel deprived. These recipes reflect that idea. The following menu selections can serve as a framework for your cleanse.

PREBREAKFAST

Begin each day by drinking the juice of half a lemon combined with a cup of hot water. (This helps cleanse the liver.)

BREAKFAST

Superfood Oatmeal (page 87)

OR

Soaked Oats and Chia (page 88)

Serve breakfast with plenty of berries, Superfood Breakfast Sprinkle (page 117), and fresh, homemade almond milk (page 74).

LUNCH

A LEGUME:

Chickpea Mash (page 70)

Simple Marinated Beans (page 70)

Lemony Marinated Lentils (page 71)

Kitchari (page 175)

SERVED WITH A VEGETABLE OR SALAD:

Steamed Greens with Zesty Flax Dressing (page 92)

Sprout Salad with Toasted Sunflower Seeds and Umeboshi Vinaigrette (page 182)

Simple Pressed Salad (page 200)

SNACKS

Soft goji berries (see the Resources section)

Toasted pumpkin seeds/spicy toasted seeds

Soaked or toasted almonds

Fresh blueberries, raspberries, or strawberries

Pomegranate seeds or pure pomegranate juice

Radishes (eaten between meals, they can help cleanse the gallbladder)

Vegetable broths (a great choice of snack if you're feeling week or hungry; try adding in sea vegetables, turmeric, and shiitake mushrooms for extra minerals and nutrients)

DINNER

A SOUP:

Creamy Cauliflower and Celery Root Soup with Roasted Shiitakes (page 168)

Pea Zucchini Soup with Dill (page 159)

Ume Shiso Broth with Soba Noodles (page 160)

Hearty Winter Miso Soup with Adzuki Beans, Squash, and Ginger (page 174)

AND/OR A SMALL PORTION OF A WHOLE GRAIN:

Simple Quinoa (page 64)

Brown and Sweet Rice or any of the variations (page 63)

Millet, Squash, and Sweet Corn Pilaf with Tamari-Toasted Pumpkin (page 138)

Quinoa Congee (page 146)

Millet Cauliflower Mash (page 90)

SERVED WITH A VEGETABLE AND STEAMED GREENS:

Arame with Carrots and Sesame (page 107)

Steamed vegetables with Black Sesame Flax Dressing (page 93)

Burdock and Carrot Kinpira (page 281)

Kabocha Nishime (page 281)

DRINKS

By increasing vegetables, soups, and broths in your diet and avoiding dehydrating substances like coffee, alcohol, and sugar, you'll find you don't need to drink as much water. Be sure that the water you do drink is filtered (page 51) and drink when thirsty or if you're sweating a lot. I suggest carrying a selection of herbal teas with you. This is a good time to try detoxifying and cleansing blends that you can find in health-food stores, or experiment with making your own. You can also drink superfood powders like goji berry or pomegranate with warm or room-temperature water, or try cereal grass powders. Both traditional Ayurvedic and Chinese Medicine suggest drinking warm or room-temperature liquids (and meals) to ensure you're not putting out your digestive fire.

organics

Daily, our eating turns nature into culture, transforming the body of the world into our bodies and minds.

—MICHAEL POLLAN, THE OMNIVORE'S DILEMMA:
A NATURAL HISTORY OF FOUR MEALS

So what does it mean to grow and raise food organically? The overarching philosophy behind organic farming is that we work in harmony with nature and improve and maintain the health and vitality of the land. This means organic growing practices strive to promote and enhance natural diversity, keeping the soil rich in nutrients and healthy with an abundance of microorganisms. Organic farms rely on beneficial insects (biological pest control) and crop rotation to maintain a balanced ecosystem and healthy soil. For this reason, synthetic pesticides, herbicides, fungicides, and fertilizers have no place on an organic farm as they wreak havoc on the environment, pollute the water supply, damage the soil, and ultimately have a negative effect on the health of animals and farm workers. Organic food is never irradiated or genetically modified.

Biodynamic farming takes organic farming a step further by nourishing and enlivening the health of the whole farm (including animals and workers) with herbal and homeopathic preparations, thus enhancing the nutrition, flavor, and quality of the food being raised. Food grown using biodynamic methods has its own certification process called Demeter. Demeter is the largest and oldest certification for biodynamic agriculture and is regarded as the highest grade of organic farming in the world—and perhaps the truest measure of organic and sustainable.

Fueled by a decline in crop vitality, seed fertility, and animal health, the concept of biodynamic farming was founded in the 1920s by the Austrian philosopher and scientist Rudolf Steiner with a group of concerned farmers. Steiner's goal was to take an ethical, ecological, and spiritual approach to agriculture, viewing the farm as a whole living organism that is responsible for creating and maintaining its own health. A biodynamic farm is built as a self-sustaining system in which soil fertility comes from recycling the organic material the system generates. All planting, weeding, and harvesting is done in harmony with lunar and solar rhythms.

A sustainable farm uses methods that protect and support human, animal, and environmental health, without compromising productivity for future generations. The reality is that it's almost impossible for any large farm to be truly sustainable. Sustainable farming is usually organic, but not all organic farms are sustainable. Sustainable agriculture doesn't have its own certification; the best way to know if your food (certified organic or not) is grown in a sustainable way is to buy directly from the farmer and ask about their farming methods.

In our increasingly cost-conscious culture, it's important to know that buying organic is not always more expensive; in fact, the true cost of organic food (especially when locally grown) is far less when you consider the hidden costs associated with the polluting chemicals used in producing conventionally grown food.

Consider, for instance, what it might take to cultivate a small pot of herbs for your kitchen windowsill: seeds, soil, a clay pot. Or perhaps you find a plant at your local farmers' market and decide to bring that home. No matter—notice how many sprigs of rosemary or thyme or basil, for example, you are able to harvest from that one plant. Even with a limited life, what it costs to purchase the same quantity of herbs from the supermarket is far greater than what it costs to raise your own. If the herbs are packaged in plastic—which they probably are—add the cost of the highly polluting, nonrenewable resources it takes to make the plastic container and the hundreds of years they take to break down once you've thrown the packaging away.

The long list of reasons why I will always go above and beyond to seek out organic and sustainable food can be narrowed down to one word: health. By this, I mean the health of the environment (soil, air, and water); the health of the farm workers; the health of the people I feed; my own health; and the health of the local economy. In my mind, it's a win-win situation—you and I seek out the best-tasting ingredients while supporting a sustainable food system that supports the planet on which we live.

Buying foods that are labeled organic at your supermarket is a great place to start, but buying organic food from your local farmers' market is where your dollars can really make a difference—to our food system and its environmental impact. Since large corporations growing organic produce are not required by the U.S. Department of Agriculture's (USDA's) organic certification process to practice sustainable methods of farming like crop rotation and diversity, water preservation, or recycling of compost for fertilization, there's no guarantee that your food was grown in a sustainable way. And then there's the question of how far it has traveled to reach your plate. In an average supermarket, organic produce is sourced and shipped from all over the world, increasing carbon emissions and draining energy resources for storage and packaging. Because of the increased time between harvest and delivery, the food loses vitality and essential nutrients as well. Buying from small organic and local farms guarantees that your food is fresher, more nutritious, and produced sustainably.

Due to the large fees and involved paperwork required to be certified organic by the USDA, many small organic farmers, some of whom have been growing food organically for generations, are unable to certify their crops. For this reason, many organic growers at the farmers' markets are not USDA-certified organic, even though (in many cases) their farming practices are far truer to the meaning of the term.

It is imperative that small farms practicing truly sustainable methods get our support. They don't get government subsidies like many conventional growers, and organic and biodynamic farming methods require more time, work, and diligence.

We have developed an underappreciation for the true cost of food or, as Michael Pollan puts it, a "cheap food mentality." Since most people have stopped growing food, we have forgotten how much work is involved, and due to cheap labor and government subsidies given to agribusinesses, we have also lost awareness of its true value. Before complaining about the cost of organic food, think about what we spend on unnecessary luxuries first (modern technology, expensive consumer goods, and restaurant meals). Still, it's true that many people cannot afford the prices of organic, sustainable food, which is why those who can must—it's the only way our broken food system can improve.

acknowledgments

My deepest gratitude goes to everyone who helped create this book:

My partner, Jacqui Kravetz: I could not have written a book without your unequivocal support and generosity. Thank you from the bottom of my heart for all that you do—for helping me find my voice and choose the perfect words, for all the time spent editing everything I write, and for giving me a most inspiring kitchen to create this book.

My parents, Pamela Shera and Will Chaplin: for bringing me up alongside a garden (and a compost!), for instilling in me a deep appreciation for good food and reverence for nature, and for giving me the freedom to follow my dreams.

Bonnie Chaplin: my sister and best food critic, for all your support, for the epic late-night tastings, long recipe-related discussions, and for helping me make hundreds of difficult recipe decisions (scones especially)!

My editor, Sara Bercholz: for allowing and encouraging me to write *my* book, for believing in it from the very beginning, and for all the work it took to make it the best it could be. And a huge thank you to everyone at Roost Books.

Stephen Johnson: for the amazing job you did designing, art-directing, and prop-styling this book—for going above and beyond for this project, for being an absolute joy to work with, and for your friendship. I really cannot thank you enough!

Johnny Miller: for the exquisite photographs. It was a true pleasure to collaborate with you, to witness your refreshing, bare-bones approach, and the ease with which you brought beauty and clarity to these images.

John Derian: for your endless generosity with both your personal and your public collection of antiques and beautiful things. This book simply would not look the same without your input! Thank you *so* much!

ABC Carpet and Home: for the use of their gorgeous props.

My agent, Brandi Bowles, and Foundry Media: for supporting and guiding this book from the beginning.

Blaine Arin: for all your dedication, enthusiasm, and hard work assisting me throughout this project and for diligently testing and retesting so many recipes.

Christina Trush and Kate Davis: for recipe testing, proofreading, and brilliantly assisting in all areas.

Miranda Van Gelder, Laura Jackson, Mike O'Malley, Kristen Esposito, Nancy Sobel Butcher, and my mother: for recipe testing and feedback.

Gabby Russomagno: for unwavering support and thoughtfulness.

Mary Wiles: for your generosity and special skills as a makeup artist.

Sarah Perlis: for exquisite jewelry and for loving everything I make.

Paul Pitchford: for inspiring me to be a better chef and for sharing the wealth of his knowledge with me.

Rosada Hayes: for all that I learned from working with you and the many years we spent cooking and laughing in the kitchen. I miss you!

The community of families and friends who fed me at their tables when I was growing up: Lynne Tarleton, Anshu Jacobs, the Lords, the Tuckers, the Parkers, the Hanleys, the Boltons, and Jillian, Lou, Kelly, Lorraine, Angie and Albert, Charlie, and my lovely Aunts. And to Guinevere and Greta for knowing me so well and bringing out the adventurer in me.

Gloria Von Sperling: for never tiring of our ongoing discussion about the healing benefits of food and herbs and for first encouraging me to teach.

Brian McCormac: for helping me define and truly confirm my path.

Natalie Portman and Liv Tyler: for ongoing support and enthusiasm for my cooking.

Seung Suh and Bob Caccamise: for being the best neighbors ever!

Tatiana Philippova and Deborah Hallahan: for keeping my qi flowing throughout this project.

Stella, Alfie, and Percy: for excellent company and endless patience.

All my past employers and coworkers in Sydney, Amsterdam, London, and New York: for sharing their knowledge and helping me grow into the chef I am today.

My ongoing gratitude goes to all the organic and biodynamic farmers who dedicate their lives to growing beautiful, sustainable food. The fruits of your labor inspire me every single day—thank you for all that you stand for.

My wonderful clients and readers: for making it possible for me to do what I love and support the causes that are most important to me. Thank you so very much!

Amy x

resources

GRAINS AND FLOURS

SHILOH FARMS
Sprouted flours and wide range of organic whole grains, including teff and amaranth.
www.shilohfarms.com

BOB'S RED MILL
Gluten-free oats and flours, whole grain flours, arrowroot powder, and aluminum-free baking powder (made without GMO corn starch).
www.bobsredmill.com

LOTUS FOODS
Forbidden black rice, Bhutan red rice, and jasmine rice.
www.lotusfoods.com

TO YOUR HEALTH SPROUTED FLOUR COMPANY
Every kind of sprouted flour you can imagine.
www.organicsproutedflour.net

BLUEBIRD GRAIN FARMS
Organic heirloom grains and freshly milled flours.
www.bluebirdgrainfarms.com

ANSON MILLS
Organic polenta and heirloom grains milled into meals and flours.
www.ansonmills.com

HEIRLOOM BEANS

NATIVE SEEDS
Nonprofit dedicated to conserving traditional agricultural heritage of the Greater Southwest. Selection of heirloom beans and seeds, dried chilies, whole grains, and meals.
www.nativeseeds.org

RANCHO GORDO
Wide range of exquisite heirloom beans.
www.ranchogordo.com

NUTS, SEEDS, AND NUT/SEED BUTTERS

NUTS.COM
Large variety of organic raw nuts, dried chestnuts, unpasteurized almonds, organic almond meal, Austrian pumpkin seeds, superfoods, and more.
www.nuts.com

MASSA ORGANICS
Organic, raw, and unpasteurized California almonds; the best toasted almond butter I have tasted, packaged in glass jars; organic short grain brown rice.
http://massaorganics.com

ARTISANA
Wide range of organic and raw nut butters, extra virgin coconut oil, and coconut butter.
http://artisanafoods.com

BLUE MOUNTAIN ORGANICS
Wide variety of sprouted nut butters.
http://bluemountainorganics.com

REAL FOODS MARKET
Truly raw cashews, Italian almonds, sprouted almond butter, sprouted almond meal.
www.realrawfoods.com

SUPERFOODS

NAVITAS NATURALS
Gelatinized maca root powder, hemp seeds, chia seeds, dried mulberries, golden berries, superfood powders, sprouted flax powder, and yakon syrup.
http://navitasnaturals.com

RICH NATURE
Goji berries for snacking and cooking, dried mulberries, golden berries, and superfood powders.
http://richnature.com

GOHUNZA
Goji berries, dried mulberries, raw nuts, Austrian pumpkin seeds, dried coconut, and unsulfured dried fruit.
www.gohunza.com

RON TEEGUARDEN'S DRAGON HERBS
Heaven Mountain goji berries that are especially moist and soft for snacking.
www.dragonherbs.com

OILS

FLORA
Cold pressed flax oil, pumpkin seed oil, and herbal tonics.
www.florahealth.com

BRAGG
Organic unpasteurized apple cider vinegar and organic unrefined extra virgin olive oil.
www.bragg.com

FRANKIES 457
Organic extra virgin olive oil—rich and grassy, perfect for dipping and drizzling.
www.frankiesspuntino.com/olive_oil.html

ANCIENT ORGANICS
Organic, grass-fed handcrafted ghee.
www.ancientorganics.com

TRADITIONALLY MADE JAPANESE PRODUCTS

EDEN FOODS
Organic Japanese and macrobiotic products, including traditionally brewed tamari, mirin, brown rice vinegar and umeboshi products, unrefined sesame oil and toasted sesame oil, BPA-free canned beans cooked with kombu, French Celtic sea salt, wild-harvest kuzu, whole-grain pastas and noodles, bottled crushed tomatoes, agar flakes, instant wakame and other seaweeds, naturally sweetened organic soy milk, kuki-cha tea, and more.
www.edenfoods.com

SOUTH RIVER MISO COMPANY
Organic, traditionally made miso sold
in glass jars. Chickpea miso, adzuki miso,
and all the classics.
www.southrivermiso.com

MISO MASTER
Organic, traditionally made miso.
https://great-eastern-sun.com

SEA VEGETABLES

IRON BOUND ISLAND SEAWEED
Dulse, wild Atlantic kombu, and wakame.
www.ironboundisland.com

MAINE COAST SEA VEGETABLES
Wild Atlantic wakame, nori, dulse,
and unique varieties of seaweed.
www.seaveg.com

SALT, HERBS, SPICES, NATURAL SWEETENERS, AND EXTRACTS

**SELINA NATURALLY
CELTIC SEA SALT**
Fine-ground Celtic sea salt and Fleur de Sel.
www.celticseasalt.com

MALDON
Flaked sea salt.
www.maldonsalt.co.uk

**FRONTIER
NATURAL PRODUCTS CO-OP**
Organic spices, maple sugar, aluminum-free
baking powder, vanilla and almond extracts,
and Earl Grey tea.
www.frontiercoop.com

MOUNTAIN ROSE HERBS
Bulk organic and sustainable herbs
and spices.
www.mountainroseherbs.com

**FLOWER POWER HERBS
AND ROOTS, INC.**
Organic rose buds, dried burdock root,
dried nettle for tea, and a wide range
of organic and ethically wildcrafted herbs
and tinctures.
www.flowerpower.net

HERB PHARM
Olive leaf extract and a wide range of
organic herbal extracts.
www.herb-pharm.com

SUZANNE'S SPECIALTIES
Traditionally made organic
brown rice syrup.
www.suzannes-specialties.com

COCONUT SECRET
Coconut sugar, coconut nectar,
and coconut flour.
www.coconutsecret.com

JUICES/NECTARS, JAMS/FRUIT SPREADS, AND BOTTLED ITEMS

BIONATURAE
Organic fruit spreads, pear nectar,
BPA-free canned tomatoes, balsamic
vinegar, and whole grain pastas.
www.bionaturae.com

ST. DALFOUR
Black cherry, raspberry, and other fruit
juice-sweetened preserves available in
health food stores and gourmet markets.
www.stdalfour.us

LAKEWOOD ORGANIC
Organic pure pomegranate juice not from
concentrate.
www.lakewoodjuices.com

JOVIAL
Organic tomatoes packaged in jars
and whole grain pasta.
www.jovialfoods.com

SEGGIANO
Organic roasted artichoke hearts, extra
virgin olive oil, and other specialty
Italian products.
www.seggiano.com

BREAD, CRACKERS, AND PASTA

EZEKIEL BREAD
Sprouted bread, English muffins,
and tortillas.
www.foodforlife.com

SAN-J
Organic black sesame crackers.
www.san-j.com

DELALLO
Organic, oven-ready, whole-wheat lasagna
noodles and biodynamic wholegrain pasta.
www.delallo.com

TEA

RISHI TEA
Sencha tea, matcha, Earl Grey, and
other high-quality organic teas.
www.rishi-tea.com

TRADITIONAL MEDICINALS
Nettle and dandelion root, and other
organic wellness teas and blends.
www.traditionalmedicinals.com

YOGI
Ginger tea and many other
organic tea blends.
www.yogiproducts.com

BEYOND TEA
Teas based on ancient herbal remedies,
including Cold Prevention Tea and
Healthy Digest Tea.
www.americanhealing.net

BELLOCQ TEA ATELIER
Specialty tea in beautiful packaging.
www.bellocq.com

LOCAL FAVORITES

REAL PICKLES
Wide range of naturally fermented
vegetables.
www.realpickles.com

HAWTHORNE VALLEY FARM
Biodynamic fermented vegetables, sourdough rye, and spelt breads.
http://hawthornevalleyfarm.org

CAYUGA PURE ORGANICS
Organic spelt berries, wheat berries, emmer,
corn grits, whole-grain flours, and pasta.
www.cporganics.com

NORDIC BREADS
Organic sourdough rye breads.
www.nordicbreads.com

DEEP MOUNTAIN MAPLE
All grades of maple syrup available in large
glass bottles, maple sugar, and maple cream.
http://deepmountainmaple.com

SAXELBY CHEESEMONGERS
Wide variety of local and regional artisanal cheeses.
www.saxelbycheese.com

LYNNEHAVEN
French style goat milk feta and fresh goat cheese.
www.lynnhavennubians.com

NETTLE MEADOW
Excellent goat, sheep, and Jersey cows milk cheeses.
www.nettlemeadow.com

ARDITH MAE
Fresh and aged goat cheese.
www.ardithmae.com

FRESH TOFU INC
Organic tofu made with locally grown soybeans.
www.freshtofu.com

THE BRIDGE
Organic tofu made with locally grown soybeans.
www.bridgetofu.com

BARRY'S TEMPEH
Handmade, unpasteurized tempeh from local organic soybeans.
www.growninbrooklyn.com

LOWER EAST SIDE ECOLOGY CENTER
Composting information and drop-off locations in New York City.
www.lesecologycenter.org

FARMERS' MARKETS

LOCAL HARVEST
A website for finding farmers' markets, family farms and CSAs (community supported agriculture) in your area.
www.localharvest.org

GROW NYC
Farmers' markets and composting in the New York City area.
www.grownyc.org

BAKING AND COOKWARE

BROADWAY PANHANDLER
Cake and tart pans, sheet pans, quality cookware, and tools.
www.broadwaypanhandler.com

N.Y. CAKE
Cake and tart pans in all sizes, as well as cellophane bags for gifting baked goods.
www.nycake.com

LE CREUSET
Enamel-coated cast-iron pots and pans in many colors.
www.lecreuset.com

KUHN RIKON
Pressure cookers in all sizes.
http://us.kuhnrikon.com

WILLIAMS SONOMA
Quality cookware, Weck Jars and organic cotton flour sack towels.
www.williams-sonoma.com

ALL-CLAD
High-quality, heavy duty stainless cookware.
www.all-clad.com

KITCHEN TOOLS

KORIN
Japanese knives, Tawashi brushes, and suribachi mortars.
http://korin.com

MINOSHARP
Ceramic knife sharpener.
www.minosharp.jp

LIVE SUPERFOODS
Fast drying mesh nut milk bags.
www.livesuperfoods.com

KYOCERA ADVANCED CERAMICS
Ceramic blade vegetable slicers.
http://kyoceraadvancedceramic.com

BENRINER
Japanese mandolines with adjustable, stainless steel blades.
www.benriner.com

MICROPLANE
Zesters and other kitchen tools.
www.microplane.com

STORAGE

SIMPLE ECOLOGY
Variety of organic cotton produce, grocery, and string bags.
www.simpleecologystore.com

ECOBAGS
Recycled and organic cotton shopping and produce bags.
www.ecobags.com

VEJIBAGS
Thick produce storage bags for keeping washed greens and produce for long periods. Made by hand in Maine.
www.vejibag.com

BEES WRAP
Beeswax coated cloth alternative to plastic wrap.
www.beeswrap.com

WECK JARS
Perfect glass storage jars, available in all sizes.
www.weckjars.com

PYREX
Heat-resistant glass storage containers and baking dishes.
www.worldkitchen.com

FISHS EDDY
Mason jars, Weck jars, and clear glass food storage containers.
www.fishseddy.com

UPRIGHT BLENDERS

VITAMIX
The most powerful blender on the market.
www.vitamix.com

WARING PRO
Affordable blenders with glass carafes.
www.waringpro.com

WATER FILTERS

CWR ENVIRO
Countertop and under-the-counter water filters that remove high amounts of fluoride, heavy metals, nitrates, and chlorine and its by-products.
www.cwrenviro.com

bibliography

BOOKS

Balch, Phyllis A. *Prescription for Dietary Wellness.* New York: Avery 1992, 1998, 2003.

Berley, Peter. *The Modern Vegetarian Kitchen.* New York: HarperCollins, 2000.

Gates, Donna, with Linda Schatz. *The Body Ecology Diet.* Carlsbad, CA: Hay House, 1996, 2010, 2011.

Katz, Sandor Ellix. *The Art of Fermentation.* White River Junction, VT: Chelsea Green 2012.

——. *The Revolution Will Not Be Microwaved.* White River Junction, VT: Chelsea Green, 2006.

——. *Wild Fermentation.* White River Junction, VT: Chelsea Green, 2003.

Kornfeld, Myra, and George Minot. *The Voluptuous Vegan.* New York: Clarkson Potter, 2000.

Kushi, Aveline, with Alex Jack. *Aveline Kushi's Complete Guide to Macrobiotic Cooking.* New York: Warner Books, 1985.

Lahey, Jim, with Rick Flaste. *My Bread: The Revolutionary No-Work, No-Knead Bread.* New York: W. W. Norton, 2009.

McEachern, Leslie. *The Angelica Home Kitchen.* Berkeley, CA: Ten Speed Press, 2003.

Murray, Michael, and Joseph Pizzorno, with Lara Pizzorno. *The Encyclopedia of Healing Foods.* New York: Atria Books, 2005.

Nestle, Marion. *What to Eat.* New York: North Point Press, 2006.

Pitchford, Paul. *Healing with Whole Foods.* Berkeley, CA: North Atlantic Books, 1993, 1996, 2002.

Pollan, Michael. *In Defense of Food.* New York: Penguin Press, 2009.

——. *The Omnivore's Dilemma: A Natural History of Four Meals.* New York: Penguin, 2006.

Wood, Rebecca. *The New Whole Foods Encyclopedia.* New York: Penguin, 1999, 2010.

——. *The Splendid Grain.* New York: William Morrow, 1997.

WEBSITES

BIODYNAMIC FARMING AND GARDENING ASSOCIATION
www.biodynamics.com

ENVIRONMENTAL WORKING GROUP
www.ewg.org

SMALL FOOTPRINT FAMILY
www.smallfootprintfamily.com

SUSTAINABLE TABLE
www.sustainabletable.com

index

M

macadamia nuts
  Roasted Red Pepper Macadamia Pâté, 216
  Summer Rolls with Macadamia Lime Sauce, 206
maca root powder, 21
  Superfood Breakfast Sprinkle, 117
main dishes, meals
  Beet Chickpea Cakes with Tzatziki, 263
  Beet Tartlets with Poppy Seed Crust and White Bean
    Fennel Filling, 243–44
  Bento Bowl, 278–281
  Coconut Curry with Tamarind Tempeh and Forbidden
    Black Rice, 274–77
  Dill Roasted Plum Tomato Tart with Pine Nut Crust,
    236–37
  Fragrant Eggplant Curry with Cardamom-Infused
    Basmati Rice, Tangy Apricot Chutney, and Cucumber
    Lime Raita, 251–52
  Heirloom Bean Bourguignon with Celery Root Mash,
    283–85
  Late Summer Stew with Heirloom Beans and Parsley
    Pistou, 247–48
  from the pantry, menu suggestions, 57
  Roasted Fall Vegetable Cannellini Bean Stew with Spelt
    Berries and Kale, 269
  Soft Polenta with Nettles, Peas, and Goat Cheese, 235
  Spicy Black Bean Stew with Crispy Sweet Corn Polenta
    and Tomatillo Avocado Salsa, 264–67
  Squash Blossom Orecchiette with Aged Sheep's Cheese
    and Red Chili, 238
  Sweet Corn Tofu Frittata with Roasted Cherry Tomato
    Compote, 259–260
  Tempeh Portobello Burgers, 255–56
mandoline, Japanese, 48
Maple Coconut Crunch, 329
maple syrup and sugar, 43
marinades
  Harissa Marinade, 187
  ingredients for, 11, 14, 24–25, 31, 45, 56
  Spicy Sesame Marinade, 188
Marinated Beans, Simple, 70, 359
Marinated Beets, 57, 104
Marinated Goat Cheese, 98, 116
matcha tea, 354
Mayonnaise, Miso, 114
Medjool dates, 43
Melnyk, Georgia, 347
milk, nut, 49, 74. *See also specific nuts*
millet, 10
  cooking instructions, 142
  health benefits, 138

Millet, Squash, and Sweet Corn Pilaf with Tamari-
    Toasted Pumpkin Seeds, 138
Millet Cauliflower Mash, 92, 359
Plum Millet Muffins, 10, 142
mirin, 26
miso, 36
  Hearty Winter Miso, 174, 359
  Miso Mayonnaise, 114
  Spring Miso Soup with Lemon, 158
mixing bowls, 49
The Modern Vegetarian Kitchen (Berley), 236
Muesli, Amaranth, with Toasted Seeds, 130
muffins
  Blackberry Cornmeal Muffins, 132
  Herbed Black Quinoa Muffins with Sweet Potato and
    Caramelized Onions, 152
  Plum Millet Muffins, 142
mulberries, dried, 20, 87, 359
Mulled Concord Grape Juice, 229
mung beans, 14, 175
mushrooms
  dashi, 158
  Creamy Cauliflower and Celery Root Soup with Roasted
    Shiitakes, 168
  Tempeh Portobello Burgers, 255–56
  Ume Shiso Broth, 160
mustard, Dijon, 26
  Dijon Mustard–Marinated Tempeh, 105
  Mustard Dressing, 199
  The Pantry Sandwich, 109
My Mother's Spelt Almond Waffles, 131

N

nettles
  Soft Polenta with Nettles, Peas, and Goat Cheese, 235
  tea, 354
The New Whole Food Encyclopedia (Wood), 221
nishime-style cooking, 281
noodles/pasta, whole-grain
  Butternut Squash Lasagna with Whole-Wheat Noodles, 270
  as ingredients, 11
  Squash Blossom Orecchiette, 238
  Ume Shiso Broth with Soba Noodles, 160, 359
  Whole-Wheat Fettuccini with Kale, Caramelized Onions,
    and Marinated Goat Cheese, 98
  Whole-Wheat Udon Salad, 188
nori, 27–29
  Nori Sesame "Leaves," 171
  toasting, 210